THE COMPLETE GUIDE TO
Conservatory
Gardening

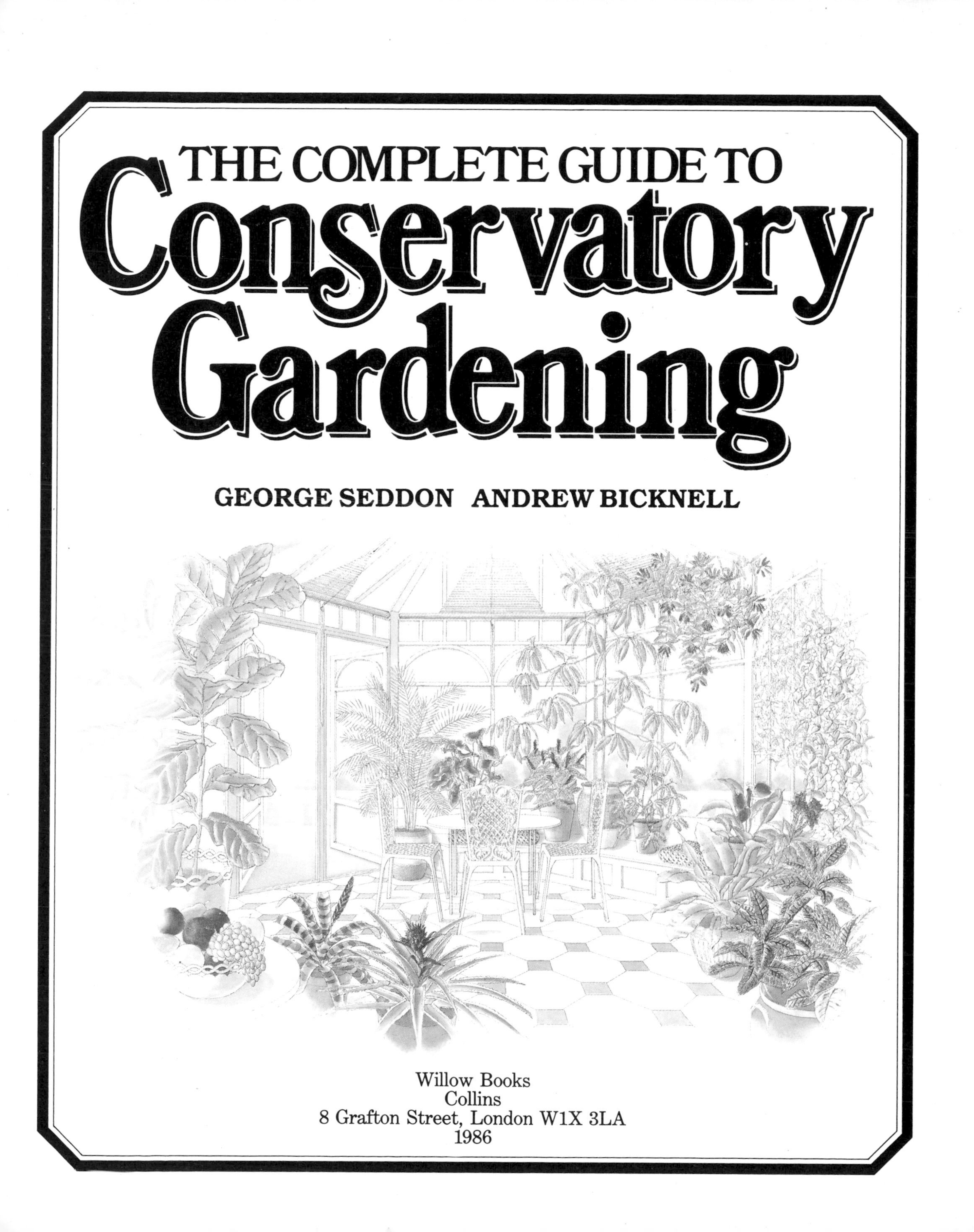

THE COMPLETE GUIDE TO Conservatory Gardening

GEORGE SEDDON ANDREW BICKNELL

Willow Books
Collins
8 Grafton Street, London W1X 3LA
1986

The Complete Guide to Conservatory Gardening was conceived, edited and designed by Grub Street, 4 Kingly Street, London W1R 5LF

Willow Books
William Collins Sons & Co Ltd
London · Glasgow · Sydney
Auckland · Toronto · Johannesburg

First published in Great Britain 1986

Illustrations by Lynette Conway (colour); Simon Roulston

British Library Cataloguing in Publication Data
Bicknell, Andrew
The complete guide to conservatory gardening.
1. Indoor gardening
I. Title II. Seddon, George
635.9′65 SB419
ISBN 0-00-218187-8
ISBN 0-00-218197-5 Pbk

Printed and bound in Great Britain by Blantyre Printing Ltd, Glasgow

Contents

Introduction

'It's the best fun I ever had' was how the famous gardening and wine writer Hugh Johnson summed up his first year as owner of a conservatory. Strange, he thought, that there were not more books about conservatory gardening. That was in the early 1980s when indeed it would have been hard to find even one contemporary book on the subject; and not surprisingly, for the current revival of the conservatory had only just got under way. Now the conservatory is flourishing again after the almost total eclipse it suffered in the years following the Second World War, when the utilitarian greenhouse largely took its place.

Conservatories are not 'greenhouses putting on airs', although some may give that impression. The distinction between the two is not so much their structures as the uses to which they are put. Greenhouses are primarily for plants; conservatories are for people and plants. The enjoyment of a greenhouse comes through working with plants, and is usually a solitary pleasure. The enjoyment of a conservatory is as much through relaxing among plants, although much work is also involved in caring for them. Moreover, it is a pleasure that can be shared; indeed the social aspect of the conservatory is very much part of its special appeal.

If the conservatory is not a glorified greenhouse, neither is it simply a home extension, as a garden room might be. In a real conservatory the balance between the needs of the plants and those of the people is tilted rather in favour of the plants; the simple purpose of all that glass is to let in as much light as possible. In a garden room, people come first. While the walls may be of glass, for the benefit of the plants, the roof will be solid, to protect human residents from the scorching heat and blinding light of summer days.

The conservatory may not offer as much scope to the interior decorator as does the garden room, but for the lover of plants the real conservatory gives the excitement of being able to grow a greater range of plants far more successfully than can ever be achieved in a mere extra room.

A major part of the book is therefore devoted to choosing the best plants for a conservatory, together with advice on caring for them. The choice of plants from the hundreds available is determined basically by how warm the conservatory will be in the winter months. Conservatories are usually divided into three types: cool, with minimum winter temperatures in the range 45°–55°F (7°–13°C); temperate, 55°–65°F (13°–18°C); and warm, 65°–75°F (18°–24°C). There are a large number of plants suitable for each type of conservatory, but the ranges of temperatures given are the *minimum* needed by the plants in each group during even the coldest spells of winter. Of course, in summer, when the natural heat of the sun takes over from artificial heat, the temperatures in the cool and temperate conservatories, and even in the warm conservatory, will be

Early in the current conservatory revival, Hugh Johnson, gardening and wine writer, had this one built. Verdict: 'The best fun I ever had'.

far higher. The problem then may be to prevent the conservatory from getting too hot, and for this, proper ventilation and shading provide the answers.

Cheapest to run is the cool conservatory, for which there is also the widest choice of plants. Many plants for the cool conservatory will do equally well in a temperate conservatory, however, and some even in a warm one, as long as they can be moved in winter to a cooler place. This is because they need the period of cool winter rest to which they are accustomed in their natural outdoor environment. A good selection of plants will also do well in a temperate conservatory all the year round, and this list can be extended by adding to it some of the species suggested for a garden room. Space may also be found for some rarer or out-of-season fruit and vegetables. By comparison the list of plants for the warm conservatory is shorter, even though there is no lack of warmth-loving plants. There are two reasons for this. Fewer warm-zone plants are available from nurseries and garden centres, and many of them need not only heat but also such high humidity that a conservatory ideally suited to their requirements would be unbearable to sit in (as a visit to a botanical garden's hot and humid glasshouse will soon confirm).

However much fun it is to own and enjoy a conservatory, choosing one is a serious business. First you must decide where it might go (the section on finding the right place, page 28, explains which sites make most efficient use of sunlight). Next comes the decision of choosing the right design of conservatory. You are about to make a considerable investment, as costly as a car, and perhaps even greater care is needed in making a choice, if only because the conservatory will last far, far longer. The section on choosing what to buy, page 36, is a basic guide to the varieties available and also gives advice on planning permission (if necessary), building regulations, preparation of site, erection and financing.

At the same time as you choose the conservatory, you have to decide what equipment is needed, so the book includes sections on how to provide the right heating, all-important ventilation, shading, watering and humidity control. There are also helpful suggestions on the display of plants and the selection of appropriate furniture.

Finally, the book examines the subject of plant care – including potting, feeding, pruning, propagation, and how to avoid or cope with plant pests and diseases.

Part 1

The Rise of the Classic Conservatory

Growing oranges became a fashionable aristocratic obsession in Europe from the 15th century. The craze spread from Italy to Germany and eventually to England. As the orange trees travelled north they required greater protection against the cold. At first temporary wooden sheds were built over the trees in winter and removed in summer. In time they were replaced by permanent buildings, which became more and more palatial, serving as annexes to stately homes, and used for banquets and the like. Orange trees went out of fashion, but the orangery survived until superseded by the conservatory. This late English example is the early 19th century orangery at Longleat, in Wiltshire.

Some two thousand years ago the Romans had greenhouses, after a fashion; evidence of such buildings was found among the ruins of Pompeii, the Roman town overwhelmed by the eruption of Vesuvius in AD 79. The Romans also enjoyed banqueting rooms which were open to the gardens beyond. Centuries later two similar architectural concepts reappeared in northern Europe and from the merging of the two the modern conservatory eventually evolved. The way in which this happened was determined by several factors: by fluctuating tastes in styles of architecture, by technical advances during the emergent Industrial Revolution, by European exploration of remote parts of the world bringing shifts of fashionable interest in newly-discovered exotic plants and, above all, by basic changes in social class structure in the 19th century.

In England it was King Henry V who started the fashion, later popular among the Tudors, of building banqueting halls in the gardens of grand estates. The first halls were of timber, but later they became more substantial, and the taste for them persisted into the 17th century. Around this time the first

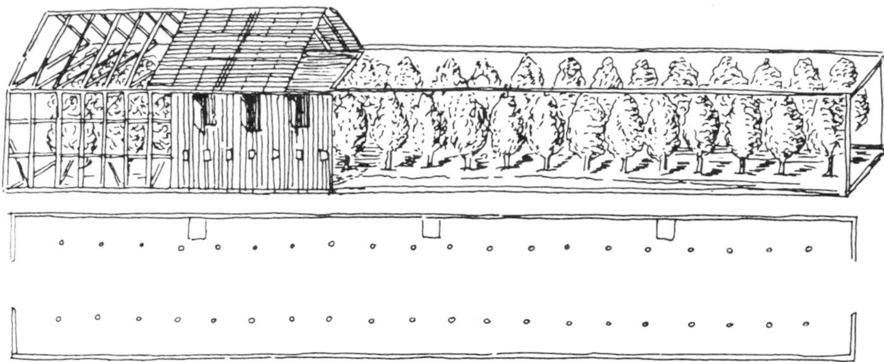

structures described as 'greenhouses' arrived in England. Copied from Germany, they owed their existence entirely to the craze in courtly and aristocratic circles for growing orange trees. The orange, a native of China, had been introduced into Europe towards the end of the 13th century and became a symbol of status and wealth. Its cultivation grew into an obsessive aristocratic pastime throughout Europe. Unfortunately, the further north orange trees spread, the more likely they were to die in severe winters. To protect these delicate trees, 'greenhouses' were built and so named because the evergreen orange trees were known as 'greens'. These early greenhouses were in fact just large sheds erected round the trees in autumn and dismantled in spring. There was no glass to let in light and the wooden shutters were removed only in mild weather. This meant that the trees inside were almost as likely to die from lack of light and the noxious fumes given off by stoves burning inside the building as they would had they been left to face the cold outside.

Ornamental orangeries

These 'wooden tabernacles' as the diarist John Evelyn called them, though the general name had become 'orangeries', were gradually replaced by permanent buildings. The reason was partly because the cost of dismantling and re-erecting them every year was stupendous,

Top left: Vast wooden framework conservatory at Chatsworth. Built 1836–40, it was demolished in 1920. Above: The early 19th-century Palm House, Bicton, Devon. Its pioneering iron framework, is a far cry from the 17th-century orangery (left).

but largely because a huge wooden shed looked out of place in the grounds of a stately home. So the architects took over and during the first half of the 18th century they built large ornate orangeries. These were often used for grand social occasions and banquets, echoing the function of the Tudor banqueting halls. The oranges, the original reason for their existence, were reduced in these performances to a walk-on role. It was the building which now stayed put, while the orange trees, in tubs, were moved out for summer and back again for winter. When fashions changed again, oranges went out altogether to make way for rarer exotic plants. These newcomers created practical problems, because they needed more light than was let into even the most advanced orangeries, which still had solid roofs and heavy stonework.

Alongside the changing orangeries, however, developments had taken place in the building of glasshouses, also called planthouses, or forcing houses. They had been in use for raising plants since the end of the 16th century, mainly in botanical gardens. Most were built with brick back walls and sides, but had fronts and roofs of glass. Since only small panes of glass could be manufactured at that time, there was of necessity a large proportion of framework, blocking out much light. The glass itself was of poor quality, with bad light transmission, yet it was costly. During the 18th century there were some improvements in the manufacture of glass, but it was not until the later stages of the Industrial Revolution in the 19th century that the transition from the Baroque orangery of the architect to the functional glass and iron conservatory of the engineer was finally possible. Even so, conflict between the approach of architect and engineer continued throughout the 19th century.

The Iron Masters

Iron was by no means a new material. The Iron Age dates from around 1100 BC, when iron-working began in the Middle East, but not until the end of the 18th century was it possible to smelt and manufacture iron cheaply and on a large scale. Glass was also an ancient material, but it was not until the 1830s that sheet glass of good quality could be manufactured; in Britain it came to be used more lavishly after the abolition of tax on glass a decade later.

What is believed to be the first iron and glass planthouse was built at Wollaton Hall, near Nottingham, in 1823 and is still in use. It has a restrained classical frontage, erected from prefabricated ironwork, but not of modular construction – that came later. The first huge functional conservatory was at Chatsworth in Derbyshire, home of the Duke of Devonshire, and was designed by Joseph Paxton, a farmer's son. The framework holding the glass was of wood, supported on iron columns. It was 277 ft (37.5 m) long; 67 ft (20 m) high; and had a carriage road through it which greatly impressed Queen Victoria when she drove along it in 1848.

The Chatsworth conservatory begat the great Palm House at the Royal Botanic Gardens at Kew, built with a framework of cast iron and wrought iron. It was the result of a combination of plans by an architect, Decimus Burton, and an engineer, Richard Turner, who had an ironworks in Dublin. Fortunately, Turner's influence appears to have been paramount, for it is a dramatic and beautiful masterpiece of engineering. Not so the Temperate House at Kew, twice the size of the Palm House, begun in 1866, and designed by Decimus Burton alone. This was a conservatory perceived through an architect's eyes. The two structures are still there to compare.

Chatsworth also inspired the Great Exhibition Building of 1851, designed by Joseph Paxton, using iron, wood and glass. It was a

marvel of prefabricated technology, which made it possible to take down, re-erect and enlarge as the Crystal Palace in Sydenham, London, where it burned down in 1936. (It is now resurrected in reproduction in the United States, in Dallas, Texas.)

Although the Crystal Palace was hardly a conservatory, its methods of prefabricated modular construction had a profound effect on the spread of conservatories through the second half of the 19th century. Until then these buildings had mainly been the preserve of hereditary landowners, dukes, earls, marquesses and the like. They were grand affairs, not only for the display of plants, but also of wealth, status and self-importance. When *The Gardener's Magazine* was founded in 1826 by the pioneering horticultural writer, John Claudius Loudon, the gardens described in it were divided into those of the 'seats' of the aristocracy and the 'residences' of the rest. But the decline of the landed gentry had already begun and their influence was to be increasingly undermined by the new-rich industrialists and

Contrasts at Kew Botanical Gardens, near London. Bottom left: Engraving of the Palm House, an engineering masterpiece. Built between 1844–48, a massive restoration began in 1985. Left: Inside the Palm House in Victorian times. Top left: Temperate House at Kew, an architect's approach. Built between 1860–62 and 1895–99, it was restored 1978–81, letting in more, much needed light. Above: Conservatory of the English mustard magnate, Jeremiah James Colman, MP, at Carrow House, Norwich. Built of teak, it is adorned with 19th-century arts and crafts stained glass.

professional men, who also took to building conservatories. Loudon looked back to the time when a greenhouse (the name was then interchangeable with conservatory) was a luxury not often to be met but 'is now become an appendage to every villa, and to many town residences'.

Some of the newcomers built their conservatories grandiosely, others more modestly, demonstrating their varying levels of wealth and good or bad taste. Conservatories were built on the profits of Sunlight Soap and Pear's Soap (by the man who introduced the 'Bubbles' advertisement) and of beer, salt, shipping, commerce and the law.

Tropical splendour

These edifices may have appeared functional structures of iron and glass from the outside, but the interiors were designed to create an illusion of far-off tropical paradises, a world away from the dark Satanic mills. Even the normally sensible Loudon was carried away by Victorian exuberance, envisaging conservatories with tropical birds and fish, and even natives of the tropics as gardeners to complete the illusion. The jungle was in; 'the rich

Lord Leverhulme, soap magnate, joined the loggia revival with this grand example along the length of his London home near Hampstead Heath.

disorder of the virgin forest', as one contemporary writer put it. Virginal it certainly was, for Victorian morality had invaded the conservatory. William Cobbett, the English social reformer, wrote: 'It is the moral effects naturally attending a greenhouse that I set most value upon. How much better during the long and dreary winter for daughters and even sons to assist or attend their mother in a greenhouse than be seated with her at cards or in the blubbering over some stupid novel or at any other amusement that can possibly be conceived?'

While the jungle décor lasted it consisted largely or solely of palms, of which there were hundreds of species to choose from. By the end of the 19th century the palm had lost its claim to be the top people's plant and had become the cliché of the middle classes, who by then had conservatories in their thousands, just as the upper classes were losing interest in them.

Britain's flourishing iron foundries were responsible for this rapid expansion of the domestic conservatory, by mass-producing standardized ironwork with which simple or elaborate conservatories could easily be built. The expensive pastime of the aristocracy had turned into a mail order business and the snob appeal of the conservatory was inevitably diminished. There were still glass and iron buildings on the grand scale, such commercial hybrids as winter gardens, winter palaces and people's palaces, for example. No upper-class hotel in city or health resort could afford to be without a winter garden. The lower orders were offered winter palaces, or people's palaces, where among the palms they would find aquaria, zoos, skating rinks, amusement parks, concert halls and restaurants, and any other entertainments that would bring in the crowds and profits for the speculators.

Decline and fall

Other influences were working against the genuine conservatory. The arts and crafts movement of the later part of the 19th century did not like iron, or mass production, or, indeed, conservatories. The objection was that conservatories cut off the house from the outdoors and that therefore the loggia was a far better alternative – fresh air having become fashionable. (It was perhaps symptomatic that Lord Leverhulme, the soap

magnate, had a conservatory at his home on Merseyside but a loggia at his London home in Hampstead.) Another change in fashion affected plants. Much of the world having been scoured for exotics over two centuries, botanists now turned to hardy plants, which did not need the warmth of the conservatory.

The First World War delivered the mortal blow to the Victorian conservatory, both ducal and domestic. It became a luxury that none could afford in cost or labour, either to run or to keep in repair. Peace brought no respite, only economic depression. Many conservatories either fell down or were demolished, among them Paxton's pioneering Great Stove at Chatsworth, although it took five explosions to flatten it. Inter-war neglect and the Second World War brought the *coup de grace* to others. The most humiliating end was suffered by the much-minareted and pinnacled extravagance erected at Enville Hall in Staffordshire by the Earl of Stamford and Warrington in the mid-19th century. It was blown up – for practice – by an army demolition team stationed there; a fate it probably deserved.

Towards the end of the 19th century the once upper-class conservatory was taken over by the prosperous middle classes. Conservatories and greenhouses were mass produced to provide 'hothouses for the million' as one firm advertised. Contemporary photographs featured domestic respectability among the make-believe jungle.

Part 2

The Conservatory of Today

A conservatory added to an old building (or, as here, to a group of venerable buildings) can easily look out of place. Two factors help the new to fit in with the old here. The windows of the conservatory and adjoining door follow, and indeed emphasise, the pattern of the house windows, while the white brick walls of the house and white woodwork of the conservatory blend easily together.

A lean-to conservatory with a single slope roof built against a house has many practical advantages. Some types have little character, but those above and opposite show that lean-tos can have great appeal and individuality.

The eclipse of the conservatory lasted throughout the economic disasters of the second post-war period. When glass did begin to reappear in the garden with the arrival of the affluent 1960s, it was as the strictly utilitarian, prefabricated greenhouse. This was as likely to be an adjunct of the vegetable garden as of the flower garden, although what was grown was often less important than the pleasure of growing it. Then in the 1970s the conservatory began to creep back, almost unnoticed at first, but by the start of the 1980s the trend had become inescapable. What had been the seemingly idle dreams of thousands turned into reality. Not since Victorian times has such a wide variety of conservatories been available as can be found today.

As with the previous conservatory era, many influences have been at work. One was the home extension movement of the 1950s and 60s, which started in the loft and moved down to the ground floor, where the tacked-on rooms combined comfort with warmth. Simultaneously, the enthusiasm of the houseplant revolution brought exotic plants back into favour. But the main obstacle to growing plants successfully in a living room is lack of light, since there is usually a window in only one wall. A home extension which has a glass roof as well as glass walls is the logical answer to that problem, and so the conservatory has been reinvented in a modern idiom.

Today's conservatory is almost invariably attached to the house and is a much more integral part of it than the Victorians considered healthy. While they seemed able to accept the appalling pollution of their homes from gas light and coal fires, they were suspicious of the effects of damp soil and growing vegetation. They were convinced that the air in the conservatory, contaminated by vegetable matter, was unfit to breathe for any length of time and destructive of the furniture. Therefore many of their conservatories, though attached to the house, were built with no access from indoors, while others had a corridor separating the conservatory from the house, a kind of *cordon sanitaire*. The greenhouse was held to be particularly menacing at night and was on no account to be used for dining, since in the evening the plants were giving off carbon dioxide. One could safely lunch there, however, because at midday the plants were breathing out oxygen, providing also a suitable atmosphere for a promenade, or a proposal of marriage on bended knee, as in the best romantic novels. Today we have no such fears of unhealthy dampness and the conservatory is firmly and sensibly part of the house.

Types of conservatory

The probability is that the modern conservatory will be a lean-to built against one or sometimes two walls of the house, or as an attached wing. Because the lean-to has a considerable amount of solid wall through which heat escapes from the house, it gains in warmth, but loses out on light. The wing conservatory, having a far higher proportion of glass, suffers greater heat losses, but gains light. These differences are much the same whether the conservatory is designed as part of a new house or whether it is added to an existing home. When designing a new house, however, it is easier to place the conservatory where it will receive the maximum light. (See the section on siting the conservatory, page 28.)

Lean-tos with a difference, thanks to unusual roof design. Left: Angular aluminium roof combined with a porch-like entrance in wood. Above: Attractively curved roof with glazing bars of wood.

The materials used for building the modern conservatory vary from those in traditional examples. Aluminium has replaced iron and much of the wood, although some steel may be used in larger buildings. Aluminium structures are not universally liked, so wooden versions, which look more like the accepted image of a conservatory, remain popular and may fit better visually with older houses. Even in traditional buildings modern materials may be employed. These include glass fibre, often for ornamentation, and PVC for guttering. PVC is little used for glazing, since glass lets in more light and is no more expensive, although it is sometimes chosen for models with curvaceous roofs.

The inside appearance of the conservatory has altered too, through changes in taste and advances in technology. The jungle look has gone. Now the greatest effect is achieved by restraint, under- rather than over-crowding, to maintain a feeling of space and light.

Modern technology has made possible thermostatic heat control and automatic ventilation, shading, watering and humidifying. How much of such equipment you want to instal will depend on your taste for automation, and even more on how much you want to spend. A thoroughly modern conservatory is never a particularly cheap pleasure and can be – although it need not – an extremely expensive one. It is false economy to try to reduce the initial cost by buying a small conservatory, however, for the smaller it is the greater the danger of overheating and poor ventilation (as explained in the section on ventilation, see page 48). Instead it is better to buy as large a conservatory as you can afford and can find space for; labour-saving refinements can be added later, after a period of time to decide whether or not they are necessary.

Running costs, more than capital outlay, will determine both your use of the conservatory and the plants you can grow. Way above all other running costs are the expenses of

heating during the winter months. The comfort level of most humans sitting about indoors doing nothing is within a narrow range around 65°F (18°C), while the range of temperatures in which different plants can live is much wider. Some need a minimum average temperature of only 45°F (7°C), while others must have 70°F (21°C). It may be possible quickly to heat a bitterly cold conservatory to the level of human comfort just for the occasions when humans want to be in it, but this will not do for the plants. They have to live there all the time and any drop below their minimum temperature needs is liable to damage or kill them. So a constant temperature, never falling below the minimum requirements what-

Conservatories by degrees. Above left: Cool — mainly annual flowers, tomatoes and somewhere to sit in summer. Above: Temperate — giving more human comfort for more of the year. Left: Warm all year — with a lush, exotic atmosphere in which to relax.

ever the temperature outdoors, must be maintained. If it is a few degrees higher than the minimum, that is usually so much the better.

Temperature ranges

By convention, conservatories are divided into three categories – cool, temperate and warm – according to their minimum winter temperature levels. Plants do not, of course, fit altogether neatly into these categories; overlapping occurs at the margins of each range, but on the whole the system works reasonably well.

The Cool Conservatory is for plants which need winter temperatures in the range 45°F (7°C)–*and no lower*–to 55°F (13°C). This is the cheapest heated conservatory to run, but is obviously no place for humans to loiter in winter and must be accepted as a part-time, not a year-round, pleasure. Perversely, the widest choice of plants for conservatory-growing is to be found among those which will survive these low winter temperatures. For while plants for the warm conservatory have probably originated in the tropics, where there is little variation in temperatures all year round, those for the cool conservatory have come from parts of the world with cold winters, even though the summers might be baking hot or temperate.

The Temperate Conservatory is suitable for the wide range of plants which need a winter temperature between 55°F (13°C–the minimum–to 65°F (18°C). A selection of these plants provides a continuous show in the conservatory during late spring, summer and autumn. In northern latitudes, considerable artificial heating is necessary to reach the recommended winter minimum, but still far less than is needed to support plants in a warm conservatory. With the temperature kept at the low end of the range, little incentive is given for using the conservatory in the winter months without boosting the temperature for short periods, say with an electric fan heater, and letting it fall again at night.

The Warm Conservatory is for the tender plants which need winter temperatures between 65° and 75°F (18°–24°C). How much artificial heat has to be provided depends on how big is the gap between the temperature outside and the minimum temperature needed by the plants. In very clement latitudes it will be small, but the gap widens the further north you go and the more daunting becomes the cost of filling it, whatever fuel is used. The recompense is to enjoy the exotic plants which cannot be grown in a cooler conservatory, or in the house itself, with certainty of success. The extra advantage of a warm conservatory, of course, is that it adds another, permanently warm, room to the house. So in reckoning the cost, not all of it should be accounted to the plants; the more warmth in the conservatory, the more it is adding to your own comfort.

The Garden Room

The solid roof of this magnificent garden room cuts out glare for humans, but the expanse of glass gives plenty of light for plants. Blinds grant shade to all occupants.

Alongside the development of the modern conservatory has flourished the garden room. This hybrid – a cross between a conservatory and an ordinary living room – is also described as a 'plant room', a 'sun room' and even 'winter garden'. Plants and people still live in close proximity, but with the balance shifted in favour of people. In northern Europe, especially in Scandinavian countries, the garden room provides a substitute for the weatherbound and inaccessible garden during the long winter months. In the warmer parts of Italy and the United States, on the other hand, the garden room, open to the garden for much of the year, acts as a bridge between outdoors and indoors.

Bringing Nature right indoors is an ancient concept. A famous example of a so-called garden house is that of Livia, wife of the Emperor Augustus, who around 30 BC had a subterranean building near Rome, its walls painted with pomegranate, quince and strawberry trees on which perched magpies, jays and flycatchers, while poppies, roses and periwinkles blossomed beneath. Turning to the real thing, and more modern times, room plants and the inevitable books about them have been known since at least the 17th century. It was then Sir Hugh Platt, in his book *The Garden of Eden*, recommended bringing into the house such herbs as rosemary, basil and marjoram (as well as cucumbers pierced with growing barley to keep flies off the oil paintings). But it was the popularity of the conservatory in Victorian times that encouraged the spread of plants into the house. Many were the hardy annuals and bedding plants which materialized indoors as pot plants.

Just as William Cobbett had emphasized the moral aspects of the conservatory, so the pompous Shirley Hibberd in his *Rustic Adornments for Homes of Taste* (1856) extolled the moral virtues of houseplants. They strengthened family ties, cheered the lonely, and helped 'the soul in its aspirations by conducting it away from disturbing scenes'. He insisted that 'taste is the application to Nature of the same faculty which in morals enables us to distinguish between right and wrong'.

It is doubtful if the current obsession with houseplants has such moral foundations. The basic reason would appear to be the remarkable spread of central heating in the last quarter of a century, making more practical the cultivation of exotic plants. And to the surge of home extension building over a similar period, itself encouraged by the installation of central heating, the modern garden room owes much; there is little point in adding another cold room to a chilly house, but another warm room makes sense. So although garden rooms are increasingly a feature of new houses, many have also been created as home extensions.

An extension garden room is usually built against the wall of the house, having three sides of glass and a solid flat roof. Although the roof deprives the plants of some light, it has the advantage of making the room a more comfortable place in which to sit on glaringly hot summer days. The base of the walls may be of brick or wood, perhaps two feet high, with glass above, but if the view from the room is particularly attractive, all-glass walls – perhaps in the form of large sliding windows – make a better alternative and further break down the barrier between indoors and out. The garden room can be a stylish, comfortable and charming alternative for those who do not want, or do not have room for, a full-blown conservatory.

Selecting the site

Having considered whether to have a cool, temperate or warm conservatory, the next thing to decide is where to build it. The choice will obviously be most affected by the layout of the house, and that may limit the range of plants you can grow; for instance, a north-facing site would be unsuitable for the kind of plants at home in a warm conservatory.

The basic reason is simple. A plant needs both warmth and light to live and grow. In a conservatory in summertime it will get warmth and light, perhaps too much; but not in winter. Then there will be too little natural warmth and too little light. The plant can be provided with as much artificial warmth as the owner has a mind to pay for, but substituting artificial light for inadequate sunlight is not yet practical. All that can be done is to make the most of the limited light available. This will depend on several factors:

1. The structure of the conservatory: how much light will it let in?

2. Its position: is there anything in the way to obstruct the winter sun, low in the sky?

3. Its orientation: should it run east-west, north-south, or something in between?

Enough research has been undertaken over the past fifty years to give answers to such questions. Unfortunately, it is not always possible to put them into practice.

Structure

Two factors in the design of a conservatory affect the amount of light falling on the plants – the roof's framework and its slope.

Since it is the glass that lets in light and the framework that blocks it, the conservatory should have no more than the minimum amount of wood or metal necessary to hold fast the glass and withstand strong winds. A heavy frame can shut out up to half the available light, especially in winter, for when the sun is low in the sky the glazing bars cast very long shadows.

Not all the light that falls on glass passes through it; some is reflected back. How much is reflected – and therefore lost to the plants – depends on the angle at which the sun's rays fall on the glass at different seasons of the year. This is known as the angle of incidence. Maximum sunlight is transmitted through glass if the sun's rays hit it perpendicularly; the light diminishes slowly until the angle of incidence is more than 40 degrees and after that it plummets rapidly. This fact has been known for over 150 years and led the famous John Claudius Loudon to design dome-shaped conservatories, or half-domes if built as a lean-to. Theoretically, a hemisphere is without doubt the ideal conservatory shape, since the sun's rays will hit some areas of the glass vertically at some time of the day, whether winter or summer. But such hemispherical conservatories are totally impractical nowadays, both because of the cost – which even Loudon saw as a drawback – and the incongruity of their appearance when joined to a modern, medium-sized house. Many of today's conservatories are designed with multi-angled roofs on top of vertical walls, especially if they form a mini-wing to the house, but lean-tos usually have a simple sloping roof. The degree of slope is determined more by design and cost rather than concern for its effect on the angle of incidence; generally it will be in the region of 30 degrees. The taller the south-facing wall of the conservatory can be, so much the better, for when the winter sun is low above the horizon its rays hit the glass at a very low (efficient) angle of incidence.

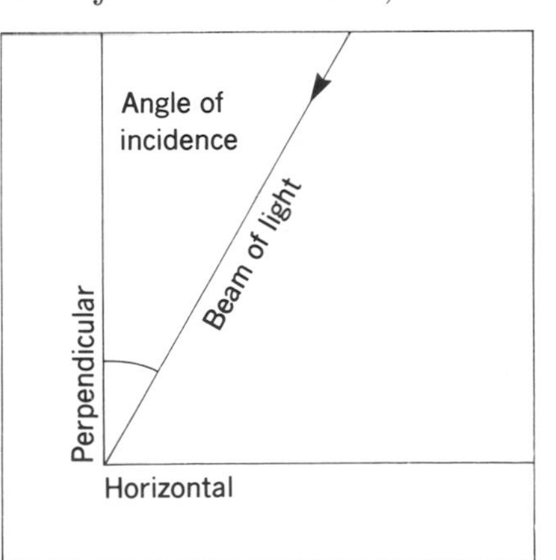

The angle of incidence (above) is the angle made by a beam of light with a line perpendicular to the glass surface at the point of incidence. Light will hit a multi-angled roof (right) at a variety of angles at different times of the day and of the year.

Position of the conservatory

A north-facing lean-to conservatory would be without direct sun for about three months of winter. A lean-to built against a south-facing wall receives most winter sunlight, always assuming that there is no shading from nearby houses or trees. If the south-facing position is impossible, the next best sites are against walls facing south-east to east or south-west to west. These will receive winter sun in either the morning or afternoon. (Whether morning sunlight is stronger than afternoon light at this time of the year is a debatable point.)

The amount of direct sunlight available naturally varies from place to place, and in many parts of northern Europe the sun may be obscured by cloud for up to three-quarters of the day during the three darkest months of winter. The resulting diffused light is far less intense than direct sunlight; in fact, during these three winter months the weakest direct sunlight is stronger than the brightest diffused light. Nonetheless, diffused light is better than none at all and heading the table for light are south-facing conservatories, followed by those on the east and west, with the north-facing site only a little way behind the west.

The great superiority of a south-facing conservatory is based on the assumption that it has a clear view of the southern, south-eastern and south-western skies, with no nearby houses or trees getting in the way. There may be no offending obstruction when the summer sun is high above, but the low winter sun can easily be blotted out. The seriousness of the problem depends on latitude. At 52 degrees latitude N (London) the mean height of the sun during 16 weeks of winter is only 12 degrees above the horizon

Finding a place in the sun

Of the many points to consider when choosing the site for a conservatory, one of the most important is how much light it will receive in winter. This basically depends on which way the conservatory is to face — north, south, east, west or somewhere in between. The more winter sunlight available, the healthier the plants and the lower the heating costs.

Facing south

Facing southwest and southeast

Facing west, east, southwest to west, southeast to east

Facing north and northeast

Colour key to relative amounts of winter sunshine

1. **West-facing wall** *A quite promising position, if for any reason the south-facing wall is not available. Not much winter sun will fall on the roof, but a west-facing conservatory gets good diffused light in the darkest months of the year, and plenty of summer sun in afternoon and evening.*

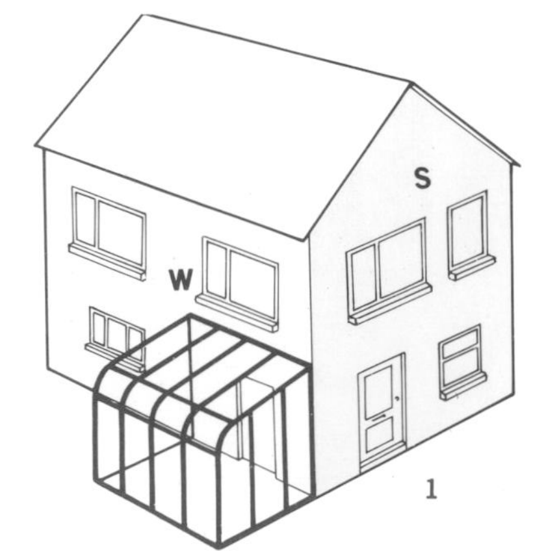

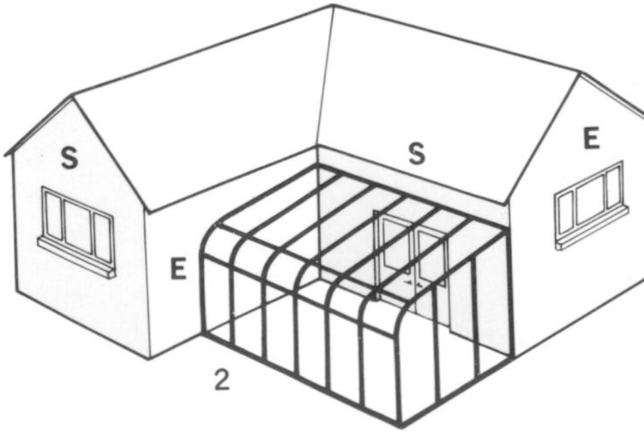

2. **South-facing wall** *The best position for a warm conservatory. As shown here, it would receive good winter sun from south-east and south, though none from the west. In summer it would have western sun until the evening, when the roof of the house would block it out.*

3. **South-east facing wall** *A perfectly good site for a temperate conservatory and reasonable for a warm one, as far as light is concerned. The exposed north-easterly side would increase heating costs in winter.*

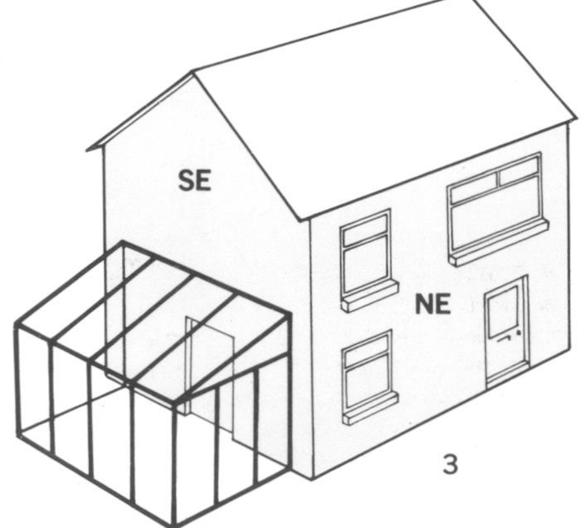

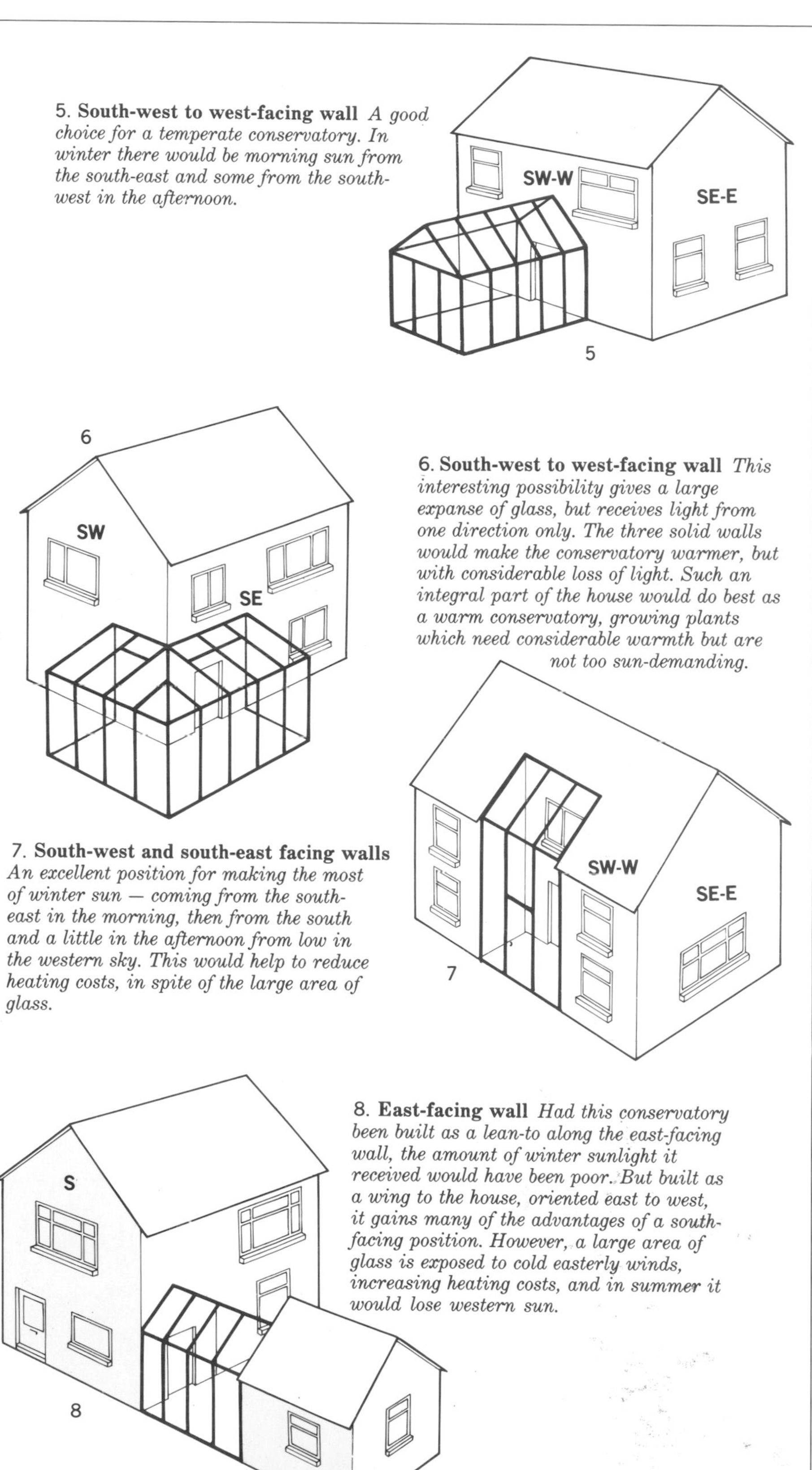

5. **South-west to west-facing wall** *A good choice for a temperate conservatory. In winter there would be morning sun from the south-east and some from the south-west in the afternoon.*

6. **South-west to west-facing wall** *This interesting possibility gives a large expanse of glass, but receives light from one direction only. The three solid walls would make the conservatory warmer, but with considerable loss of light. Such an integral part of the house would do best as a warm conservatory, growing plants which need considerable warmth but are not too sun-demanding.*

7. **South-west and south-east facing walls** *An excellent position for making the most of winter sun — coming from the south-east in the morning, then from the south and a little in the afternoon from low in the western sky. This would help to reduce heating costs, in spite of the large area of glass.*

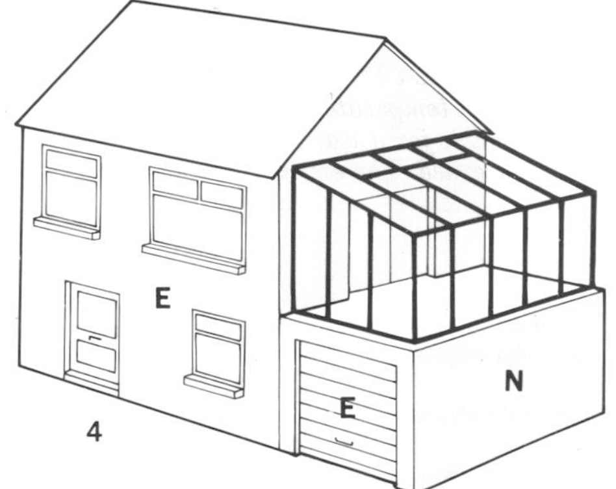

4. **North-facing wall** *This conservatory would be without direct sun for about three months in winter, making it expensive to heat and still short of light. Only a cool conservatory should be considered for such a site, stocked with plants which need a cool winter rest and not much sun in summer.*

8. **East-facing wall** *Had this conservatory been built as a lean-to along the east-facing wall, the amount of winter sunlight it received would have been poor. But built as a wing to the house, oriented east to west, it gains many of the advantages of a south-facing position. However, a large area of glass is exposed to cold easterly winds, increasing heating costs, and in summer it would lose western sun.*

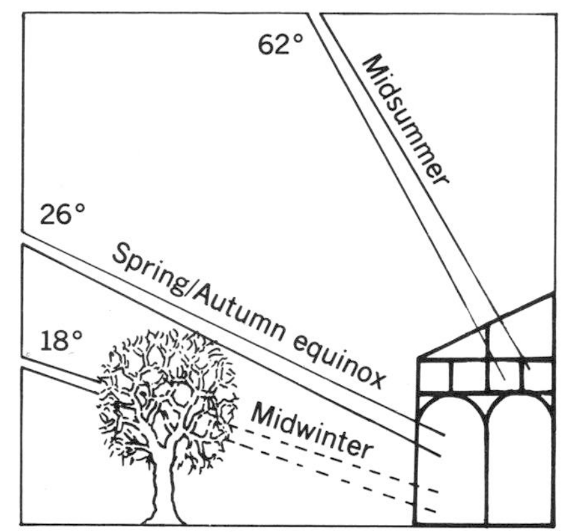

The diagram above shows the elevation of the sun at different times of the year and illustrates how even a bare tree obstructs some winter sun. But the appeal of the conservatory on the left depends far more on the trees framing the panoramic view than on anything that might be grown inside.

(the degree of elevation). In northern Finland, the sun will scarcely rise above the horizon. Conversely, the problem diminishes the further south one travels in the northern hemisphere.

Orientation of the conservatory

A south-facing lean-to is, of course, oriented east-west, which is the best position for winter sunshine. When building a conservatory wing against a west or an east wall, it is best if its length runs east-west. This will transmit more winter light, in spite of the fact that any north-sloping roof is contributing little. On the other hand, a conservatory running north-south will transmit more sun from early spring until autumn – though that is not necessarily the time when you want it most.

The summary below, though necessarily ignoring many of the more complicated factors, indicates the best positions for the three categories of conservatory – cool, temperate and warm.

Cool A cool conservatory *could* be attached almost anywhere to a building, but it deserves the best feasible site. Facing south would give it most light and warmth, reducing further the cost of already low winter heating. A north-facing position should be used only for a cool conservatory, to grow plants accustomed to colder rest periods in winter, when they need less light, and avoiding sun-loving plants in summer. A cool conservatory is basically for summer use by its owners.

Temperate Plants in a temperate conservatory need more winter warmth and light than those in a cool conservatory. Structures facing south, south-east and south-west would be fine and those with more westerly or easterly aspects would be reasonably good. Temperate conservatories can be shared with plants for a large part of the year.

Warm Plants for a warm conservatory need considerable warmth, matched with as much light as possible in winter. Therefore the only suitable sites for a warm conservatory are those with a predominantly southern aspect, preferably facing due south, oriented east-west, and unobstructed. Such a warm conservatory would be a delight to use all year round.

Building regulations

Other considerations may affect the siting and building of a conservatory, whether cool, temperate or warm, but have nothing to do with the angle of incidence, the angle of elevation or the transmission of light through glass. These are planning and building regulations. Each country has its own rules, some of which are stricter than others. The conservatory manufacturer should be able to give help and guidance with any problems.

In England and Wales, planning permission rests with the planning department of the local authority under the Town and Country Planning Act of 1971. For some conservatories and garden rooms built on to a house, permission may not be necessary. Ask your local planning department for a free copy of *Planning Permission: A Guide for Householders*, which gives a general guide as to when permission may or may not be needed. It is as well to check with the authority before making definite commitments, for powers exist to make you move or dismantle any extension which contravenes the Act. If planning permission is needed, many manufacturers will give advice or help in drawing up applications; or if your local builder is erecting the conservatory you can turn to him.

You will certainly need to apply for planning permission if your house is a listed building, or if you live in a flat or maisonette.

You will not need planning permission if the extension to your *house* meets the conditions laid down under the following terms.

Permitted increase in volume An increase is allowed of up to 70 cubic metres or 15 per cent of the original volume of the house (with a maximum of 115 cubic metres), whichever is the greater. If the house is terraced, or is in a conservation area, the permitted increase without need for planning permission is only 50 cubic metres or 10 per cent of the original volume of the house (again with a maximum of 115 metres). These allowances are cut if there has already been an extension to the house.

Permitted increase in area Not more than half the original garden area is to be covered by the existing buildings plus the extension. No part of the extension is to project beyond the front of any part of the house which faces the highway.

Permitted height The extension must be no higher than the highest part of the original house. Any part of the extension within two metres of the boundary of the property must not be higher than four metres.

It is also wise to check the terms

of any lease or tenancy agreement and the deeds of the property, as appropriate, to make certain that there are no restrictions on what you are allowed to do, even with planning permission.

If you live in a flat or maisonette, start by seeking the advice of the planning officer of your local authority.

In Scotland, planning controls are in the hands of the planning department of the district council, which will advise you.

Building regulations in England and Wales are separate from planning controls, and come under the building control department of the local district surveyors. They vary from authority to authority and are of such labyrinthine complexity that they are best unravelled by professionals. The regulations mainly concern how the extension is to be built – questions of safety of the structure, foundations, drains, ventilation and the like. Ignoring or contravening building regulations gives the authority power to make you remove or alter the new building or to impose other penalties. So before starting work you must have building control approval as well as planning permission, where necessary. Building inspectors have powers to inspect the work while it is in progress and to give or withold their approval. (More information on this subject is given in the section on building the conservatory, page 40.)

It is interesting to note that for the purpose of the building regulations, a conservatory is a conservatory only if it has a clear or translucent roof. A solid roof turns it in the eye of the law into a 'habitable room'.

The beauty of surrounding trees and dappled sunlight more than compensates for the shade that requires careful choice of plants in this airy conservatory.

Choosing the conservatory

By the simple use of arched windows this modern lean-to comfortably co-exists with the Victorian house to which it is attached.

Having decided that you would like a conservatory, and having selected the best site for it, you are ready to proceed with choosing a particular type. The basic choices are between conservatories with frames of wood, or of aluminium, or a combination of both.

What kind of material?

Most traditional-looking conservatories are made of wood, although apart from the most expensive, made-to-order conservatories it is only the appearance which is traditional. Others start life as a large assortment of modules so designed that they can be arranged to produce almost any shape and size of structure a customer could want. One recent development has been the use of a computer to design a conservatory from some 300 components in a matter of a few minutes. A Victorian architect might have sweated for weeks to produce the same result.

In many people's eyes timber has more appeal than metal, but it has disadvantages. A framework of wood excludes more light – and therefore radiant heat – than one of slenderer aluminium. Wood is organic and so liable to rot, especially the cheaper sort of softwoods, while hardwoods are expensive. Whatever the wood, it will require more maintenance than aluminium. Traditional-type timber conservatories are often designed to stand on a brick base. The base cuts out much of the view of the garden for people sitting inside and reduces potential light for the plants but, if there is no view worth looking at and people rather than plants are the priority, a base wall does make the interior feel cosier.

Aluminium conservatories are cheaper than good timber ones; they let in more light and need less maintenance, although some people feel that they look too clinical, especially from the outside (inside a profusion of plants can tone down the functional appearance). But when used as a simple lean-to along the whole or most of one side of a house they are hard to fault.

Some combination of wood and aluminium is an excellent idea, making use of some of the advantages of both materials. One effective design incorporates an aluminium framework for the roof. This increases the amount of light entering the conservatory and reduces maintenance costs by cutting out the need to repaint the timber on the roof, the trickiest part to reach. The framework of the sides is of wood, and can be designed to match the style of the house.

More and more manufacturers of greenhouses have turned to building conservatories to meet the rapidly-growing demand, so there are plenty of styles to choose from. Some firms specialize in custom-built timber conservatories, but the cost of these is high. Aluminium conservatories, and most timber ones, are built from prefabricated modules; the permutations and combinations possible in their assembly can therefore produce a structure that the makers are pleased to call 'near custom-built'. Start by writing for manufacturers' catalogues; addresses can be found by buying a few gardening papers. Study the claims with care and some scepticism and beware being seduced by the glossiness of the brochures. Many will leave a lot of questions unanswered and some probing will be necessary – even more than when investing in a car. Manufacturers exhibit at large shows; scrutinize their products and cross-examine the staff.

Here are some guidelines to the kind of information you should be given.

What kind of structure?

Wood It should be hardwood. Of the once-popular hardwoods, teak is now entirely out of the question because of its cost, but mahogany is sometimes offered. Good prefabri-

Materials for today's conservatory

Sections showing three typical examples of modern conservatories, and the various materials most commonly used in their construction.

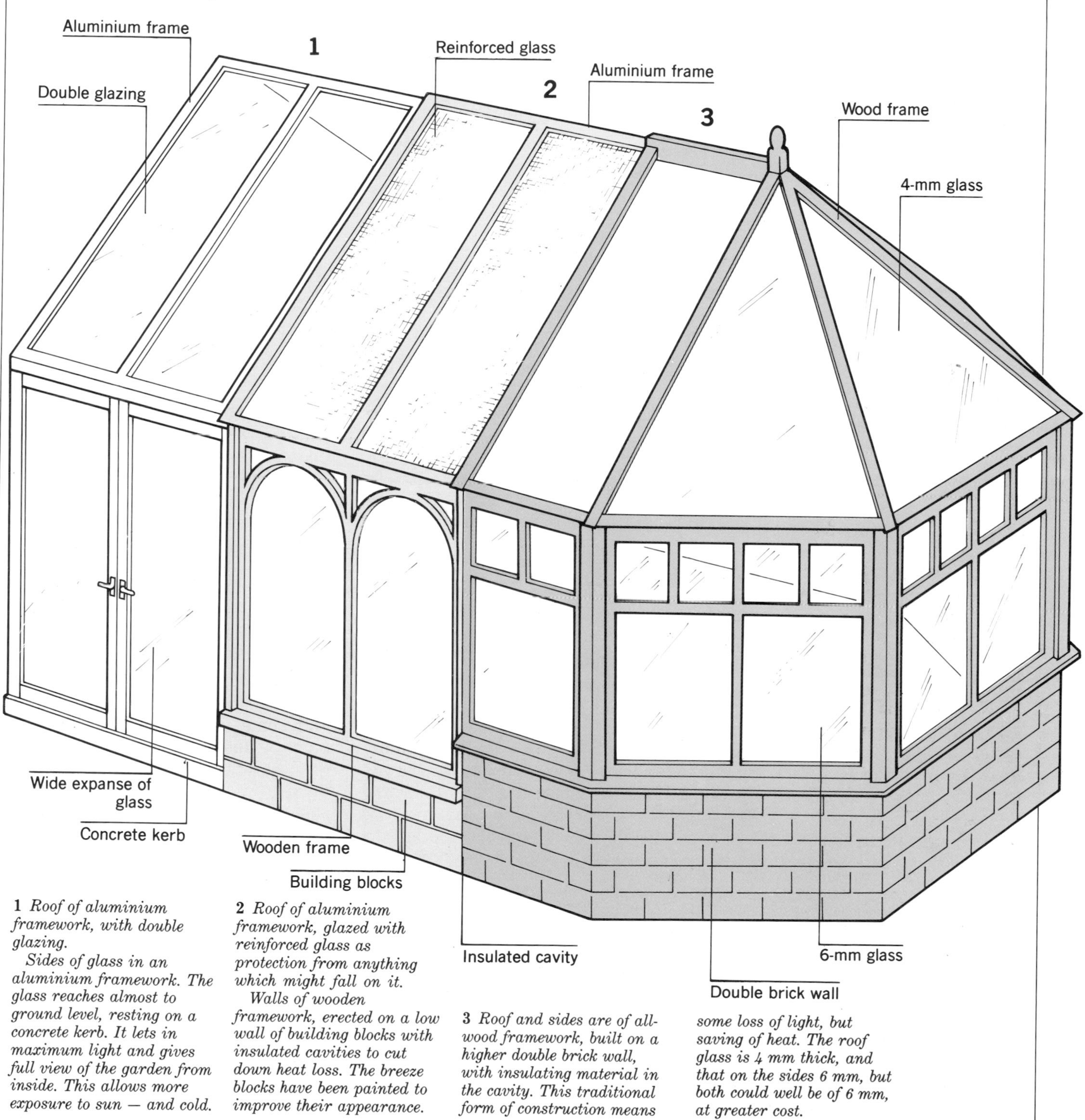

1 *Roof of aluminium framework, with double glazing.*
Sides of glass in an aluminium framework. The glass reaches almost to ground level, resting on a concrete kerb. It lets in maximum light and gives full view of the garden from inside. This allows more exposure to sun — and cold.

2 *Roof of aluminium framework, glazed with reinforced glass as protection from anything which might fall on it.*
Walls of wooden framework, erected on a low wall of building blocks with insulated cavities to cut down heat loss. The breeze blocks have been painted to improve their appearance.

3 *Roof and sides are of all-wood framework, built on a higher double brick wall, with insulating material in the cavity. This traditional form of construction means some loss of light, but saving of heat. The roof glass is 4 mm thick, and that on the sides 6 mm, but both could well be of 6 mm, at greater cost.*

cated wooden conservatories are now likely to be made of Western Red Cedar *(Thuja plicata)* or Scots Pine *(Pinus sylvestris)*. Western Red Cedar, while not a particularly strong wood and therefore not the best for very large structures, is quite suitable for a domestic conservatory. Whatever anyone claims, it is not indefinitely durable outdoors, even when treated with a preservative and it will need treating again every four to five years. The chief wood to avoid is whitewood, the timber of Norway Spruce *(Picea abies)*. It is only moderately strong and not resistant to damp.

Is the conservatory structurally sound? Whether made of wood or aluminium, it should have been built to comply with building regulations, but it is best to check.

Glass Ordinary horticultural glass as used for small greenhouses and frames is only 3 mm thick. Glass 4 mm thick is often used for conservatories, but 6 mm glass is better for doors and for long panes of glass on the sides. Where there is a risk of slates or tiles falling onto the roof of a lean-to, wire-reinforced glass may be advisable. Sealed double glazing units add to the capital outlay but reduce heating costs. An alternative form of double glazing involves fitting two separate pieces of glass on top of each other. One piece is ordinary 3 mm flat glass, and above it is laid a piece of patented 'Hortisave 34' glass, moulded to create a cushion of air between the two sheets. The transmission of light is slightly reduced, but the heat lost through it may be 30 per cent less than with single glass. If the glazing bars are suitable, the moulded glass may be added to existing flat glass.

To cut down glare from the sun, various types of glass are available. These include rough cast glass, anti-sun glazing and solar control glass. They will not necessarily make other shading devices superfluous, however.

Opposite: Small conservatory perched on a ground floor extension blends with the old brick of a town house. Above: Popular style of aluminium and glass-to-ground lean-to, set against a spick-and-span red-brick suburban house.

Glazing bars hold the glass in place. Those made of aluminium are narrower than wooden bars and so keep out less light. They are also easier to glaze. Ingenious clips hold the glass in place, whereas with most wooden bars the glass is secured by metal sprigs and putty, which deteriorates. When metal bars are used, the glass may be bedded into strips of mastic or neoprene (a synthetic rubber) to avoid direct contact with the glass and so reduce the risk of breakage or, for the same reason, the edge of the glass may be covered with plastic.

If the sides of the conservatory have a wooden framework, the glass may be held in place by hardwood beading.

Bases Unless it is built of glass to ground level, the conservatory will need some kind of low base wall. Always choose bricks rather than wood. Wood near ground level is particularly exposed to rain and rot, especially alongside a path from which falling rain bounces up. To keep a wooden base clean involves constant washing and, to preserve it, constant painting. A brick base, which weathers rather than rots, can also keep a conservatory warmer. If possible, choose a double wall with insulating material in the cavity; or alternatively a wall of building blocks with insulated cavities. The blocks can be painted on the outside to make them more attractive. The width of the walls will decide the width of the foundations.

Will it give adequate ventilation? Building regulations require that a minimum amount of ventilation must be allowed for. If a room in the house leads directly into the conservatory then the area of ventilation must be one-twentieth (5 per cent) of the combined floor area of the room and the conservatory. It is better to be more generous than that, for the plants may need more ventilation than the law demands. (See the section on ventilation, page 48.)

Erecting the conservatory

The structural problems may have been dealt with, but there are still questions to ask about preparing the site, laying the foundations, erecting the framework and glazing it.

Queries for the manufacturer

Will the manufacturer excavate and lay the foundations? Some manufacturers do; many will not. If they do not oblige, the alternative is a local builder, either recommended by them or chosen yourself. The manufacturer will help with information about the foundations needed and may advise on planning and building applications, together with drawings required for submission to the local authority. Building permission usually goes through the bureaucratic machine faster than planning permission, but you must wait for both; changes in the plans may be asked for.

You might, of course, think of doing the excavating yourself, but having removed soil to a depth of some 10 in (25 cm) over the whole of the area, and from trenches 24 in (60 cm) deep or more for the foundations, you will be left with an enormous mound of earth to dispose of. If you then thought of laying the floor and the foundations, you would be advised to think twice about it, unless you are an extremely experienced handyman. Before any concreting is done, water and gas pipes and electric cables have to be laid; these are jobs strictly for professionals.

Furthermore, there are important building regulations to comply with at this stage. Any drain under the site has first to be exposed, so that local building control inspectors can look at it if they wish. Only then may it be buried again, this time protected by a layer of concrete, before the floor is laid over it. Any manhole within the conservatory must be moved or raised to the level of the new floor and fitted with a watertight and airtight cover. Air bricks on the house wall may have to be moved. The damp course of the house must not be covered.

The do-it-yourselfer also often has problems in getting the foundations dead level, and a perfect level is essential for a mainly glass structure. The framework of a conservatory, whether metal or glass, has a considerable amount of 'give' and needs the glass to firm it up. A classic demonstration of this fact occurred in 1827, when an enormous domed conservatory was being built at Bretton Hall in Yorkshire. Loudon records that when the ironwork was in place, but before glazing, 'the slightest wind put the whole of it in motion from the base to the summit' to the great alarm of a Mrs Beaumont for whom it was being built. 'As soon as the glass was put in it was found to be perfectly strong and firm.' But if the modules of a modern conservatory are laid on to uneven foundations or base, the framework will be distorted and the glass will simply not fit. Laying the foundations is therefore another job best left to an expert.

Will the manufacturer erect the conservatory? Some will (there will be extra erection charges), and some will not. Again the best alternative is a local builder, for although some of the work may be simple for two pairs of hands, there are several tricky operations. These include making waterproof the abutment against the wall, which becomes doubly difficult if there are soil or down pipes in the way. A builder could also be responsible for any brick base or alterations necessary for making an entrance from the house into the conservatory.

Will the manufacturer glaze the conservatory? Some do, and include it in the quoted cost. Others will charge extra. Some advise using a local builder, while some insist it is child's play and can be done by anyone. In fact, manufacturers are much more likely to be willing to glaze their conservatories than to prepare sites or erect the structures. Since glazing is the key to keeping out the rain and keeping in the heat, the more

Left: It is best to use a reputable builder for all but the simplest of conservatories. However, some manufacturers will do the all-important glazing.

obvious it is that it should be done professionally. Moreover, having professionals responsible for all the operations means that you are relieved of the bother of dealing with planning and building controls.

What makes a good finish for the floor? The concrete slab which is laid along with the foundations is hard and impervious, as a conservatory floor should be, but is hardly attractive. Brick paviors or quarry tiles laid on top of the concrete are equally impervious and hard-wearing, but you may prefer tiles of a colour other than red. Whatever the colour, choose ceramic tiles which are non-slip, and plain rather than those with a pattern, since the early attraction of the pattern may soon pall. Vinyl tiles are a perfectly acceptable alternative. Walking on them makes less clatter than on ceramic tiles; they are also cheaper, but choose the best quality so that they will last.

What exactly does the price include and what are extras? This final, and most important, question to the manufacturer should be answered in writing.

What will it cost? There is one query that only you can answer – whether or not you can afford the conservatory you have chosen. If you need help with finance you can turn to a building society for a mortgage, or to a bank for a home improvement loan. No general rules apply but building societies at most times would look favourably on an advance for a conservatory if it is an extension to a house already mortgaged with them. Bank home improvement loans are more expensive than building society mortgages and ten years is the general length of the term of a loan. If the bank had already given a mortgage on the house your application would probably be looked on favourably, but the question of whether the improvement would add as much to the value of the house as it had cost would also be taken into account.

Flooring should be not only attractive, like these flagstones, but also hard wearing and impervious to water.

Florid designs on the floor soon pall. Above are three suitable materials – vinyl (top), wood coated with polyurethane (left) and ceramic tiles (right). Carrying the floor pattern through to a patio (far right) gives a feeling of greater space.

Heating

It is always warmer inside a conservatory than it is outside. On a cold winter's night the difference may be only a degree or two. But on a hot summer afternoon the difference in temperature can make the conservatory intolerably hot.

The reason why the air inside is warmer is simple. Glass allows through a large part of the short waves radiating from the sun (both light and heat) but keeps in the long-wave heat rays which are given off by anything under 212°F (100°C). The incoming short waves warm the soil, walls, plants and other solid objects in the conservatory; but when these objects start losing heat, the long waves given off cannot pass straight through the glass – so the temperature of the air inside rises. This happens both when the sunlight is direct and – to a lesser extent – when the light is diffused. As already explained in the section on siting (see page 31), an east-west oriented conservatory lets in most light in winter. It therefore also traps more radiant heat and this can be of significant help in cutting heating costs. Another contribution to warmth can be supplied from the wall of a lean-to, through which heat from the house escapes and is trapped in the conservatory.

Of course, some heat is lost by conduction through the glass, or simply by escaping, since no building is airtight and a conservatory should certainly not be. The rate of heat loss depends largely on the surface area of the building, the difference between the temperature inside and outside, and the strength of the wind. Before thinking about how to heat a conservatory, therefore, think first about how to keep heat loss to a minimum, to save both on capital and running costs of heating.

A verdant dinner on a balmy summer night. But a well-heated conservatory affords this pleasure in winter too.

Reducing heat loss

The smaller the conservatory, the more expensive it is to heat in relation to the floor space it gives you; for the surface area of the glass, through which heat is lost, is high in relation to the ground area. To cut down in size, therefore, is not the simple answer it might seem. Unit costs drop as the surface area decreases in relation to the ground area.

Insulation Insulation can achieve a positive cut in the actual cost of heating. The double glazing of glass surfaces on the sides and roof can reduce heat loss by up to 40 per cent compared with single glazing. But there are drawbacks. It will cost some 40 per cent more than single glazing and, being heavier, will need a more substantial and more expensive framework if used on the roof. Double glazing also lets through rather less light. Many common or garden greenhouses are insulated in winter by lining the glass with polythene film, the cellular type giving better results than single sheet film. This cuts the light entering the greenhouse by at least 20 per cent. Other objections to film are that by reducing ventilation it may also cause condensation and that it impedes the view from inside, which is hardly desirable in a conservatory.

If the conservatory has solid base walls, of brick or wood, these could be insulated by covering the inside wall with ½in (13mm) thick polystyrene sheeting. An alternative is to erect another interior false wall, filling the cavity between with insulating material. Or the conservatory base could be built of 9in (23cm) blocks with a built-in cavity that could be filled with insulating material.

Some heat is lost through the floor. When laying the concrete floor base, spread ¾in (19mm) thick polystyrene immediately under the damp course. This will prevent much heat from escaping into the soil below. As the temperature in the conservatory falls during the night, the heat stored in the floor during the day will be given out into the building.

Protection from wind A strong wind on a cold day causes far greater heat loss than on a day which is just as cold but calm. As a long-term project, a quick-growing windbreak of trees could be planted on the exposed side of the house. Plant far enough away from the conservatory so that winter sun is not obscured. This will mitigate heat loss and also help reduce the risk of gale damage. Multiply by four times the probable eventual height of the trees, and this gives you the distance at which they must be planted from the conservatory. If that is not possible, forget the idea.

Which form of heating?

Whatever steps you take to cut down heat loss, heat has to be generated in the first place. How is it to be provided? One of the early methods tried was a hot bed, in which heat for the plants came from the fermenting manure among which they were planted. In the earliest lean-to glasshouses, of the 17th century, the rotting dung was piled against the back wall. Neither method is now practicable – through general shortage of dung – or appropriate for a conservatory (although anyone with a herd of cattle could manufacture methane gas and have a marvellous fertilizer as residue). Developments since those early days have included open fires or stoves in the building itself; stoves underneath it; and ducts under the floor carrying hot air and smoke from furnaces. The smoke flues lasted into the 19th century, but from the 1820s they were overtaken by hot water systems. Coal was then the only fuel, yet now it would be the last choice, if only because of the labour involved in stoking and clearing out the ashes. Today mains gas, if available, is the obvious choice on grounds of convenience and cost, though the price is always rising. If there is no gas supply, oil is an alternative. Electricity, though the most convenient, is now ruled out for most people because of the prodigious cost.

Gas If the house itself has gas central heating and if the central heating boiler has spare capacity, by far the best arrangement is to extend the system to the conservatory. However, the conservatory must be on a separate piping circuit, direct from the boiler, to run it independently of the time and thermostat controls in the house. This is because heating must be kept on for the plants in the conservatory even if it is turned off in the house. Night heating need not be as high as in the daytime, but the temperature must never fall below the minimum the plants need. The conservatory should therefore have a separate thermostatic control, and if that can be reset in the house – lower at night and higher in the morning – it will save having to trail out to the conservatory to do it. Even this routine can be avoided by installing in the conservatory (at some expense) an electronic thermostat with an extremely sensitive temperature sensor, plus a light sensor which, when night falls, switches the thermostat to a chosen lower temperature.

If the boiler in the house has no spare capacity, or if you prefer it, a small gas boiler can be installed in the conservatory with a balanced flue outside and pumped hot water circulation through small bore pipes. Modern types are unobtrusive and around 70 per cent efficient (allowing for heat lost through the flue). There are flueless heaters which use piped natural gas (methane) or bottled gas (propane). Since they have no flues, none of the heat is simply lost to the outside air.

Though cold and bare outdoors on this early spring morning, inside there is warmth enough to linger over breakfast and the Sunday papers.

They are comparatively cheap to buy and run (although bottled gas will be dearer than natural) and there are few installation costs.

Gas heaters have become popular for small greenhouses, but they have drawbacks. They do not give such an even distribution of heat as can be achieved with a circulating hot water system. The burning gas produces a lot of moisture, and humidity in the conservatory can become too high and cause condensation. Although neither methane nor propane gives off carbon monoxide when burning, both release nitrogen oxides and a build-up of these can seriously damage plants. Increased ventilation will avoid condensation and pollution, but with consequent loss of heat, which may equal that lost via a flue.

Oil An oil-fired boiler heating a hot water system is the best choice if mains gas is not available. If the house is already heated by oil it may be possible to extend the system to the conservatory. As with gas, a separate circuit will be necessary so that the conservatory can be heated independently of the house.

If a separate oil boiler has to be installed it should be sited in a building adjoining, but not inside, the conservatory. A storage tank will also be needed and is subject to building regulations. Installation costs for oil are therefore higher than for gas.

Flueless paraffin heaters are used in small greenhouses, but are not to be recommended for conservatories. They cannot be automatically controlled and, when adjusting the flame, you have to forecast what the weather is likely to be until you can attend to the heater again. They need constant refilling and there are also problems of condensation from the water vapour produced by burning paraffin and of pollution from sulphur dioxide.

Electricity is clean, efficient, easily controllable and prohibitively ex-

pensive. Electric tubular heaters were once popular for small greenhouses because they were cheap to buy, but now they are costly to run. The tubes themselves are far hotter than hot water pipes, making the areas immediately around them very much warmer than elsewhere. Fan heaters have become popular in recent years, both inside the house and in greenhouses and conservatories. They can indeed produce a considerable stream of heat, but it is not well distributed and any plants in the direct flow of hot air will be dehydrated. It is essential to buy a model specially designed and heavily insulated for use in a more humid environment than is found in a room in the house.

A fan heater usually has a fitted thermostat, but this is unlikely to be very accurate. Replacing it with a more reliable rod-type thermostat is a sound investment.

In spite of its drawbacks a fan heater is excellent for briefly boosting the temperature of the conservatory for the benefit of human occupants. With the heating elements switched off, the fan can also help to cool the air in summer but must not blow on to the plants.

As always, treat electricity with great caution. Installing electric cables and fittings in a conservatory is a job for professionals.

How much heat?

How much artificial heat each conservatory may require to bring it into the cool, temperate or warm categories depends on many variables – including latitude, altitude, orientation, and exposure to wind. It cannot be decided by guesswork – that way you could easily instal an appliance which cannot cope, or something with an output far beyond what you would want in even the severest weather. Seeking expert advice before buying a heating system is essential, but there is a formula by which you can roughly assess the conservatory's needs. The equation is:

> Heat requirement (in British thermal units per hour or Btu/h) is equal to the exposed surface area in square feet (roof, sides, ends) multiplied by the difference in degrees Fahrenheit between the inside and outside temperatures divided by 1.4 Btu/h (the assumed average rate of loss of heat per square foot).

On the other hand, you may prefer to leave such calculations to your heating engineer expert, and you could well be right. Getting this sum correct is the first vital step in choosing a heating appliance.

A conservatory for the future: solar panels collect heat to warm the whole house in this energy-saving home in Suffolk, designed by the owner. Heat from the panels is conveyed by a duct to the heat pump (left) which feeds the domestic heating.

A wing conservatory, with its larger area of glass, loses more heat than a lean-to of the same size, and so costs more to heat.

Temperature checking

Many thermostats controlling boilers have an unacceptably high margin of error, adding considerably to fuel costs. A rod type thermostat, though not the cheapest, is the best for conservatory use. As a check on the performance of the boiler and the efficacy of the thermostat, a reliable thermometer is essential. Choose a maximum and minimum thermometer to mark – and keep – a daily record of how high the temperature rises by day and how cold it becomes when you are in bed. On cold winter nights an unreliable thermostat could let the temperature fall too low; if you discover this margin of error, readjust the thermostat accordingly. Traditional maximum and minimum thermometers have to be reset by magnets which tend to get mislaid, but convenient push-button models are only a little more expensive.

Among the plethora of gardening equipment and gadgetry on offer are two items concerning temperature which may not be top priority. One is a device which claims to warn you of approaching frost several hours ahead. Another sets alarm bells ringing when the temperature in the conservatory rises higher or falls lower than you want – just the thing to wake you in the middle of a cold winter's night.

Ventilation

Whereas in winter the problem is to keep the conservatory warm, in summer the difficulty may be to keep it cool enough – both for the health of the plants and the comfort of people. On a summer's day when the sun beats down from a clear sky, the conservatory rapidly becomes unbearably hot, as heat waves are increasingly trapped inside. Plants transpire through their leaves, losing water more rapidly than their roots can replace it, and they wilt and collapse. Similarly, humans sweat and wilt, though seldom as dramatically.

Since heat rises, provision must be made for it to escape through the roof and for cooler air to be drawn in from ground level, creating the so-called 'chimney effect'. This circulation of air is the more gentle indoor version of a breeze outdoors.

Keeping fresh air moving inside the conservatory is important for two other reasons. During daylight hours the leaves of plants absorb carbon dioxide from the air; this is essential for the process of photosynthesis by which plants manufacture their food. Only minute amounts of carbon dioxide are present in the air and there is a danger when the air is stagnant that the supply of carbon dioxide around the plant will gradually be used up and the rate of photosynthesis slowed down. Lack of ventilation on warm days also increases relative humidity in the conservatory, and moist, *still* air is the perfect environment for fungal disease. High relative humidity is likely to cause condensation on the glass as the temperature falls in the evening.

The importance of ventilation in keeping plants healthy has been increasingly recognized in recent years, but many conservatories and greenhouses are still grossly underventilated. The smaller they are – with large glass surface areas in proportion to the ground area – the better ventilation is needed. Remember also that building regulations stipulate that, when a conservatory leads straight into a room in the house, both are treated as one room for the purposes of ventilation, with the minimum ventilation area not less than one-twentieth of the combined floor area. This may still leave the conservatory under-ventilated and it is better to provide for ventilation well above the minimum, even if a few of the ventilators seldom need to be opened during cool summers.

The natural escape route for hot air is through the top of the structure, and is provided by roof ventilators. The more exposed to sun the conservatory is, the more roof ventilators are needed, maybe one every 4 to 5 feet (1 to 1.5 m) depending on the width of the modules from which the conservatory is built. So that the heat can readily escape, the ventilators should be constructed to open at least as far as a horizontal position.

Automatic controls

Opening and closing roof ventilators by hand is by far the most time-consuming and boring operation in looking after a conservatory and is therefore frequently over-

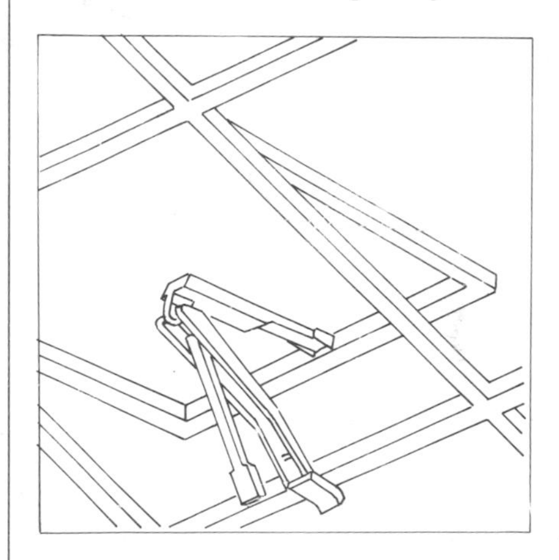

The comfort of occupants (and building regulations) demands adequate ventilation in a conservatory. Cool air enters the building near ground level and hot air escapes through roof ventilators. These can be operated by hand or automated by a device (as above), activated by temperature changes.

looked. Fortunately, the job can be done automatically with greater efficiency but without great cost. Banks of ventilators in large-scale glasshouses are operated by electric motors controlled by a thermostat, but this method is too expensive, distractingly noisy and ugly for a home conservatory. Instead there is a simple device, a fairly unobtrusive and silent autovent fitted to each roof ventilator and operated by the heat of the sun alone. Some types are activated by a cylinder containing mineral jelly, which expands and contracts with different temperatures, operating a lever arm to open or close the ventilator. A few are operated by contracting and expanding metal springs. Each ventilator can be pre-set to open and close within a range of temperatures. There is a limit to the weight of glass that the device can cope with; a large model could manage up to 30 pounds (13.5 kg), but many can operate only half that weight. Such devices are not expensive and are often offered as extras, already fitted, when a conservatory is ordered. They are simple to fit to existing ventilators. Being operated by the sun they cost nothing to run, and very little can go wrong. They should certainly top the list of automatic equipment for the conservatory.

Moving air is cooler than stagnant air, but modern electric fans can cause harmful draughts; the leisurely fan in the conservatory above is more acceptable. Opposite: Louvred windows allow hot air to escape.

How to provide for incoming fresh air at ground level depends on the construction of the conservatory. If it is built on a brick or wooden base you can use box ventilators with sliding panels which can be closed. If the conservatory has glass to ground level, use louvred panel ventilators. These can also be operated by autovents similar to

those for roof ventilators. Many conventional-looking wooden conservatories have windows which open at waist level. These are not the most effective way of ventilating the conservatory from the plants' point of view, although they may pass muster with humans.

It is quite possible that on some hot summer days the 'chimney effect' alone cannot change the air rapidly enough to cool the conservatory down; at times a change of air once a minute, or even more frequently, may be necessary. The flow of air can be boosted by an electric fan, either permanently fixed above head height and switched on by thermostatic control, or by a portable fan placed so that it is not blowing directly on the plants. Alternatively, and more effectively, instal an extractor fan high in the side of the conservatory to remove the hot air.

There remains one more obvious way of increasing air circulation – leaving doors open (and door areas are included in the minimum requirements laid down in building regulations). The snag is that if you are not in the conservatory to keep an eye on things, the doors will be wide open also to insects, pests, birds, cats and sudden changes of weather.

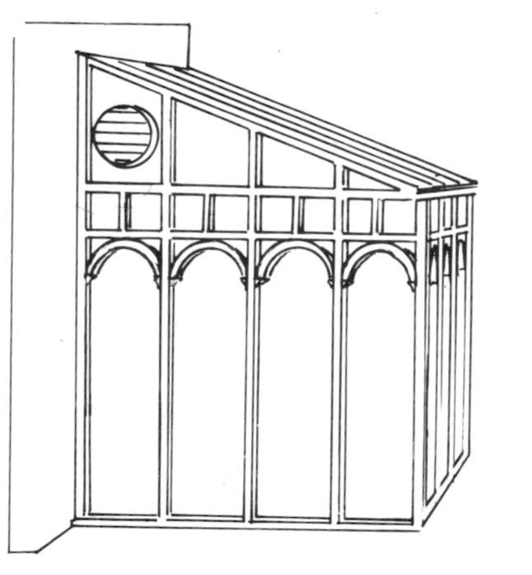

Forcing hot air out. An extractor fan draws out hot air more rapidly than a simple open ventilator.

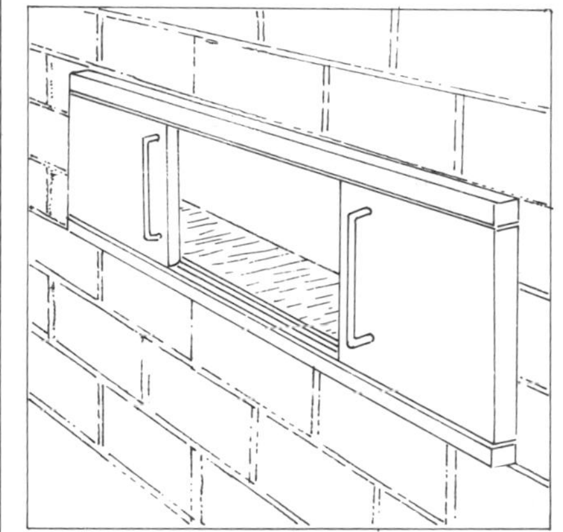

Letting cool air in. Box ventilator in brickwork base, to be opened and shut according to need.

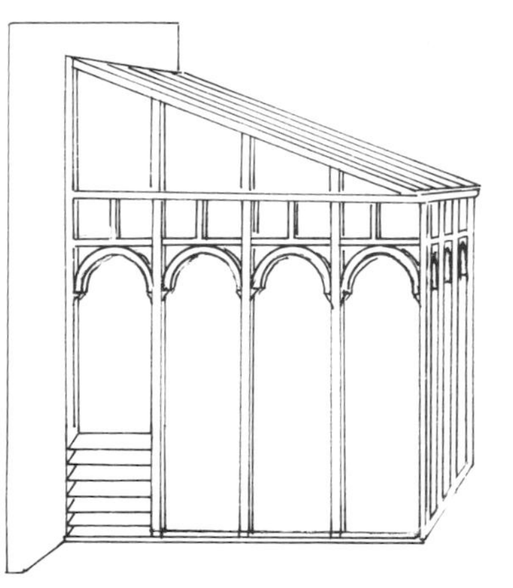

Letting cool air in. Glass louvred window at ground level; this can be automated, like roof ventilators.

Keeping the conservatory cool

Sun beating down on the glass can quickly make the conservatory too hot for plants and people. Adequate ventilation and shading must be provided.

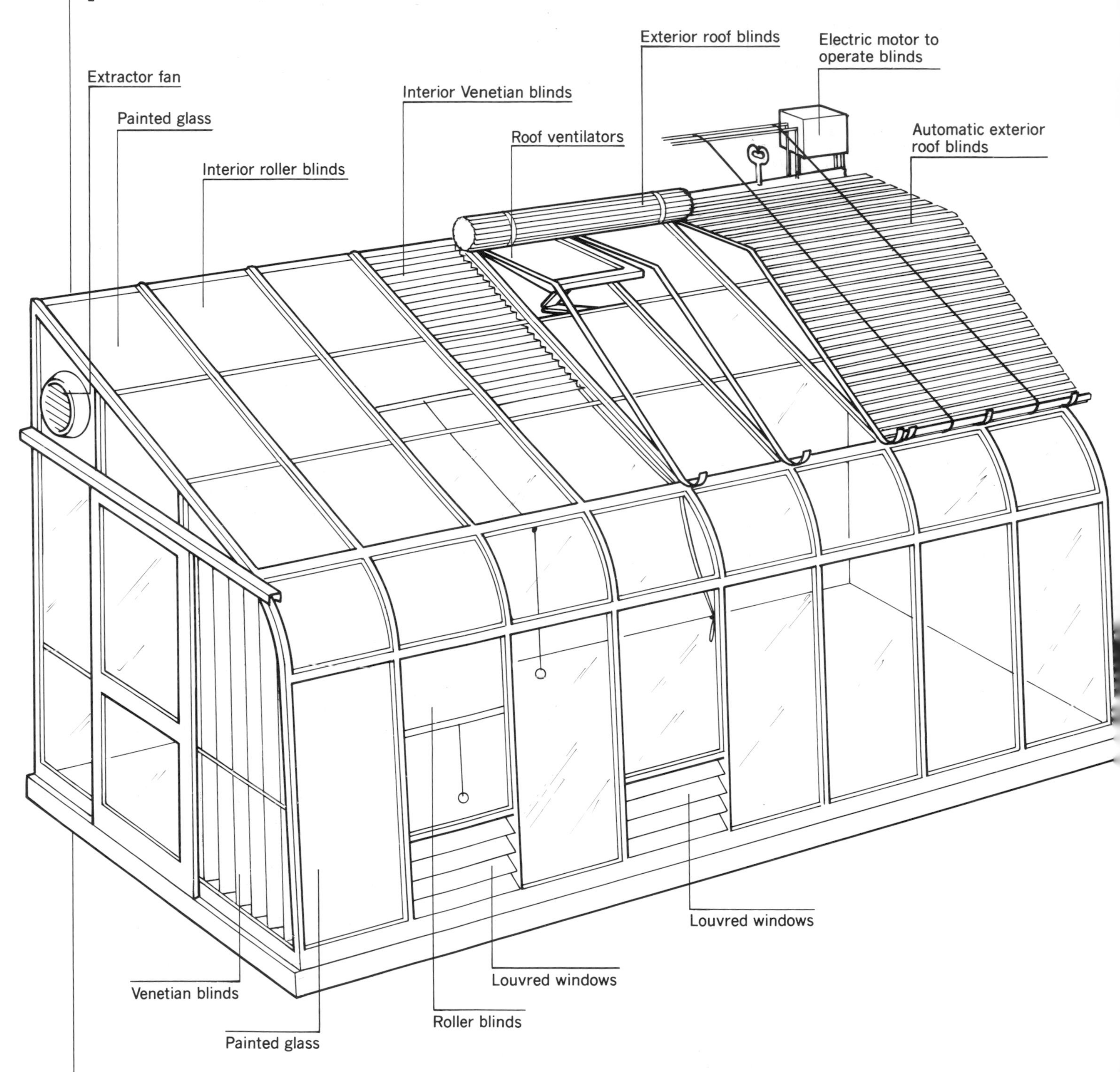

Shading

VENTILATION *Cool air enters near ground level by the louvred windows spaced along the length of the conservatory. As the air warms it rises and escapes through the roof ventilators, one every 4–5 ft (1.2–1.5 m) along the roof. Louvred windows and roof ventilators which open automatically as the temperature rises are available. The natural 'chimney effect' circulation can be assisted by an extractor fan placed near the apex of the conservatory.*

SHADING THE ROOF *There is a wide choice. Painting the glass for the summer is cheap and simple, but cuts out valuable light on dull days. Spring roller blinds fitted inside the roof are inexpensive, but the drawback is that they have to be operated by hand. The more expensive interior Venetian blinds can be automated so that the angle of the slats is altered to shut out or let in the sun. Exterior roof blinds block out more heat than blinds inside, but have drawbacks. Some have to be operated by hand. Others are automatically worked by an electric motor which has to be housed on the roof.*

SHADING THE SIDES *The glass walls of the conservatory can be painted, shaded by roller blinds or by Venetian blinds with white translucent vertical slats.*

Internal blinds are a better way of subduing fierce sun than painting the glass. Many are made either of plastic net or pinoleum fabric.

The more effective that ventilation is in keeping the conservatory cool in summer, the less there is need for shading to shut out the sun. Even so, some shading may be necessary both to supplement the ventilation and to protect plants from exposure to direct scorching sun. The need will be greatest in a conservatory facing south or west.

Unfortunately, while ventilation can easily be controlled automatically to respond to changes in temperature, automatic shading to react to varying intensities of light is more cumbersome and expensive. Eventually the solution may be to use glass treated like spectacle lenses, which darkens according to the brightness of the sun. But this is not yet available. For now we can 'paint' the glass to exclude some of the sunlight, or use blinds inside or outside the conservatory (some blinds can be operated automatically). Neither of these choices is without drawbacks.

Painting the glass is the cheapest and simplest shading method. Shading compounds may be powders or liquids which, after mixing with water, are painted or sprayed on to the glass. Choose a white compound rather than a green one because white surfaces reflect heat, whereas dark surfaces absorb it. The compound should not be applied before late spring and should be removed by early autumn; for the rest of the year the plants will need all the light they can get. While the 'paint' is admirably efficient on bright, hot days, on the many dull days of summer it shuts out light. This inherent drawback is somewhat minimized by using a liquid compound called 'Vari-shade', which is white and opaque when dry but translucent

Imaginative shading can add to the attractiveness of a conservatory. Light filters gently through fluted open-weave fabric (left). Other styles include lively awning-type blinds (above) and Venetian blinds (above top); the angle of the slats controls the light entering.

when wet, so at least on dull days when it is raining, more light is let in.

Interior blinds are certainly effective in shutting out light, but less so in keeping the conservatory cool, because heat has already passed through the glass before encountering the blinds. The cheapest roller blinds are made of plastic and are usually an unnatural green, a colour which fails to make the blind more efficient and spreads a ghastly hue over plants and humans. A pale linen blind would reflect more light and look more attractive. Such blinds are virtually impossible to automate and on days of alternating sun and showers, either the tedious chore of frequently lowering and hoisting the blinds by hand has to be faced or, more probably, neglected. The more expensive slatted Venetian roof blinds are more easily automated. Instead of having to be let down and raised, all that is needed is to alter the angle of the slats. This can be done with an electric motor, controlled by a photoelectric cell or a thermostat.

Watering

Exterior blinds, if fixed about 9 in (23 cm) above the glass, prove far better than interior blinds since they block out sunlight before it hits the glass. If they must be operated by hand they may be as much of a chore, or more, than interior blinds, but they can be automated. Automation does not exclude other drawbacks, however. An exterior blind, even when fixed well above the glass, does restrict the opening width of the ventilators. Also, the blinds are fitted on metal runners, therefore permanently adding to the amount of light already blocked out by the framework of the roof. While slatted blinds of wood can look quite attractive, the motor and other associated fittings perched on the top of the roof hardly add to the conservatory's aesthetic appeal. That, as well as the cost, is the penalty to be paid for the benefit of a labour-saving device.

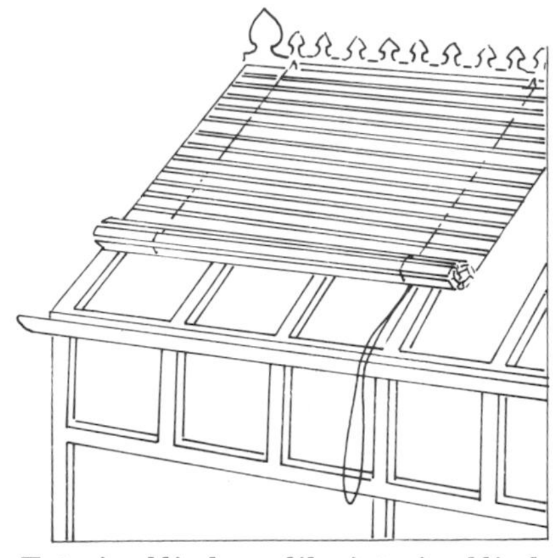

Exterior blinds, unlike interior blinds, intercept the heat of the sun before it hits the glass.

Shading the sides Depending on the siting of the conservatory, some shading of the sides as well as the roof may be desirable, although probably more for the comfort of people than the plants. Venetian blinds with white translucent vertical slats are the answer. No more hardship is involved in manipulating these by hand if the sun's glare becomes excessive than in drawing curtains inside the house.

On everything a little rain must fall, except, of course, on plants growing under glass. They therefore have to be watered and at times this can be a great burden. In commercial glasshouses automation has taken over from the watering-can – inevitably, to cut labour costs. But automation, however useful in heating and ventilating the conservatory, is basically both unsuitable and impractical for watering the plants in it, just as it is for houseplants in a living room. The obvious advantages of watering by hand are that a plant receives individual attention and can be given just the amount of water you judge it needs. Plants can also be placed where they look most pleasing, instead of being regimented to conform to a watering system with its unprepossessing paraphernalia of trays, tubing and cisterns.

There are three main types of 'automatic' watering systems in use – capillary, trickle and spray.

Capillary watering For this system, plant pots are grouped in plastic trays, standing on plastic matting which is kept permanently wet either from a cistern or by hand. (An alternative to matting is wet sand.) As the compost in the pot is used up by the plant and dries out, water is drawn up from the matting by capillary action. The system works best with plastic pots which have many holes in the base in close contact with the matting. If a clay pot is used, a capillary wick must be pushed into the drainage hole, with the other end pressed against the matting. It is clear that this method cannot be used if the pots are within another, less utilitarian, container. Algae may build up on the matting, which will have to be scrubbed.

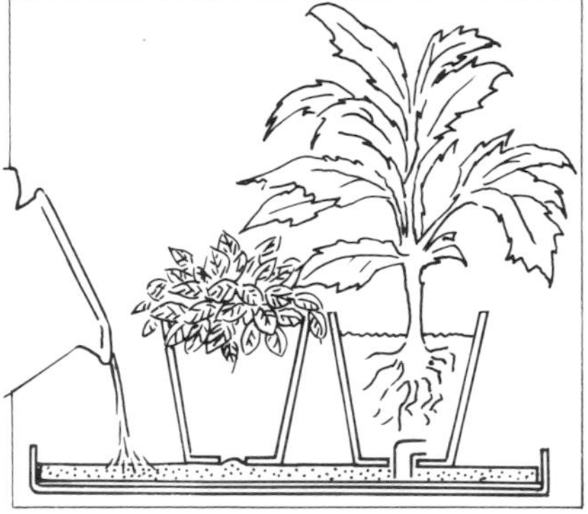

Plants draw up water from wet capillary matting lining their trays.

The idea behind this system is that the plant always has an adequate supply of water, but not an excessive amount. For the majority of plants, however, it is preferable if the compost dries out a little between waterings, a cycle which ensures a better supply of air to the roots to provide the vital oxygen. Nonetheless, capillary matting is the best simple way of leaving plants to water themselves.

Trickle irrigation By this system a trickle of water is fed to each pot through a network of very small bore tubing. The rate of flow can be adjusted and may be automated so as to turn on for shorter or longer periods, depending on your judgment of the weather. The built-in drawback is that whatever the rate of flow, each pot will receive the same amount of water. On a commercial scale this is acceptable enough if you are growing, say, two hundred tomato plants in similar conditions, but in a conservatory with a mixed bag of plants some will inevitably get too much water and some too little; nor are the plastic tubes worming their way round the plants a pretty sight.

Spray lines These are perforated pipes, slung from the roof, for overhead watering of plants. Although fine for commercial glasshouses they are unsuitable for conservatories, unless you have a penchant for damp floors.

The art of watering

The method left is watering by hand, and there is no denying that this can be as repetitively burdensome as making beds, cleaning the car or taking the dog for a walk. But if you choose to have a bed, car or dog you must do these things and, if you choose to have living (not plastic) plants around you, they have to be watered. Since watering must be done it is worthwhile knowing how to do it, for there is also no denying that some people's watering can be as indiscriminatingly lethal as any unsuitable automated watering system.

The commonest failing is to water too frequently, and the second commonest is not to water enough at any one time. In general the rule is to water well and then leave the compost to dry out to some extent – by how much depends on the plant. (Guidance is given in the growing instructions for individual plants in the second section of this book, from page 74 onwards.)

How dry the compost is can be judged in part by looking at the surface. But this dries out quickly and to discover whether the dryness extends below, stick your finger an inch (2.5 cm) or so into the compost, depending on the size of the pot. If it is dry this far down, it should be watered thoroughly and then allowed partially to dry out again. Some plants, however, do better if they are kept moist always and these should be watered again when the compost an inch down is still just moist, but not if it is still wet. A compost which is permanently sodden cuts off oxygen from the plant's roots.

When watering is needed, water thoroughly. You are more likely to do this if water is laid on in the conservatory. Use a can with a long and narrow spout. The long spout will enable you to direct the water exactly where you want it – on to the compost and not on to the leaves – and a narrow outlet makes it easier to control the flow of water. Continue pouring until water starts to come through the drainage hole into the saucer on which the pot is standing, or into the container. Then move on to the other plants in need of water. When you have finished, go back to the first plant and empty any water still standing in the saucer or container. Never leave a plant standing in water, unless it is a marsh plant such as the Umbrella Plant *Cyperus alternifolius*.

Plants with leaves which are easily marked if splashed by water are more safely watered from below. Put the pot in a shallow bowl of water and leave it until the surface of the compost shows little beads of moisture. This method is advisable for plants with velvety, felt-like or hairy leaves.

The most thorough, and time-consuming, way of watering is by immersing the pot in water. This is easier to do in a kitchen sink than in the conservatory, because the pot must be left to drain for 20 minutes or so after immersion and the draining board is a better place than the conservatory floor. In summer, of course, this could be done outdoors, using a bucket of water. The water must be just deep enough to cover the surface of the compost. At first air will bubble up. When the bubbles stop, remove the pot to drain. As the water rushes out through the drainage hole, air is sucked in through the compost, so providing a fresh supply of oxygen for the roots.

In winter, water drawn straight from the mains can be very cold and a sudden lowering of the temperature in the compost will produce a state of shock in a plant's roots. To avoid this risk, keep a couple of full buckets standing in the conservatory to take off the chill. If you are carrying water from the house, mix some from the hot tap with the cold. Plants always flourish better with slightly tepid water.

Holiday watering

Watering plants may be tedious, but leaving them unwatered while you are away is worrying. There

Improvised capillary matting keeps plants watered in your absence.

are two ways to lessen the anxiety. One is to get a neighbour to take over. The second is to resort to make-shift capillary watering, which may be more reliable. A simple non-permanent capillary system can be set up on the draining boards of the kitchen sink. If there is a single draining board only, buy a capillary tray to stand on any flat surface at the opposite side of the sink. The two mats should be long enough to go right down to the bottom of the sink and to cover the draining boards or tray. Make absolutely certain that the sink plug is watertight and fill the sink with water. A neighbour might be willing to drop in occasionally to see that the sink is kept full.

Even if you have a neighbour anxious to take over a normal watering routine, it would be sensible in summer to remove the plants from the conservatory to some less scorching part of the house, preferably the kitchen, where water is at hand. Even a conservatory fitted with fully automated ventilation and shading systems will at times become hotter than rooms in the house, and there is no point in drying out the compost faster than need be.

Hydroculture

All the work and worry of watering plants can be eliminated simply by growing them in water (plus fertilizer) without soil or compost. That is *hydroculture*. An Englishman, John Woodward, had the idea at the end of the 18th century; French and German biologists experimented with it in the 19th century and it was commercially developed by a Californian in the 20th century. In the last twenty years it has inevitably spread to the glossier end of the houseplant scene. Much is to be said for it in a conservatory.

A plant growing in compost can be suffocated or drowned by water, since water-sodden compost deprives the roots of oxygen. A plant brought up to growing in fertilized

A pot for hydroculture. The inner container supports the plant in an inert aggregate. Roots grow into the solution of essential nutrients below.

water has developed a different root system. The roots, fleshier in appearance, absorb oxygen from the water instead of from the air. Many plants which have been grown in compost can be converted to hydroculture, if taken fairly young, but there is always a setback. It is better to buy plants which have been reared hydroponically, but, as yet, fewer varieties of such plants are available.

Instead of being rooted in soil or compost, the hydroponic plant is anchored in an inert aggregate and the roots grow into water in which are dissolved all the elements it needs for growth. What is known as the double container method is the better choice. The outer container, usually of plastic since metal corrodes, holds the fertilizer solution. The inner container, holding the plant in the aggregate, is suspended from the rim of the outer container so that it reaches a little way into the fertilizer solution. The solution, into which the roots grow, has to be topped up from time to time; a gauge shows maximum and minimum levels.

There is no danger of overwatering with hydroponic culture, but there is a risk from build-up of mineral salts in the aggregate. The excess salts have to be washed away at least every two months. This is done simply by lifting out the inner container and holding it under a running tap.

Outer containers are generally square or cylindrical, and on the whole have so far escaped over-decoration. Although made of plastic, if they are plain and unfussy or in white or the palest cream or black they are quite agreeable. They blend with both functional metal conservatories and the neo-Victorian structures beloved of many architects. The containers take up more room than ordinary pots and so look best if planted with one large plant or with a group of smaller ones.

Humidity

Plants need moisture in the air around them as well as at their roots. It is important to maintain an adequate level of humidity in the conservatory and equally to avoid an excess.

Humidity is measured in two ways. 'Absolute humidity' records the number of grams of water in a cubic metre of air; we can forget about that here. It is, however, important to understand 'relative humidity' (RH). This indicates the amount of water in the air at a given temperature as a percentage of what the air could hold at that temperature. The warmer the air, the more moisture it is able to hold. If the temperature in the conservatory rises and no more moisture is provided, the *level* of humidity falls and the air draws moisture from the foliage of plants. On hot days this drying out process could make the plants droop and wilt whenever their roots cannot make good the loss of water quickly enough. How is this to be avoided?

Ventilation is the first step because it will lower the temperature and so automatically increase relative humidity – in other words, make the air less dry. It is also possible to provide more moisture. The old and effective greenhouse

Maintenance

method was to hose down the floor and benches, but this is hardly feasible in the modern conservatory. An alternative is an electric humidifier. These are efficient, but they will need refilling with water at least once a day unless they are attached to a cistern with a mains water supply. It is vital that cables and plugs are fully protected against moisture.

There are also automatic misting systems which give off the finest of sprays. Some incorporate a humidstat controlling an electronic water valve which sets off the mister according to the level of moisture in the air. Others have a timing system which turns them on for short bursts as pre-set. All these electric appliances need full protection from water.

Maintaining a suitable level of humidity in a conservatory in summer is complicated by unpredictable changes in the weather. A hot day with a relative humidity of about 30 can easily turn into a cooler but still warm night with a relative humidity of 100, which is saturation point. The result will be condensation on the glass, with droplets of water falling on the plants. If the automatic ventilators have then closed themselves because of the falling temperature, the plants will be left in moist, stagnant air, in which fungal diseases can thrive. The way to mitigate this danger is to instal a small electric fan and run it all through the summer. Its purpose is not to cool the air, but to keep it moving.

Cacti and succulents can tolerate lower levels of humidity than most other plants. In very general terms, foliage plants fare best with a level around RH 60 per cent, but higher for plants with thin leaves which dry out more rapidly.

RH levels are far more easily measured than controlled. The simplest device is a hygrometer, which measures and displays percentages of relative humidity from RH 0 per cent to RH 100 per cent.

To prevent the conservatory from deteriorating, both as a building and as an investment, it will need regular care.

Types of material

Timber Western Red Cedar will have been treated with preservative right at the start but may not have been painted. When new, this timber is a rather raw red but it turns silvery grey as it mellows, and this is perfectly natural. However, unpainted cedarwood should be treated every four or five years with another coat of preservative. Any wood which has been painted after the initial preservative coat needs repainting at least every three years. As soon as there is any crack in the coating of paint, fungi can find a way in.

When repainting wooden glazing bars, make sure that any cracks between the putty and the wood are filled in and given extra coats of paint.

The interior of a cool or even temperate conservatory should need painting less frequently than the exterior. Much will depend on the degree of condensation; the more ventilation, the less there is likely to be. A warm, humid con-

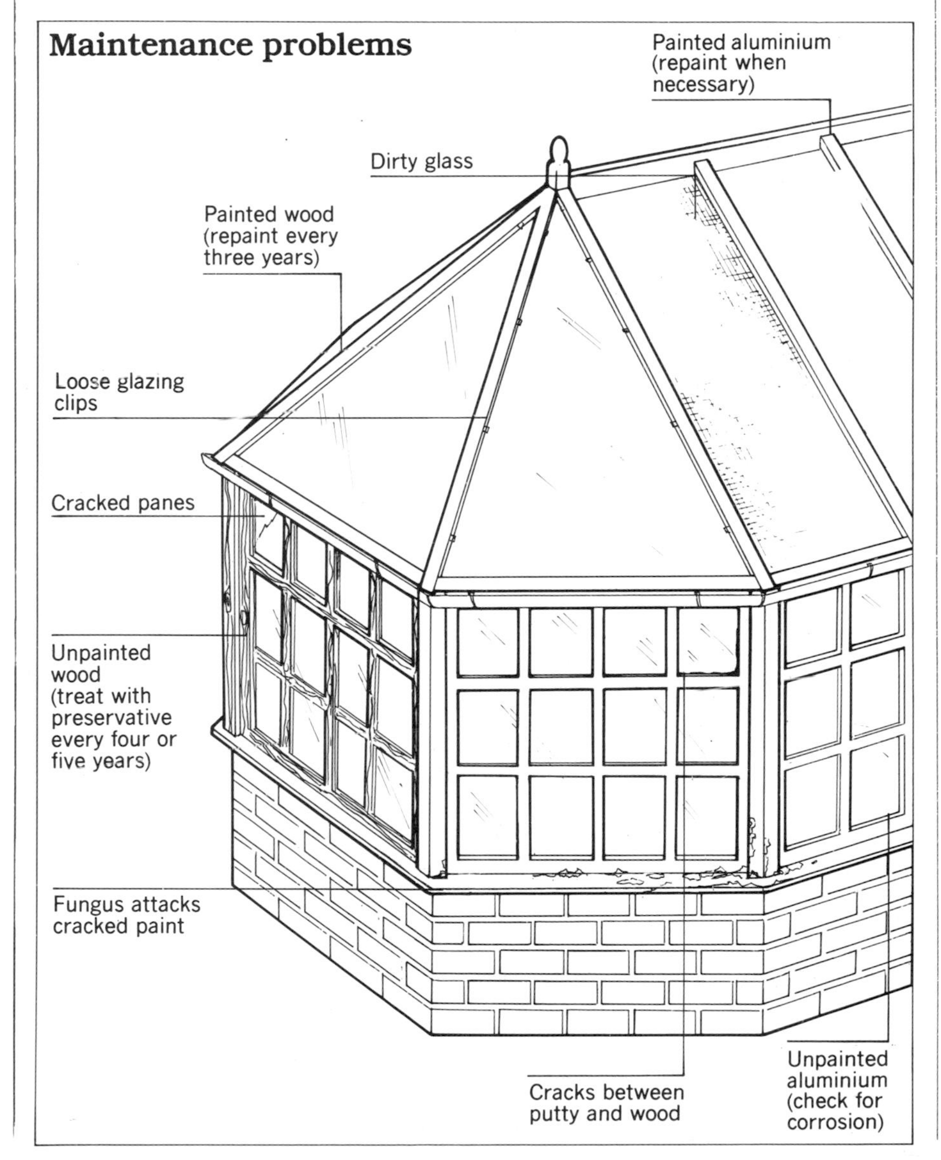

servatory is a promising target for fungi in search of a biodegradable meal.

Aluminium Unpainted aluminium needs little attention. It corrodes slightly to begin with, producing a dusty deposit on the surface – the main result of which is to take the shine off the metal. If the aluminium has been painted, it is the paint which will start to deteriorate and in time repainting will be needed to smarten it up.

Check each year that the glazing clips holding the glass are securely in place; it is best to do this at the end of summer before the winter gales begin. A supply of spare clips is advisable. Anyone working on the roof (preferably only one person at a time) should do so from boards.

Glass As well as frequent cleaning of glass, cracked or broken panes should be replaced as soon as possible. They let in rain, let out heat, and suggest neglect.

When considering the subject of light, it should be pointed out that up to 40 per cent of daylight may fail to penetrate the conservatory simply because the glass is filthy. The build-up is insidious – a small percentage loss each week, progressively increasing as the dirt thickens. Within a few months a brand-new conservatory can be losing 20 per cent of the light it should be receiving. The atmosphere is especially murky in winter and dirty glass at this time means the loss of precious light and, in turn, of expensive heat.

The roof is particularly affected since there more dust settles and sticks than on the side walls. In town the pollution from cars and chimneys turns the dust into a sticky film, hard to remove. In the countryside algae has the same effect; country dust is just as dirty and hard to get rid of as city dirt.

It is easier to prevent the build-up of dirt than to remove it. Hose down the exterior of the conservatory regularly, before the sticky film has a chance to take hold. If it does, a stiff brush and detergent will be needed.

The interior of the conservatory will not get as dirty, but since the glass there cannot be hosed down it will have to be cleaned by hand, with at least the same regularity as windows in the house. It is a bore, but whoever wanted the conservatory most in the first place might reasonably be expected to do it. It is obvious that someone must.

Renovation

Renovating an old conservatory which has been neglected for years can present problems. A rotten, sagging roof is beyond hope, but if it is structurally sound it could be reglazed either with new glass, or by replacing only the cracked and broken panes. Remove the old flaking paint and give the frame three coats of paint, finishing with a good quality gloss. If the roof is useless but the sides sound, it may be worthwhile fitting a new roof, using aluminium modules. These are available in so many shapes as to fit almost anything. Doing this oneself, with a bit of advice from the manufacturer of the modules, might be more within the range of skills of the amateur handyman than building a conservatory from scratch.

The sides, if (as most likely) of timber, should have the flaking paint removed. Before repainting, replace all defective putty and renew broken glass. The iron gutters of an old conservatory may have collapsed. Replace them with PVC guttering, which is lighter and rustproof. A renovated conservatory, while not brand-new, is at least likely to work out cheaper than starting all over again. It might be best to use it as a cool conservatory with minimal heating, or even as a cold conservatory for human use only in summer. If you want to put in heating where none exists, that would be a job for professionals.

Plant display

The most basic and cheapest of plant containers are plastic or clay pots. Plastic pots are cheapest and lightest, but the standard pale brown colour is not particularly pleasing, unlike the warm orange-red of clay. Since clay is porous, the outside of the pot can be stained with unpleasant deposits of lime in hard-water areas, and by mineral deposits as a result of overfeeding plants. They will need to be wiped regularly to keep them looking good. Plastic, being non-porous, does not suffer such disadvantages and pots are increasingly available in colours other than pale brown.

If plastic or clay is not to your liking, pots can be concealed by inserting them in pottery containers, cane or wicker baskets. The disadvantages here are that water can collect in pottery containers, making the compost in the pot sodden, and that wicker and cane will rot if a saucer is not placed beneath the pot. This device precludes the use of capillary or water matting.

You will not want all your pots at ground level, so some form of bench is desirable. This may run along part or all the length of one or more sides of the conservatory. Slatted wooden benches are the simplest and cheapest, but will never win a good design award. They also suffer from the disadvantage that, if not constructed from hardwood, they will quickly rot. Hardwood benches require treatment to keep them in good condition, but not such frequent attention as ones made from softwood.

On this extensive floor space many plants are displayed in pots at ground level because they look better from above; green leaves turn uppermost and flowers face upwards to the light. Variegated plants with dramatic marking on the underside of leaves, and pendulous flowers, are more effective at, or above, eye level. Trailers need to hang down and climbers to reach up. The art of plant display is to let each plant be seen at its best.

Aluminium staging is more robust and durable, requiring little or no maintenance. There are systems sold in basic size units to which you can add as the plant collection increases. Some are luxury versions of aluminium greenhouse staging, designed specifically with the conservatory in mind, with painted surfaces in a satin anodized finish. Tiered aluminium staging can enhance the display of plants and provide easy access to them. It is also a way of covering the back brick wall of lean-to conservatories. Some staged units incorporate plastic troughs, similar to window boxes, in which plants can be grouped. There are also free-standing aluminium units with plastic trays for displaying groups of plants just above ground level. For large specimen plants, any number of suitable stone containers or urns are sold for garden use which look equally effective in the conservatory.

A large group of alpine plants will require a bench, preferably constructed of aluminium, with a deep tray into which the pots can be plunged. The tray should be filled with coarse gravel to ensure good drainage and the pots inserted almost to their rim.

Epiphytic orchids can be grown

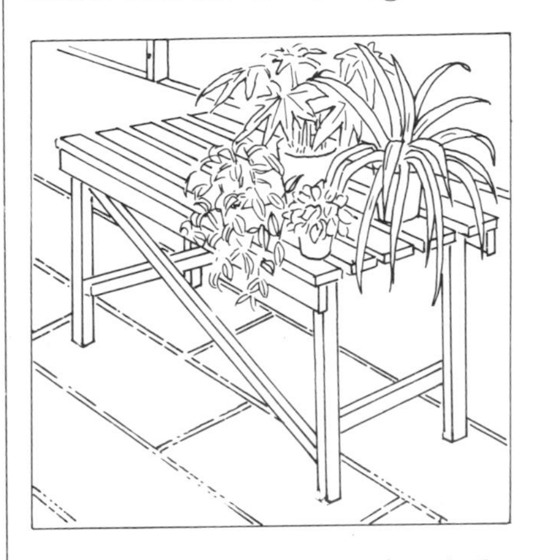

Above: A slatted bench is a practical way of showing an orchid collection. Right: Slatted bench in wood, less long lasting than aluminium.

Aluminium bench with deep trays in which pots can be plunged in peat (to boost humidity) or in gravel, for cacti and alpines.

Aluminium bench for display of plant groups.
Opposite: Greenery overhead, with climbers, trailers, hanging baskets.

on bark or osmunda fibre, mimicking the conditions in which they grow in the wild. Even better for displaying them would be an old tree branch on which several could be grouped. Sphagnum moss should be placed under the rhizome and the roots spread over it, the whole being secured firmly to the support with nylon cord or thin plastic-coated wire. Take care not to damage the roots.

An alternative is to display such plants in a glass case, providing the controlled environment of temperature and humidity which they require for successful flowering. The framework of the case may be of wood or aluminium, incorporating a deep tray containing peat into which pots can be plunged. The case can be landscaped with the addition of a small tree branch to which orchids could be attached. Soil-heating cables embedded in the peat would provide additional heat if necessary and the case, being enclosed, would be humid. Ventilators should be installed for essential air movement.

Bromeliads are another group of epiphytic plants which can be displayed on a tree branch. Cover the roots of plants completely with sphagnum moss secured with nylon cord and attach them to niches on the branch with plastic-coated wire. Spray regularly to keep the sphagnum moss moist always and keep the central 'cups' of the plants topped up with water.

Climbers and trailers

Climbing plants can be planted against a back wall where they will cover the brickwork. Annual climbers can be planted in pots and perennial climbers may progress to

Plants with trailing and arching foliage look best displayed in hanging containers. The problem here is access for watering, especially in hot weather, when the plants may have to be watered every day. The higher and more out of easy reach they are, the more likely are they to be neglected, with disastrous results. If they can be positioned where they will not be a nuisance in banging heads, they can be hung low for greater effect. If they must be high up, attach the chains supporting the pot to a rope and pulley so they can be lowered for easy watering without trouble. Take care that the container is not too near the glass roof.

There are problems in attaching hanging containers to the roof of a conservatory, because the glazing bars of both aluminium and wooden conservatories are not strong

Plants hang from containers attached to roof and wall, while climbers frame the glass.
Right: How training wires can be fixed to aluminium glazing bars.
Left: Angle bracket on a lean-to wall supports a hanging basket.

tubs. All climbers need support of some kind, such as strong canes, lengths of wire, or netting. Plants which throw out tendrils – such as cissus, ipomoea and rhoicissus – are better trained against netting, over which they will spread quickly to form a blanket of greenery.

enough to carry the weight of hanging containers. It may be possible to attach them to more solid parts of a wooden framework, but aluminium roofs are trickier. For safety's sake it is best to confine hanging containers to the solid wall of the conservatory, where it will be possible to fix angle brackets securely. Trailing plants can also be shown to advantage in semi-circular pots fitted flush against such a wall; or several plants could be grouped together to provide an overall wall covering.

Furniture

Conservatory furniture should not only be attractive, but also functional and practical for its environment. Choose materials which can stand up to a sometimes humid atmosphere, but also to the scorching direct rays of sun shining through glass. Everything should be easy to clean and require little maintenance. The most practical, if not always the most appealing materials, are plastic and glass-fibre. There are many ranges of tables and chairs either moulded in one piece of plastic or glass-fibre or constructed from steel, coated in rot- and corrosion-proof polythene. Furniture of these materials is usually white, often treated so that it does not turn an unsightly yellow. It will require only wiping with a damp cloth to keep it sparkling.

Wooden tables and chairs in natural finish add a feeling of warmth. Choose a hardwood such as teak which will stand the most punishing atmospheric changes and needs only the occasional application of oil to keep it in good condition. Softwood furniture is far cheaper, but needs regular treatment of either oiling or painting about every two years to prevent the wood from rotting.

Cast aluminium furniture is light in weight and does not rust. It is available in modern styles, as well as in ornate designs copied from Victorian cast-iron furniture. (Cast-iron itself should be avoided; it is extremely heavy, prone to rust, and requires frequent painting.) The painted finish to cast aluminium is often baked on to give a durable surface, which will need only wiping down. One great advantage of aluminium chairs and tables is that they are light enough to carry about and so, if carefully chosen, they can be used not only in the conservatory but also on a patio or on a lawn.

Cane, wicker, rattan and bamboo furniture give a 'colonial' touch to the conservatory. All these materials have a tendency to rot and

Today's look: The deep yellow of chairs, cushions and beakers is in brilliant contrast to the dull grey framework of the conservatory (left). Victorian look: The cast-iron past revived in lightweight aluminium (top). Colonial look: Nostalgia for the heyday of wicker, bamboo, rattan (above).

leaving them in the conservatory all year round will bring a speedy end to their useful life. Treat with a preservative for added protection.

Some types of conservatory chairs and benches are more comfortable to sit in than others, but all can be improved with the addition of foam-rubber cushions. These can be taken into the house when the conservatory is not frequently used, and in winter especially. Choose plain or simply patterned washable and removable covers – avoid loud floral or jungle foliage designs which tend to compete with the plants.

The garden room does not present the same atmospheric problems as the conservatory. Here there may be normal living-room furnishings, carpeted floors, with comfortable chairs and sofas, chosen according to taste.

Propagators

Propagation on any large scale is more suited to a greenhouse than a conservatory, where the comfort demands of people make it difficult to provide the best conditions for raising plants. The paraphernalia of propagation also hardly accords with the conventional image of a conservatory – although now that such structures are being designed by computer it is possible to foresee the fully hi-tech conservatory. There all operations will be fully computerized and robotized while the owner relaxes among the wonders of science rather than those of nature. The new plants will be raised in the most hygienic conditions by *in-vitro*, or micro, propagation; in this system, sterilized plant tissue grows into a plant within a sterilized, sealed glass jar in a sterile jelly which contains nutrients and hormones.

Until that day, the urge which many of us have to grow something from seed or cuttings can best be satisfied by use of a propagator, which need not impinge too much on the rest of the conservatory. (It is when propagation is very successful and room has to be found for the resulting plant explosion that problems begin.)

Some cuttings and many seeds need high temperatures to root or germinate, so it is best to have an electrically heated propagator. These give gentle bottom heat, are thermostatically controlled, economical to run and need not be expensive to buy. The covers are of clear plastic; those used for propagating cuttings must be taller than those used for raising seed.

More sophisticated – and expensive – versions include a misting unit. This can be operated by hand or may be electronically controlled to give bursts of mist spray over the seeds or cuttings, more frequently in sunshine, less often when the weather is dull. In a conservatory where there is enough warmth for cuttings to strike without extra heat, mist propagation makes success more likely. Such a unit is also automatically controlled by the intensity of light in the conservatory.

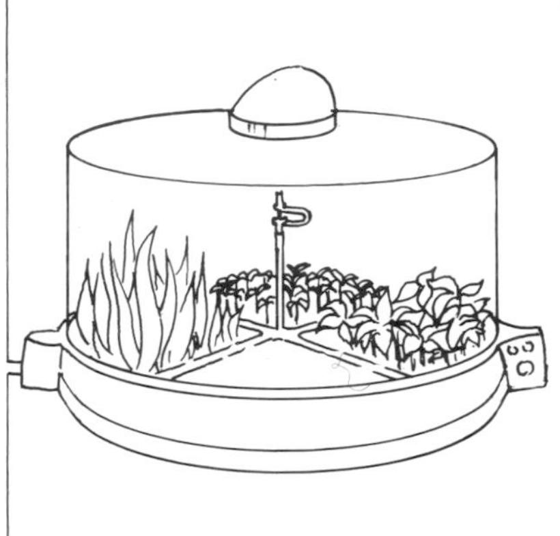

Above: Giving seeds and cuttings the best start in life — in a small propagator with thermostatically-controlled heat and electronically-controlled mist-spray.
Right: Even in this conservatory — as far from the jungle look (bar potted palm) as one could get — comes evidence that the owner cannot resist the appeal of propagation. Note the trolley with trays of flourishing seedlings.
Left: Zealous propagation can sometimes create problems of fecundity and space.

Part 3

Choosing Plants for the Conservatory

All the recommended plants for growing in various kinds of conservatory and garden room are grouped in the pages which follow according to their type. The plants in some groups have particular characteristics common to them alone and may, for example, have special feeding or atmospheric requirements. Being aware of these plants' special needs helps the plant owner to care for them.

THE MAIN PLANT GROUPS

ALPINES

Alpines are killed not by cold but by wet winters. They are found growing naturally in scree and rock crevices where soil is free draining. If their roots become wet they will quickly die. For best results indoors they should be grown in a mixture of loam compost to which coarse sand or grit has been added. Standing pots on gravel is an aid to good drainage. Very often the top surface of the compost is covered with a thin layer of fine grit. The drawback to this is that it prevents you from telling at a glance how dry the compost is, but it does keep the foliage from contact with moist compost and shows off plants to good effect. In periods of very hot sun, plants should be lightly shaded.

BROMELIADS

Most bromeliads are epiphytic plants, living on nutrients from the air, and in their natural surroundings are found growing attached to tree branches or in rock crevices. The leaves grow in rosette formation, producing either a broad or narrow cup in which water and food are collected to supply the plant's needs. Even though most cultivated bromeliads have adapted to living in compost, these 'cups' should be kept topped up with water, except during the plant's winter rest. Water in the cup at this time is likely to rot the plant. The exception among epiphytic bromeliads is *Tillandsia usneoides*, which absorbs its water through the stems and will require daily spraying if the conservatory atmosphere is dry. *Ananas comosus*

'Variegatus' is the one bromeliad which is terrestrial, absorbing all its water and food from the compost.

CACTI

Cacti are easily recognized by their fleshy stems covered in areoles, or small protuberances, from which spines and flowers grow. The stems of terrestrial cacti (those rooted in soil) are globular or cylindrical, while the epiphytic (air-nourished) jungle cactus, epiphyllum, rhipsalidopsis and schlumbergera have narrow flattened stems.

Most cacti are found in desert areas where rainfall is limited and, when it comes, appears in short torrential showers. So water is stored in the stems of cactus plants and held in reserve for future use. Such plants will therefore stand a little neglect, but should never get so dry that stems begin to shrivel.

Cacti require a cool winter rest for successful flowering. The exceptions are the jungle cacti schlumergera and rhipsalidopsis, which require consistently warm temperatures. Pests should not be a great problem but watch for mealy bugs which suck the sap of plants. Their eggs are easily spotted since they are surrounded with white fluff.

ORCHIDS

Like bromeliads, most orchids are epiphytic plants found growing on tree branches in the wild, firmly attached by the creeping rhizome. From the rhizome they throw up pseudobulbs, which may be bulb-shaped or look like flattened stems. These store food and water, especially important at times of drought. If the growing medium is allowed to dry out the plant will begin to draw on its reserves until the pseudobulbs start to shrivel. This is to be avoided since permanent damage and even death may result. Calanthe and paphoipedilum are terrestrial orchids with roots firmly anchored in the ground.

These are the main groups of plants which grow in unusual ways. The specific needs of individual plants are dealt with in the individual entries which follow.

SUCCULENTS

Many succulents also originate in desert areas with hot summers and cold, frosty winters. Rainfall is limited and usually confined to one season; in between, the fleshy

leaves act as water storage reservoirs. Care must be taken in watering succulents since too much water results in bloated, soft leaves, whereas too little water causes leaves to shrivel.

The Cool Conservatory

Winter temperatures: 45–55°F (7–13°C)

The cool conservatory is for plants which need, or will tolerate, chilly winters. The drawback is that for those months it will be no place for the owners to relax in. But from late spring to early autumn it can be glorious, because the plants suitable for such an environment are legion.

More than 150 of all types of cool conservatory plants appear in this section. And even when the plants are resting in winter they still need looking after. So while the cool conservatory may be only a part-time room for lounging, it provides a full-time hobby, most of all for lovers of alpines.

1 *Chamaerops humilis* (Palm) 2 *Bougainvillea buttiana* (Flowering) 3 *Ferocactus latispinus* (Cactus) 4 *Echeveria derenbergii* (Succulent) 5 *Aeonium howorthii* (Succulent) 6 *Cereus peruvianus* (Cactus) 7 *Opuntia microdasys* (Cactus) 8 *Petunia × hybrida* (Flowering) 9 *Lobelia erinus* (Flowering) 10 *Laurus nobilis* (Herbs) 11 *Pelargonium × hortorum* (Flowering) 12 *Lilium longiflorum* (Flowering) 13 *Fatshedera lizei* (Foliage) 14 *Chlorophytum vittatum* (Hanging) 15 *Cissus antarctica* (Climber) 16 *Aracauria excelsis* (Foliage)

Foliage plants

Some of the foliage plants to choose for the cool conservatory are long-time favourites – aspidistra, spotted laurel, fatsia, fatshedera and yucca – all with a bold impact, whether plain or variegated. Others are strikingly graceful – araucaria and the tall *Cupressus cashmeriana* and *Grevillea robusta*, for instance. With their lacy foliage they make a good background against which to display smaller, possibly flowering, plants. There are varieties enough of ivy to overrun the whole conservatory, and two scented pelargoniums – lemon or peppermint, as you prefer.

What these plants have in common is the need for a cool, but frost-free, rest period in winter. Though recommended for the cool conservatory, most would also do well in the temperate conservatory as long as they could be removed for a cool winter rest, perhaps to a spare room in the house.

—— *Araucaria excelsa* ——

Norfolk Island Pine

Pyramid-shaped conifer with a straight woody stem from which grow layers of horizontal bright green branches covered in tiny needles, giving the plant a delicate feathery appearance. Grows slowly to 5 ft (1.5 m) at the rate of about 5 in (12.5 cm) a year.

Likes bright light, but shade from direct sun. In summer the pine should be in a well-ventilated spot, kept as cool as possible to prevent the needles from turning yellow and falling.
Temperatures around 50°F (10°C) in winter are also necessary to avoid needle fall on the lower branches. In warm weather it benefits from humidity.
Compost should be moist always during the growth period, but in winter months allow the surface to dry out between waterings. Over-wet compost in winter is another cause of leaf fall.
Feed every two weeks in spring and summer. Pot-on every three years in spring in loam compost. Change old compost for fresh in intervening years.
Propagate from seed sown in spring, but plants will grow very slowly.

—— *Aspidistra elatior* ——

Cast Iron Plant

Leathery, lance-shaped, dark green leaves up to 2 ft (60 cm) long, carried on short stems. Inconspicuous purple flowers may appear at compost level. *A.e.* 'Variegata' has white or creamy vertical stripes on the leaves; not as widely available as the plain green aspidistras.

Tolerates a shady spot, but not too dark or growth will be poor. Keep out of direct sunlight. Variegated forms require bright light to keep the markings; in deep shade they will quickly revert to plain green.
Compost should be just moist throughout the year; allow the surface to dry out between waterings. Roots will rot if a plant is overwatered and the compost allowed to become sodden.
Feed once a month in spring and summer. Pot-on once every three years in spring in loam compost, changing exhausted compost for fresh in intervening years.
Propagate by division when potting-on or repotting. Roots bearing small buds may break off during this operation and these can be planted in compost, with the buds facing upwards. If several pieces are planted in a pot, a good show of leaves should result in time.

—— *Aucuba japonica* 'Variegata' ——

Spotted Laurel

Shiny, oval leaves up to 6 in (15 cm) long, with notched edges and splashed with bright yellow. Small maroon flowers appear in summer, followed by bright red berries. Only female plants have berries, but male plants are needed to pollinate the female. Grows to 6 ft (1.8 m) but can be pruned.

Tolerates a somewhat shaded spot, although yellow colouring will be brighter in good light.
Compost should be moist always.
Feed every two weeks in spring and summer. Pot-on each spring in loam compost. Prune plants in spring to check growth.

Propagate from stem cuttings taken in late summer.

—— *Cupressus cashmeriana* ——

Kashmir Cypress

Elegant pyramid-shaped tree with graceful arching branches bearing scaly, blue-green leaves. Will grow to about 10 ft (3 m) indoors, but only slowly. May not be easily available.

Likes bright light all year round, and direct sun will do no harm.
Compost should be moist in growing season, but allow surface to dry out between waterings in winter months.
Feed every two weeks in spring and summer. Pot-on every two years in spring in loam compost, renewing compost in intervening years.
Propagate by sowing seed in spring or take stem cuttings in summer.

—— *Eucalyptus gunnii* ——

Gum Tree

The grey-green, circular to heart-shaped leaves grow in pairs from the stems – they have no stalks. The leaves are covered in a white powder and when young may be tinged with pink if in good sun. In the wild a eucalyptus tree can grow to an enormous size and do it very rapidly, adding several feet to its height every year. This variety is more modest, growing only 12 in (30 cm) or so a year.

Likes bright light with direct sun to bring out the best leaf colour.
Compost should be thoroughly moist in the growing period, but allow surface to dry out before watering again. In winter, keep the compost just moist.
Feed every two weeks in spring and summer. Pot-on every year in spring in a loam based compost.
Propagate from seed in spring. Bottom heat of 75°F (24°C) will be needed.

—— *Euonymus japonicus* ——
'Aureo-Variegata'

Japanese Spindle Tree

Dark green oval leaves with serrated edges about 2 in (5 m) long and blotched with yellow. Grows to 4 ft (1.2 m). *E.j.* 'Microphyllus Variegatus' has leaves with silvery white edges, about 1 in (2.5 cm) long. Grows to 18 in (45 cm).

Needs good light, but shade from direct sun.
Temperatures should be cool in winter, otherwise scale, red spider mite and mildew are likely to attack.
Compost should be well watered in the growing period, but less frequently in winter.
Feed every two weeks in spring and summer. Pot-on each spring in loam compost. Pinch out growing tips in spring for bushy growth and prune stems to shape.
Propagate by taking stem tip cuttings in summer.

—— *x Fatshedera lizei* ——

Ivy Tree

Cross between *Fatsia japonica* and *Hedera helix hibernica*. Dark green glossy leaves similar to those of *Fatsia japonica* but with fewer lobes and smaller, up to 6 in (15 cm) across. x *F.l.* 'Variegata' has dark green leaves with white to cream edges. Both grow to about 4 ft (1.2 m).

Likes good light, but with a certain amount of shade; variegated forms lose their markings in poor light.
Compost should be kept moist in the growing period, but in winter allow the surface to dry out between waterings.
Feed every two weeks in spring and summer. Pot-on each year in spring in loam compost. In spring prune back to 4 in (10 cm) any leggy stems which have lost lower leaves, a tendency with this plant. New shoots will appear, and once growth is well established, pinch out growing tips for bushiness.
Propagate by taking 4 in (10 cm) stem cuttings in summer. Bottom heat of 65°F (18°C) is necessary.

—— *Fatsia japonica* ——

Japanese Fatsia

Large, shiny, dark green leaves up to 12 in (30 cm) across. In late autumn puff balls of white flowers appear. *F.j.* x 'Variegata' has leaves with white or cream edges and blotches of colour here and there. Grows to 5 ft (1.5 m) and with spreading foliage may have a similar girth.

Likes bright light, but no direct sun. Variegated forms need good light throughout the year to maintain their colour.
Temperatures too high in winter cause leaves to shrivel and turn brown.
Compost should be kept moist in the growing period, but in winter months allow the surface to dry out between waterings. If the compost dries out completely, however, lower leaves will fall.
Feed every two weeks in spring and summer. Pot-on each spring in loam compost. Plants may be kept under control by pruning them to half their size in spring.
Propagate by sowing seed in spring or from cuttings taken in summer. *F.j.* 'Variegata' can be propagated only from cuttings.

—— *Grevillea robusta* ——

Silk Bark Oak

Lacy, fragile-looking fern-like leaves up to 18 in (45 cm) long. When new they are light green, turning dark as they mature. Grows to 6 ft (1.8 m) at a rate of 1 ft (30 cm) a year or more, but can be checked by pruning.

Likes bright light with as much direct sun as possible. Benefits from a humid atmosphere in high summer temperatures.
Compost should be kept moist during the growing period, but allow the surface to dry out in winter months. If compost dries out completely, lower leaves are likely to turn yellow and fall.
Feed every two weeks in spring and summer. Pot-on each spring in loam compost. In spring plants may be pruned by as much as half.
Propagate from seed sown in spring with bottom heat of 60°F (16°C).

—— *Hedera helix* ——

Ivy

Three- to five-lobed leaves, with a central lobe more prominent than the others. Most are self-branching, but they will grow more vigorously if growing tips are pinched out.

Many cultivars available, among them *H.h.* 'Glacier' with small bright green leaves edged with white and pink. *H.h.* 'Chicago' has dark green leaves with purple markings and *H.h.* 'Chicago Variegata' has cream edges. The leaves of *H.h.* 'Sagittifolia' are slim, arrow-shaped and bright green; a variegated form has cream edges. *H.h.* 'Lutzii' has leaves with yellow marking; this ivy is not self-branching so will need regular pinching out to make it bushy. *Hedera colchica* has dark green, heart-shaped leaves up to 10 in (25 cm) long. *Hedera canariensis* 'Variegata' (Gloire de Marengo) has leathery leaves about 6 in (15 cm) long, with a broad band of cream and white around the edge.

Ivies grown for display on tables can be kept small by regular cutting back; otherwise they can be trained up supports as climbers, or allowed to trail from hanging containers. Most ivies grow vigorously.

Likes good light in a somewhat shaded spot, but variegated forms should be only lightly shaded if leaf colour is to be maintained.
Compost should be moist in the growing period, but allow the surface to dry out between waterings in winter.
Feed every two weeks in spring and summer. Pot-on in spring each year in loam compost with added sand. Pinch out growing tips regularly in spring and summer and prune back over-long stems.
Propagate by taking stem cuttings in summer; these can be planted straight into compost or rooted first in water.

—— *Pelargonium crispum* ——

Lemon-Scented Geranium

Bright green, lobed leaves with crinkly edges and a velvety surface; if rubbed they smell of lemon. Some variegated forms have cream-edged leaves. Insignificant pale pink flowers appear from spring to autumn.
P. tomentosum, also with velvety, lobed leaves, smells of peppermint. It produces modest flowers over the same period as *P. crispum*. Both grow to about 2 ft (60 cm).

Likes good light with direct sunlight, but shade from scorching sun.
Compost should be moist always in the growing period, but barely moist in winter.
Feed every two weeks in spring and summer. Pot-on each year in spring in either a loam or peat compost. Pinch out growing tips in spring and summer for thicker growth and cut back any leggy stems by half in spring.
Propagate by taking 4 in (10 cm) stem cuttings in summer.

—— *Podocarpus macrophyllus* ——

Buddhist Pine

Stems covered with densely packed, narrow, sword-shaped leaves, up to 4 in (10 cm) long. Foliage is pale green at first, but gradually darkens. The plant will grow to 5 ft (1.5 m), but stems can be cut back to make the plant bushier.

Likes good light with a little, but not fierce, direct sun.
Compost should be thoroughly watered in the growing period, but allow surface to dry out between waterings. In winter, keep compost just moist.
Feed every two weeks in spring and summer. Pot-on every spring in a peat compost.
Propagate by stem cuttings in spring.

—— *Yucca elephantipes* ——

Spineless Yucca

Yucca cane plants are grown from sections of stem of *Y. elephantipes* which have been induced to sprout. The sections may be anything from 18 in (45 cm) to 6 ft (1.8 m) tall and none will grow any taller than its original size. The taller the stem, the more expensive it will be. Each stem may have several rosettes of leaves and there are often two or more stems to a pot.

Y. aloifolia has a rosette of dark green, sword-shaped leaves with savagely toothed edges, about 2 ft (60 cm) long, carried on top of a thick trunk up to 4 ft (1.2 m) tall.
Y. elephantipes is similar to *Y. aloifolia* but without the toothed edges to leaves. Grows to a similar height. Given plenty of light and sun, both may produce a spectacular 2 ft (60 cm) flower spike with cream, bell-shaped flowers in summer and autumn.

Needs bright light with plenty of direct sun if the plant is to flower well, but must also have good ventilation.
Compost should be always moist in the growing period, but barely moist during the winter rest.
Feed every two weeks in spring and summer. Pot-on every two years in spring in a mixture of two parts of loam compost to one of sand. Change compost for fresh in intervening years.
Propagate by removing offsets at base of plant when potting-on or repotting, or sow seed in spring.

Flowering perennials

Perennial plants can bring colour to the cool conservatory at one time or another during the whole year. Winter blooms include camellia, cyclamen, erica and primula; spring has clivia and azalea and the bracts of bougainvillea, which last through to early autumn; plants which go on flowering from spring to autumn include abutilons, fuchsias and pelargoniums, joined for part of the time by showy hydrangeas, the curious callistemon (Bottle Brush) and the pungent-smelling myrtle.

If winter flowering plants are to bloom well and last, they must be consistently cool. Resist the temptation to move them from the comparative coolness of the conservatory to the warmth of a centrally heated house or you may well find the buds and flowers dropping rapidly. Spring and summer flowering plants must also be kept cool in winter if they are to flower successfully later. During this resting period they should not be in temperatures above 55°F (13°C).

Abutilon pictum 'Thompsonii'

Flowering Maple

Dark green, lobed, elongated leaves dappled with yellow, similar in appearance to maple leaves. Orange, lantern-shaped flowers with red veins appear from spring to autumn. Grows quickly to 4 ft (1.2 m).
A. megapotamicum is a trailing abutilon, with dark green, heart-shaped leaves, while *A.m.* 'Variegata' has yellow dappled leaves. Both have red and yellow flowers. *A. hybridum*, developed from various strains, has either yellow, white or pink flowers.

Likes a well-lit spot with some direct sunlight, but not searching sun. Yellow markings on variegated leaves will fade if light is poor.
Compost should be moist throughout the growing season, but barely moist during winter months. If plants are watered too frequently or pots left standing in water, roots will rot.
Feed weekly in spring and summer; lack of food makes lower leaves fall. Pot-on each spring in loam compost, and again later in the year if roots appear through drainage hole of pot. Cut back plants in spring to about 18 in (45 cm) to encourage bushy new growth.
Propagate variegated forms from stem cuttings in summer; this is the only way to get young variegated plants. For plain green abutilons, sow seed in spring.

Bougainvillea buttiana

Paper Flower

Small oval leaves and tiny cream flowers surrounded by brilliantly coloured bracts, paper-tissue thin. These last for many weeks, appearing between early spring and early autumn. Bracts may be purple, red, orange, pink, yellow and white, depending on the hybrid. *B. buttiana* itself has crimson bracts; *B.b.* 'Kittie Campbell', orange bracts; and *B.b.* 'Mrs Butt' (or 'Crimson Lake'), rose-crimson bracts. All these forms remain a compact 18 – 24 in (45–60 cm). *B.glabra* is a climber, growing to 10 ft (3 m). It has bright green leaves and purple bracts surrounding yellow flowers. *B.g.* 'Variegata' has white or cream leaf margins.

Needs excellent light with direct sun if it is to flower well; poor light causes leaf fall.
Compost should almost dry out between waterings.
Feed every two weeks in spring and summer. Pot-on each spring in loam compost. Train the stems round a hoop of plastic wire pushed into the compost.
Temperature below 50°F (10°C) in winter will lead to rapid leaf drop. In late winter cut back main stems by a third and side shoots to within 1 in (2.5 cm) of main stems.
Propagate by taking 4 in (10 cm) stem cuttings in spring; bottom heat will be needed.

Callistemon citrinus

Bottle Brush

Cluster of 3 in (7.5 cm) long, narrow leaves, coppery when young, turning bright green when they develop. Stems covered with silky hairs which disappear as the plant matures. Flowers appear in summer and look like brilliantly coloured bottle brushes – bright red, filament-like stamens tipped yellow and carried on 6 in (15 cm) stems. Grows to 6 ft (1.8 m) but cultivar *C.c* 'Splendens' stays around 4 ft (1.2 m).

Needs bright light with direct sun for good flowering.
Compost should be kept moist in the growing season but barely moist in winter.
Feed every two weeks in spring and summer. Pot-on each spring in loam compost until a 10 in (25 cm) pot is reached. Every year after that replace top 3 in (7.5 cm) of compost with fresh.

Winter rest between 45° and 50°F (7° – 10°C) vital for successful flowering the following year.
Propagate from 4 in (10 cm) cuttings with a heel (small piece of stem from which cutting is taken) in spring.

Camellia japonica

Camellia

One of the few plants with colourful flowers in deepest winter. Evergreen shrub with glossy, leathery, dark green oval leaves, about 4 in (10 cm) long. Single, semi-double or double rose-like flowers appear from late winter to late spring. Of the many named cultivars, 'Adolphe Audusson' has semi-double blood red flowers; 'Alba simplex' single white flowers; and 'Gloire de Nantes' semi-double rose pink flowers. Plants grow to 5 ft (1.5 m), but are best kept pruned to about 3 ft (90 cm).

Likes bright light, but shade from direct sun.
Temperatures from late autumn to mid-winter must be 45° – 55°F (7° – 13°C) otherwise buds will drop.
Compost should be kept moist in growing period, but barely moist while the plant rests for about six weeks after flowering. Avoid hard water which turns the leaves yellow; use rainwater in hard water districts.
Feed every two weeks with an acid fertilizer from early summer until flowering stops. Pot-on each year after flowering in a lime-free loam compost.
Propagate by taking stem cuttings in late summer, but bottom heat will be needed.

Clivia miniata

Kaffir Lily

Strap-shaped, dark green, leathery leaves up to 2 ft (60 cm) long, in layered opposite pairs. The leaves arch, making the plant spread to about 3 ft (90 cm) with a height no more than about 2 ft (60 cm). Clivias produce one or sometimes two tall flower stems, usually in late winter or early spring. As many as 20 trumpet-shaped orange flowers are borne on each stem.

Likes good light with direct sun, but shade from fierce sunlight; plants will often not flower through lack of light.
Compost should be kept moist in the growing period, but during the winter rest period, water about once a month.
Feed once a month in spring and summer. Pot-on in loam compost, after flowering, usually every two or three years when roots begin to push above the surface. Change compost in intervening years. A cool rest period in late autumn or early winter is essential if the plant is to flower. When flowers have all fallen, cut off the flower head only, leaving the rest of the stem to wither completely before removing.
Propagate by removing offsets thrown up by parent plant when potting-on. Do not remove them until well established, with at least six leaves, and disentangle enough roots from the parent plant to support the offsets.

Cyclamen persicum

Cyclamen

Heart-shaped light or dark leaves with silvery markings, carried on short stems. Masses of shuttlecock-shaped flowers ranging in colour from white to shades of pink and red appear on 8 in (20 cm) stems from autumn to late winter. Grows no more than 15 in (37.5 cm).

Likes a well-lit spot, but shade from direct sunlight. Provide a humid atmosphere in the weeks prior to flowering period.
Compost should be just moist while the plant is in growth. After flowering, the plant will produce new leaves but during spring these will turn yellow and die down completely. When no more leaves are produced, reduce watering and stop altogether when leaves turn yellow. Remove all leaves cleanly at compost level and store the corm dry, in compost, in a cool, dark place. Bring out to a light spot in summer and start watering again, increasing the amount as leaves appear. Compost should be just moist or the corm is liable to rot. Always water around the corm, never directly on it.
Feed every two weeks after new growth appears until flowering is over. Pot-on each year before corms are started into growth in summer. Corm should show just above surface of compost. Too high temperatures in autumn and winter make the leaves turn yellow and buds and flowers drop.
Propagate from seed sown in autumn or spring.

Erica gracilis

Cape Heath

Erect stems with tiny, pale green, needle-like leaves no more than ¼ in (0.6 cm) long. Clusters of equally small, bell-shaped and long-lasting, rose-pink flowers from late autumn to early winter. Grows to 18 in (45 cm). *E.g.* 'Alba' has white flowers. *E. hyemalis* has larger leaves, about ¾ in (1.8 cm) long, and similar-sized tubular flowers, white flushed with pink, which appear from early to late winter. Grows to 2 ft (60 cm).

Likes bright light with some direct sun, but fierce midday rays can cause leaf fall. Benefits from humid atmosphere, especially in summer.
Compost should be kept moist; if it dries out, the leaves become brittle and the plant dies. Use either distilled or rain water if tap water is hard, because most ericas cannot tolerate lime. Pot-on each spring in a lime-free, peat

compost. Cut back stems by half after flowering.
Propagate from stem cuttings taken in late summer; bottom heat of 60°F (16°C) is required.

Fuchsia magellanica

Lady's Eardrops

Oval, mid-green leaves and bell-shaped flowers with flared-back sepals. Many hybrids developed from *F. magellanica* have different flower colours – plain reds and pinks or combinations of white and pink, purple and red, and white and red, from late spring to autumn. Flowers are single or double, ranging from 2 in (5 cm) to 5 in (12.5 cm) long. Can be grown as a standard to 4 ft (1.2 m), a shrub to 2 ft (60 cm), or an 18 in (45 cm) trailer.

Likes good light with some direct sunlight, but shade from fierce sun. In warm weather provide a humid atmosphere to discourage red spider mites.
Compost should be kept moist in growing period. When flowering is over, cut back stems to 6 in (15 cm) and water about once a month until new growth appears.
Feed once a week in spring and summer. Pot-on in early spring in a peat or loam compost. Except for standards, a pot no larger than 6 in (15 cm) should be necessary. Remove dead flower heads and seed pods regularly to concentrate plant's activity on producing more flowers.
Propagate from 4 in (10 cm) stem cuttings taken in spring and summer.

Hydrangea macrophylla

Hydrangea

Oval, pointed leaves with serrated edges, growing to 6 in (15 cm) long and 3 in (7.5 cm) wide. From mid-spring to early summer, the plant produces large mopheads of red, pink, blue or purple flowers, up to 8 in (20 cm) across, depending on the cultivar. Blue- and purple-flowered forms retain their colour only if grown in lime-free composts; otherwise they revert to pink or red. Lime composts can be treated with aluminium sulphate or special blueing mixtures. Grows to 2 ft (60 cm) with a similar spread.

Likes good light, but keep out of direct sun. Benefits from humidity in hot weather.
Compost must be kept moist during flowering period; if it dries out completely the plant will totally collapse. It may be revived by immersing the pot in a bucket of water, but this is not always successful. During winter rest, the compost should be barely moist.
Feed every two weeks in spring and summer. Pot-on each year when flowering is over. Cut back stems by about half some three weeks or so after potting-on: doing both operations at the same time is too much of a shock for the plant.
Propagate from 4 in (10 cm) stem cuttings taken when pruning. Bottom heat of about 65°F (18°C) is needed.

Myrtus communis 'Microphylla'

Myrtle

Combines pungent foliage, fragrant flowers and fruit. Narrow, oval, pointed, leathery leaves, about 1 in (2.5 cm) long. White flowers with thick clusters of yellow stamens appear from late summer to early autumn. Red berries follow the flowers. Grows to about 3 ft (90 cm), but can be kept smaller by pruning.

Likes bright light with some direct sunlight, but shade from fierce sun. In poor light the plant will refuse to flower and fruit.
Compost should be evenly moist during the growing period. When plant is resting, allow top surface of the compost to dry out between waterings. In hard water areas use rainwater, since myrtus is a lime-hater.
Feed every two weeks in spring and summer. Pot-on each spring in peat based compost. Pinch out growing tips for bushy growth and prune lightly to maintain good shape.
Temperature should be cool, even in summer, but if the conservatory is well ventilated the plant will tolerate higher temperatures. Cool winter temperatures are vital for successful flowering and to prevent leaves from falling.
Propagate in summer from cuttings about 4 in (10 cm) long. Cuttings should be taken with a heel, a sliver of the stem from which they are cut.

Pelargonium x *domesticum*

Regal Pelargonium

Round, mid-green leaves with serrated margins. Large, colourful, sometimes blousy, funnel-shaped flowers of white, pink, scarlet or lavender with petal veins picked out in a darker shade. Some bicoloured cultivars. Flowers about 2 in (5 cm) across appear in thick clusters from late spring to late summer. Grows to 2 ft (60 cm). *P.* x *hortorum*, usually called the geranium, has mid-green rounded leaves with brown-red rings. Clusters of white, pink or red flowers are carried on long stalks from spring to late autumn and often well into a mild winter. Grows to 3 ft (90 cm) but some hybrids reach only 1 ft (30 cm).

Likes bright light with direct sun in a well-ventilated spot.
Compost should be kept moist in growing period. When flowering is over and plants are resting at low temperatures, compost should be barely moist. Watering about once every three weeks should then be sufficient.
Feed once a fortnight in spring and summer. Pot-on each spring in either a loam or peat compost, but after a 6 in (15 cm) pot has been reached, merely change the compost for fresh each year or, better still, replace ageing plants with younger ones. Cut back stems in early spring to 6 in (15 cm) and pinch out growing tips when new growth is established.
Propagate from 4 in (10 cm) stem cuttings taken in summer. If compost is too wet, cuttings will rot. *P.* x *hortorum* may be raised from seed sown in winter.

Penstemon barbatus

Beard Tongue

Bright green, lance-shaped leaves. Spikes of tubular purple, pink, red, lavender and white flowers, with bearded throats, bloom from early summer to early autumn. Grows to 3 ft (90 cm), but dwarf forms may be 15 in (37.5 cm).

Likes good light with direct sun, but protect from fierce sun.
Compost should be always moist in growing period, but barely moist in winter.
Feed every two weeks in spring and summer. Pot-on each spring in a loam compost.
Propagate by sowing seed in spring. Or take cuttings in summer, using non-flowering stems.

Primula malacoides

Fairy Primrose

Pale green, oval leaves with serrated edges. Tall, slim stems carry tiered clusters of starlike red, pink or white flowers from mid-winter to mid-spring. *P. obconica* has round to heart-shaped bright green leaves covered with short hairs. Flowers are pink, through shades of red to mauve and white, and carried in clusters on 12 in (30 cm) stalks from mid-winter to late spring. *P. kewensis* has oval, light green leaves covered with fine white bloom. Yellow, sweet-smelling flowers appear from mid-winter to mid-spring. The leaves of *P. sinensis* are lobed and hairy. Large pink or purple flowers with a yellow eye are carried from mid-winter to early spring on short stems which lengthen as flowers develop. These small plants give welcome winter and spring colour. All forms grow to about 15 in (37.5 cm).

Likes good light with direct sunlight, but shade from scorching sun. Benefits from humidity in warm weather.
Compost to be kept moist.
Temperatures much above 55°F (13°C) will cause flowers to fade rapidly.
Feed every two weeks from appearance of flower stems to end of flowering. Remove dead flower heads to encourage further blooms. Pot-on *P. obconica* and *P. sinensis* in a loam or peat compost after flowering, but these plants are usually kept for two years only. The other species are best discarded after flowering.
Propagate by sowing seed in spring.

Punica granatum 'Nana'

Dwarf Pomegranate

Narrow, shiny, bright green, lance-shaped leaves about 1 in (2.5 cm) long. Orange to scarlet funnel-shaped flowers from summer to autumn, possibly followed by small orange fruits which will not ripen. During winter the plant loses most, if not all, of its leaves. Grows to 2 ft (60 cm), spreading its branches.

Likes bright light with direct sun for successful flowering and fruiting.
Compost should be moist always in growing period, but once leaves have dropped it should be kept barely moist until new growth starts.
Feed every two weeks in spring and summer. Pot-on every other spring in loam compost. Change compost for fresh in intervening years.
Propagate in summer by taking 3 in (7.5 cm) stem cuttings with a heel, a small piece of bark from the main stem.

Rehmannia angulata

Chinese Foxglove

Bright green, oval, pointed leaves with serrated edges. Beautiful foxglove-like flowers, pink to pale purple with throats marked red and yellow, appear throughout the summer. The plant grows to 24 in (60 cm).

Likes bright light with direct sun but strong summer sun causes scorching.
Compost should be moist in the growing period and barely moist in winter.
Feed every two weeks in spring and summer. Pot-on every year in spring in loam compost
Propagate from seed sown in spring. Or take cuttings of non-flowering stems in summer.

Rhododendron simsii

Indian Azalea

Dark green, oval, leathery leaves about 1 in (2.5 cm) long. Red, purple and white single or double flowers, 2 in (5 cm) across, appear in late spring, but plants in flower are often on sale before Christmas. Grows to about 12 in (30 cm).

Likes bright light, but shade from direct sun. Does best in a humid atmosphere.
Temperature in winter should be no more than 55°F (13°C) otherwise buds and leaves will drop.
Compost should be kept moist always, but not with hard water as this eventually turns leaves yellow.

Feed every two weeks in spring and summer using an acid fertilizer. Remove dead flower heads to encourage new flowers. Prune stems to shape after flowering has stopped. Pot-on each year after flowering in a peat compost.
Propagate by taking 3 in (7.5 cm) stem cuttings in summer. Bottom heat required.

Sparmannia africana

African Hemp

Heart-shaped, bright green, hairy leaves up to 8 in (20 cm) carried on short stems. Clusters of white flowers with yellow and purple stamens appear from late spring to early summer. Individual flowers do not last long, but new ones keep coming. Grows to 6 ft (1.8 m).

Likes good light, but should be slightly shaded to prevent leaf scorch. Leaves turn pale yellow in poor light.
Compost must always be moist during growing period but in winter keep barely moist.
Feed every two weeks in spring and summer. Pot-on each year in spring in a loam compost. When new growth is well under way, pinch out growing tips for bushiness. Old plants can be pruned by half after flowering.
Propagate by taking 6 in (15 cm) stem cuttings in late spring.

Flowering annuals

The great virtue of annuals is that they provide brilliant colour in summer and autumn, when the cool conservatory will be most frequently used. It is also inexpensive colour, whether bought in as young plants in late spring or, far more cheaply, if raised from seed. The seed of most annuals benefits from a little gentle heat to speed up germination. If the temperature in the conservatory is at the top end of the scale, about 55°F (13°C), this should be sufficient.

Spring flowers can be obtained by sowing seed the previous autumn and overwintering plants in the cool conservatory. Plants suitable for this treatment are indicated in the following selection of annuals.

Calceolaria multiflora

Slipperwort

Mid-green, oval leaves. Produces pouch-like pink, orange, red, yellow and often multi-coloured flowers, spotted or blotched, from summer to autumn. Grows to 18 in (45 cm), but many hybrids are only 9 in (22.5 cm).

Likes bright light but shade from direct sun.
Compost should be moist always.
Feed every fortnight after flowers first appear. Pinch out growing tips for bushiness.
Sow seed in late winter and early spring, or previous autumn for early flowers.

Calendula officinalis

Pot Marigold

Spoon-shaped, narrow, somewhat sticky, bright green leaves. Double or semi-double yellow to orange daisy-like flowers (depending on cultivar) produced from summer to autumn. Grows to 2 ft (60 cm).

Likes bright light with direct sun.
Compost should be moist always.
Feed every fortnight after first flower buds appear. Remove fading blooms to ensure continuous flowering.
Sow seed in spring, or previous autumn for earlier flowering.

Catharanthus roseus

Periwinkle

Oval, pointed, bright green leaves. Funnel-shaped red, pink and white flowers with spreading petals produced in summer and autumn. Grows to 12 in (30 cm).

Likes bright light with direct sun for plenty of flowers.
Compost should always be moist, but never waterlogged.
Feed every two weeks after flower buds appear. Pinch out growing tips for bushy plants.
Sow seed in early spring.

Celosia argentea 'Pyramidalis'

Cockscomb

Oval, bright green leaves. Showy and gaudy plumes of densely-packed small, bright red or yellow flowers forming a pyramid shape appear from summer to autumn. Grows to 2 ft (60 cm).

Likes excellent light with direct sun.
Compost should be kept well watered.
Feed every fortnight from first appearance of flower buds.
Sow seed in early spring.

Cineraria maritima (syn. *Senecio cineraria*)

Dusty Miller

Silver grey, woolly, deeply incised long leaves. Yellow heads of flowers produced in late summer and autumn. Grows to 15 in (37.5 cm), but there are smaller cultivars to 8 in (20 cm).

Likes bright light with direct sun.
Compost should always be moist.
Feed every two weeks once strong growth is established.
Sow seed in early sping.

Clarkia elegans

Rocky Mountain Garland

Lance-shaped, mid-green leaves with serrated edges. Double pink, red, purple and white flowers appear in summer from leaf axils of stems. Grows to 2 ft (60 cm).

Likes good light with direct sun.
Compost should always be moist.
Feed every two weeks after flower buds appear. Pinch out growing tips for bushiness.
Sow seed in early spring or in previous autumn for earlier flowers.

Exacum affine

Persian Violet

Shiny, oval, dark green leaves. Five-petalled violet flowers with deep yellow stamens produced from summer to late autumn. Bushy but compact plants growing to 9 in (22.5 cm).

Likes bright light but keep out of fierce midday sun.
Compost should always be moist.
Feed every two weeks after flower buds appear. Remove faded blooms for continuous flowering.
Sow seed in early spring, or in previous autumn for spring flowering.

Lobelia erinus

Lobelia

Lance-shaped, narrow leaves. Red, white or blue fan-shaped, five-petalled flowers produced from summer to autumn. Grows to 6 in (15 cm) and looks particularly effective in a hanging container.

Likes good light with direct sun.
Compost should always be moist.
Feed every fortnight after flowers appear. Chop off dead flowers for prolonged flowering.
Sow seed in early spring.

Lobularia maritima

Sweet Alyssum

Tiny, narrow leaves and equally tiny red, purple or white densely-packed fragrant flowers produced from summer to autumn. Grows to 6 in (15 cm) tall, but spreads to 10 in (25 cm).

Likes bright light with direct sun.
Compost should always be moist but never waterlogged.
Feed every fortnight after flowers appear. If plants become straggly, cut them back and fresh flowers will soon appear.
Sow seed in early spring.

Nemesia strumosa

Nemesia

Pale green, lance-shaped leaves with toothed edges. Pink, red, orange, white, yellow, blue and purple trumpet flowers appear from early to late summer. Some cultivars have multi-coloured flowers. Grows to 10 in (25 cm).

Likes bright light and a well ventilated position. Shade from direct hot sun.
Feed every fortnight after flower buds appear. These plants are rather lanky, so pinch out growing tips to make them bushier. Cut off fading blooms for prolonged flowering.
Sow seed in late winter and early spring.

Nicotiana hybrids

Tobacco Plant

Large, oval, pale green leaves, slightly sticky to the touch. White, pink, red and greenish-yellow tubular flowers ending in five flaring petals appear in summer and autumn. Very fragrant in early evening. Some grow to 3 ft (90 cm), but others are dwarf hybrids of only 10 in (25 cm).

Likes bright light with direct sun.
Compost should always be moist; may need daily watering in hot weather.
Feed every two weeks after flower buds appear. Remove faded flowers to ensure that more appear.
Sow seed in early spring.

Petunia x *hybrida*

Petunia

Bright green, oval leaves. Double and single white, yellow, blue, purple, red and pink trumpet flowers produced in summer and autumn. Grows to 12 in (30 cm).

Likes bright light with direct sun for plenty of flowers.
Compost should always be moist.
Feed every two weeks when flower buds appear.
Sow seed in early spring.

Reseda odorata

Mignonette

Light green, lance-shaped leaves. Spikes of small, close-packed, sweetly fragrant yellow, white or red flowers appear in summer and autumn. Grows to 15 in (37.5 cm).

Likes good light with direct sun.
Compost should always be moist, but never sodden.
Feed every two weeks when flower buds appear.
Sow seed in spring. Take care when transplanting to remove each seedling with some of the compost around the roots. Prefers a limy compost.

Salpiglossis sinuata

Painted Tongue

Narrow, bright green, elliptical, somewhat sticky leaves. In summer and autumn produces trumpet-shaped, velvety red, yellow, pink, and purple flowers, with veins picked out in contrasting colours. Grows to 3 ft (90 cm) but some compact hybrids grow to only 12 in (30 cm).

Likes bright light with direct sun.
Compost should be well watered, but not sodden, since plants are likely to rot if the compost is too wet.
Feed every two weeks after flower buds appear.
Sow seed in spring.

Salvia splendens

Scarlet Sage

Bright green, oval, pointed leaves with serrated edges. Spikes of bright scarlet, tubular flowers appear in summer and autumn. Grows to 12 in (30 cm).

Likes bright light with direct sun. Keep well watered.
Feed every two weeks after flower buds appear. Pinch out growing tips for bushy growth.
Sow seed in early spring.

Schizanthus pinnatus

Butterfly Flower

Delicate, bright green, fern-like foliage almost swamped by masses of two-lipped white, pink, red, blue and purple flowers with contrasting shading and marking on the throat. These orchid-like flowers appear in summer. Grows to 4 ft (1.2 m) but dwarf cultivars are available, growing to 12 in (30 cm).

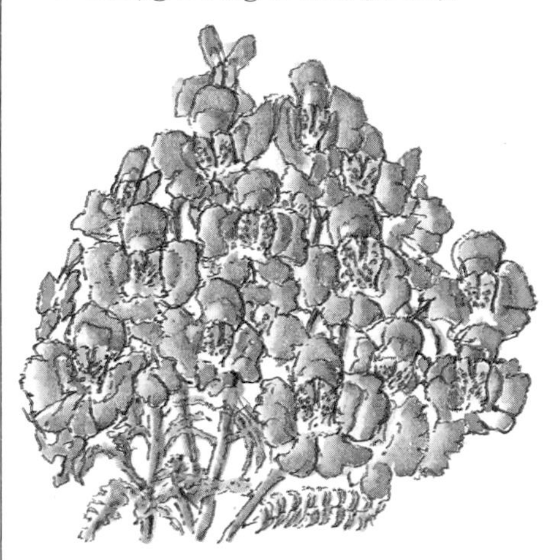

Likes good light with direct sun.
Compost should be moist always.
Feed every two weeks when flower buds appear. Pinch out growing tips of taller plants to keep them bushy and to increase flowering.
Sow seed in spring or in previous autumn for earlier flowers.

Senecio cruentus

Cineraria

Coarse, bright green, heart-shaped leaves. Daisy-like red, yellow, pink and purple flowers with contrasting white markings on the petals produced in summer. Grows to 12 in (30 cm).

Likes bright light with direct sun.
Compost should always be moist.
Feed every two weeks once sturdy growth is established. Very susceptible to attack by pests, especially greenfly. Cut off dead flower heads to encourage new growth.
Sow seed in early spring.

Tagetes patula

French Marigold

Dark green, feathery, incised leaves. Maroon and yellow, or crimson and yellow, single and double pom-pom flowers appear in summer and autumn. Grows to 12 in (30 cm).

Likes bright light with direct sun.
Compost should always be moist.
Feed every two weeks when flower buds appear. Pinch out growing tips for bushier plants and more flowers. Remove dead flower heads.
Sow seed in spring.

Torenia fournieri compacta

Wishbone Flower

Bronze-green, bushy foliage, about 8 in (20 cm) high, but may almost be hidden by mass of bloom. Velvety, gloxinia-like flowers, pale blue with lavender lips and yellow throat; the stamens are in the shape of a wishbone. Flowers appear in summer and continue over a long period.

Likes a partly shaded position and needs humidity; flowers fade in dry air.
Compost should always be moist, but not wet.
Feed every fortnight after buds form.
Sow seed in spring. Transplant five to a 6 in (15 cm) pot.

Trachymene caerula (syn. Didiscus caeruleus)

Blue Lace Flower

Small, lacy flowers forming flat-topped umbels 2 – 3 in (5 – 8 cm) across, pale lavender blue, and sweet scented, on stems of 1 –2 ft (30 – 60 cm).

Likes bright light with direct sun, but does better in cool weather than in hot.
Feed every two weeks during the flowering period.
Sow seed in spring, preferably in peat pots to avoid the disturbance of transplanting, which they resent. Plant fairly close to get profuse blooms. Pinch out growing tips for bushier growth.

Tropaeolum majus

Nasturtium

Circular, bright green leaves on long stalks. Saucer-shaped, five-petalled, double and single, yellow, orange, red and salmon flowers appear in summer and autumn. Some grow to 6 ft (1.8 m) and can be trained to cover large areas. Other cultivars stay more compact, at 18 in (45 cm), and are best displayed trailing from a hanging container.

Likes bright light with full sun.
Compost should be moist always.
Feed every two weeks after flower buds appear. Pinch out growing tips for bushier growth and abundant flowers over a longer period.
Sow seed in spring.

Ursinia anethoides

Feathery, fern-like foliage which is strongly scented. Daisy-like flowers, about 1 – 2 in (2.5 – 5 cm) across, with vivid orange and yellow petals surrounding a deep purple centre. Each of the numerous flowers, which appear over ten weeks or more, are carried on a wiry stem about 12 in (30 cm) long. They open in full sun and close at evening, though on dull days may stay shut all the time.

Likes full sun, but needs good ventilation in very hot weather.
Compost should be well draining and kept just moist.
Feed every fortnight when flowers appear.
Sow seed in spring; flowering will start after ten weeks or so.

Viola x *wittrockiana*

Pansy

Bright green, oval leaves. Produces large-petalled, flat, red, orange, yellow, blue and purple flowers – mostly bicoloured – from late spring to autumn.

Likes bright light with direct sun.
Compost should always be moist; pansies are very thirsty plants in hot weather, and may need daily watering.
Feed every fortnight after flower buds appear. If plants grow too tall they can be cut back and growing tips pinched out.
Sow seed in spring, or in previous autumn for earlier flowering.

Palms and ferns

The palms mentioned here have fronds in open fan formation. Those of chamaerops (certainly the most elegant looking) have narrow, pointed segments, while those of raphis are oval with blunt ends. As these palms mature the fronds may begin to look unattractive with browning, ragged edges. This is often caused by air which is too dry; a humid atmosphere in warm summer months will help to counteract this. Remove any unsightly fronds.

Of the comparatively few ferns suitable for conservatories, those recommended for the cool conservatory are the most popular. They include various forms of adiantum (Maidenhair Fern) with their delicate, bright green, lace-like foliage. To keep them in tip-top condition they need a humid atmosphere all year round and cool winters, between 50°–55°F (10°–13°C).

Chamaerops humilis

European Fan Palm

Deeply dissected fronds of thin, sword-shaped, grey-green segments in open fan formation, carried on stems up to 4 ft (1.2 m) long. The lower part of the stem is covered with stout spines. New fronds are coated with a grey meal which eventually falls off. Each fan can be about 2 ft (60 cm) across. The more compact *C.h.* 'Elegans' is suitable for the smaller conservatory.

Likes bright light with direct sun; growth of plants in the shade will be slow.
Compost should be kept moist in the growing period, but let the surface dry out between waterings in winter.
Feed every fortnight in spring and summer. Pot-on every two to three years in spring in a mixture of two thirds peat to one third sand. Change compost for fresh in years in between.
Propagate by sowing seed in spring or by removing suckers when potting-on or repotting. Each sucker must have plenty of roots to become established.

Raphis excelsa

Little Lady Palm

Clumps of fronds, each consisting of several elongated oval segments about 8 in (20 cm) long and 2 in (5 cm) wide, carried on 9 in (22.5 cm) stems in fan formation. Grows to 5 ft (1.5 m). *R. humilis* has fronds with up to 20 12 in (30 cm) segments. Grows to around 7 ft (2.1 m). Both species are slow growing.

Likes bright light, but shade from direct sun. Benefits from a humid atmosphere in warm weather.
Compost should be kept moist always in growing period, but barely moist in winter.
Feed once a month in spring and summer. Pot-on each spring in a mixture of two parts peat compost and one part sand.
Propagate from seed sown in spring with a bottom heat of 75°F (24°C); or from suckers taken from the base of the palm (making sure there are plenty of roots) and planted in compost.

Adiantum capillus – veneris

Maidenhair Fern

Densely-packed, triangular leaflets with frilled edges on black wiry stems. Grows to 12 in (30 cm) usually, but the fronds can be longer and then the fern looks best displayed as a hanging plant. *A. cuneatum* (syn. *A. raddianum*) has slightly coarser leaflets and the triangular-shaped fronds grow to 18 in (45 cm) long and 2 ft (60 cm) wide. *A. tenerum* 'Farleyense' has deeply incised fronds, up to 3 ft (90 cm) long with frilled leaflets.

Likes bright light but no direct sun, otherwise leaflets pale and die. Humid atmosphere essential, especially in warm weather.
Compost should be moist in growing period, but allow the surface to dry out between waterings in winter. Compost must never dry out completely, since this is the quickest way to kill the fern. A dried-out plant may be rescued by cutting down all the fronds to compost level. Thereafter, spray the surface of the compost daily; do not soak the soil ball. New growth should appear

Ornamental fruits

eventually.
Feed once a month in spring and summer. Pot-on every other spring in a mixture of peat, loam and sand or in a peat compost. Renew compost in year between.
Propagate in spring by division or from spores, but bottom heat of 70°F (21°C) and much skill and patience are needed.

— *Pellaea rotundifolia* —

Button Fern

Dark brown stems up to 12 in (30 cm) long carry almost opposite pairs of rounded, dark green, glossy pinnae. As they mature, pinnae become oval.

Likes good light but shade from direct sun. Needs a well-ventilated position.
Temperature in winter must be around 55°F (13°C).
Compost should be moist always in growing period and just moist in winter. Do not allow it to dry out completely.
Feed every two weeks in spring and summer. Pot-on every other spring in a peat compost. Change compost for fresh in years between.
Propagate by dividing the rhizome when potting-on.

The cool conservatory is the only place where it is worthwhile growing ornamental fruiting plants. There the highly coloured fruits and berries will last for any length of time – indeed, if conditions are cool enough in winter, many will last for weeks and some for months. Some of the fruits are edible (though they may be tart or tasteless) but that is hardly the point of growing them.

All the plants listed here must have winter temperatures between 50° – 55°F (10° – 13°C); in conditions much warmer than that the fruit will fall, and at an alarming rate if moved to the warmth of the house. Winter cool is also needed to induce plants to flower and fruit successfully the following year. When plants are in flower, humidity is important to help to set the fruit.

— *Ardisia crenata* —

Coral Berry

Dark green, glossy, narrow, oval leaves with wavy edges, about 6 in (15 cm) long. Sweet-smelling red flowers appear in summer, followed by red berries. These may last for six months if the plant is kept cool during winter and spring. Slow growth to 2 ft (60 cm).

Likes a well-lit spot, but away from direct sun. Provide a humid atmosphere throughout the year.
Temperatures in winter should be no more than 50°F (10°C) or the berries will rapidly fall.
Compost should be kept moist in flowering and fruiting period, but reduce frequency of watering for the rest of the year. Pot-on every spring in loam compost. Leggy stems can be cut back to 3 in (7.5 cm) to stimulate new growth.
Propagate by sowing seed in spring or take cuttings with a heel in summer.

— *Capsicum annuum* —

Ornamental Chili Pepper

Dark green, lance-shaped 2 in (5 cm) leaves. White flowers are produced from early summer to early autumn followed by multi-coloured round or cone-shaped fruits, depending on the cultivar. When fruit first appears it is green, changing to yellow, orange and then red. All colours may be present on a single plant and combinations of different fruit shapes make a fine display. Fruit lasts for two or three months. Capsicums grow to 9 in (22.5 cm), but some cultivars to 18 in (45 cm). Treat as an annual.

Likes good light with direct sun. Requires humidity all year round.
Temperatures in winter should be between 50°– 55°F (10° – 13°C) if fruit is not to fall.
Compost should be kept moist, but not sodden. Leaves will turn yellow if it is too dry. Potting-on is not necessary – throw plants away when fruit finally shrivels and falls.
Propagate from seed sown in spring with bottom heat of 65°F (18°C).

—— *Citrus mitis* ——

Calamondin Orange

Oval, glossy leaves about 3 in (7.5 cm) long. Produces sweet-smelling white flowers, usually in summer, followed by 1 in (2.5 cm) diameter fruits, green at first and turning to orange. In cool temperatures the fruit will last for many months. Slow growth to 3 ft (90 cm).

Likes bright light with direct sun and a well-ventilated spot. Requires humidity, especially when in flower, helping fruit to set.
Temperatures in winter between 50° – 55°F (10° – 13°C).
Compost should be moist always, except during winter months when it should be barely moist.
Feed every two weeks in spring and summer. Flowers require pollinating if plant is to fruit. Insects usually do the job, but to make sure draw a soft brush over the flowers. Pinch out growing tips in spring to promote bushiness and prune the plant to shape. Pot-on every other spring in loam compost to which bone meal has been added. Change compost for fresh in years in between.
Propagate from seed sown in spring or take 4 in (10 cm) cuttings in summer. Bottom heat of 70° – 75°F (21° – 24°C) is needed for both.

—— *Duchesnea indica* ——

Indian Strawberry

Groups of three heart-shaped leaves on stems of 2 ft (60 cm) or more. This may be grown as a hanging plant in a container or trained upwards on a frame. Bright yellow flowers from early summer to early autumn are followed by red, strawberry-like fruits which are edible but tasteless.

Likes good strong light but no direct sun. Requires humidity in warm weather.
Compost should always be moist except in winter when the surface should be allowed to dry out between waterings.
Feed every two weeks in spring and summer. Pot-on each spring in loam compost. Poor specimens with straggly growth should be discarded.
Propagate by division when potting-on or by layering. Pin down the runners in compost and sever from main plant when healthy growth has been established.

—— *Fortunella margarita* ——

Kumquat

Glossy green leaves about 3 in (7.5 cm) long. White flowers in summer are followed by small round or oval fruits which ripen to orange and last for several weeks in autumn and winter. The fruit is edible and is eaten whole; a somewhat acquired taste, the skin is rather sweeter than the tart flesh and pith inside – in all, it's probably better left on the plant. Grows to 4 ft (1.2 m).

Likes bright light with direct sun.
Temperatures between 50° – 55°F (10° – 13°C) needed in autumn and winter if fruit is to last and the plant is to flower and fruit the following year.
Compost should be kept moist except in winter, when it should almost dry out between waterings.
Feed every two weeks in spring and summer. Pot-on each spring in a mixture of loam compost and leaf mould.
Propagate from seeds of fruit or from 4 in (10 cm) cuttings taken in summer.

—— *Nertera granadensis* ——

Bead Plant

Creeping stems with tiny, oval, fleshy leaves. Small white flowers in spring and early summer are followed by orange berries which last for many weeks in winter if the conservatory is cool enough. Best grown in wide, shallow pots. The plants will reach no more than 3 in (7.5 cm) high but will spread over the surface of the pot.

Likes bright light with direct sun. Provide a humid atmosphere.
Temperatures much above 50°F (10°C) will cause berries to fall.
Compost must always be moist except in winter when it should be barely moist.
Feed once a month in spring and summer. Pot-on each spring in a mixture of peat compost and sand. By using a shallow container it may not be necessary to go beyond a 5 in (12.5 cm) diameter pot.
Propagate by division when potting-on or sow seed in spring with bottom heat of 70°F (21°C).

—— *Solanum capicastrum* ——

Winter Cherry

Dark green, oval leaves covering short branches thrown out from the main stem. Small white flowers in summer are followed by cherry-sized green berries which ripen to yellow and red. Grows to 18 in (45 cm) with a similar spread.

Likes bright light with direct sun. Provide a humid atmosphere, helping to set the fruit during flowering.
Temperatures around 50°F (10°C) are needed if fruit is to last over a period of weeks.
Compost should always be moist, except in winter when it should be barely moist.
Feed once a fortnight in spring and summer. When fruits have dropped, prune back stems by two thirds. Pinch out growing tips of new growth to make plants bushy. Pot-on each spring in loam compost. Plants are usually replaced after two or three years.
Propagate from seed sown in early spring.

Herbs

Room can always be found in the cool conservatory for a few of the smaller herbs – those decorative, aromatic plants which are ultimately useful in the kitchen. Sweet bay and rosemary are larger, but have claims for space on their attractiveness alone. Basil is an annual, but the perennial herbs need cool, frost-free, conditions in winter.

—— *Allium schoenoprasum* ——

Chives

Grass-like leaves with an onion smell appear in spring and often die down late in the year. Pink to lilac flowers in thick globular heads are produced in summer. Grows to 8 in (20 cm).

Likes bright light with direct sun. Keep well watered throughout the year.
Feed once a month in spring and summer. Pot-on every other spring in loam compost, changing old compost for fresh in the year between.
Propagate by division in spring or by sowing seed.

—— *Laurus nobilis* ——

Sweet Bay

Lance-shaped, leathery, dark green leaves about 3 in (7.5 cm) long. The shrub is often trimmed to a pyramid shape or is cultivated as a standard with a rounded head. Grows to 5 ft (1.5 m).

Likes good light with direct sun.
Compost should be kept moist in growing period and just moist in winter.
Feed once a month in spring and summer. Pot-on every spring in loam compost.
Propagate in summer from stem cuttings of current season's growth.

—— *Melissa officinalis* ——

Lemon Balm

Small, lance-shaped, bright green leaves, up to 3 in (7.5 cm) long, with a strong lemon scent when rubbed. Also flavours fish and chicken dishes. Small white to green flowers bloom in summer, followed by almost black oval fruits. Grows to 30 in (75 cm); cut back to 6 in (15 cm) in autumn.

Likes bright light with direct sun; less scented in shade.
Compost should be well watered in growing season, but barely moist in winter.
Feed monthly in spring and summer. Pot-on when roots have filled the pot, in spring in loam compost.
Propagate by division or take cuttings in spring.

—— *Myrrhis odorata* ——

Sweet Cicely

Perennial herb with attractive feathery, fern-like foliage and a sweet aniseed flavour. Clusters of small white flowers form in late spring and early summer. In late autumn the foliage dies down, but emerges again in late winter, unfurling stems in a way similar to ferns. Grows to 5 ft (1.5 cm), but only after many years.

Likes bright light with full sun.
Compost should be moist always in the growing period, but barely moist when resting in winter.
Feed monthly in spring and summer. Pot-on each spring in loam compost.
Propagate by seed or division in spring.

—— *Ocimum basilicum* ——

Basil

Aromatic, oval leaves up to 3 in (7.5 cm) long. Produces small-lipped white flowers in summer. Grows to 18 in (45 cm), but there are dwarf varieties up to 6 in (15 cm). Treat as an annual.

Likes bright light with direct sun.
Compost should always be moist.
Feed once a month when foliage is well established and continue to early autumn, when foliage begins to die down. In early autumn, cut back stems to one pair of leaves above compost level; the plant will go on producing leaves for a further month or so. It is then discarded.
Propagate by seed sown in spring in temperature of 60°F (16°C).

—— *Rosmarinus officinalis* 'Seven Sea' ——

Rosemary

Sweetly aromatic, narrow grey-green leaves on spreading stems. In spring, lilac-blue flowers appear. Grows to 3 ft (90 cm).

Likes good light with direct sun.
Compost should be kept moist in growing period but barely moist in winter, when watering once a fortnight should be enough.
Feed once a month in spring and summer. Picking the growing tips for use in the kitchen will help to make the plant bushy. Pot-on every spring in

Hanging plants

loam compost.
Propagate by taking 4 in (10 cm) stem cuttings in early summer.

—— *Salvia officinalis* ——

Sage

Very pungent, lance-shaped, grey-green leaves up to 2 in (5 cm) long, with a velvety feel. Produces small purple flowers in summer. Grows to 2 ft (60 cm).

Likes bright light with direct sun.
Compost should be kept moist in growing season and just moist in winter.
Feed once a month in spring and summer. For bushy growth, cut back stems by a third in spring. Pot-on every spring in loam compost. It is best to replace plants after about three years.
Propagate by taking cuttings in summer, or sow seed in spring.

—— *Thymus vulgaris* ——

Thyme

Small, narrow leaves carried on wiry stems. Tubular, pale blue flowers appear in early summer. Grows to 10 in (25 cm).

Likes bright light with direct sun.
Compost should be kept moist throughout growing period; water about once a fortnight in winter.
Feed monthly in spring and summer. Cut back stems to about 6 in (15 cm) in late spring. Pot-on every spring in loam (and limey) compost.
Propagate by division in spring or from cuttings in summer.

The following plants are particularly suitable for hanging containers in the cool conservatory. Three – browallia, campanula and *Pelargonium peltatum*, the Ivy-leaved Geranium – will between them produce colourful flowers from spring to early winter. Tradescantia and chlorophytum add to the mixture with their variegated leaves. *Saxifraga stolonifera* (Mother of Thousands) and *Tolmiea menziesii* (Piggybank Plant), along with the chlorophytum (Spider Plant), provide extra interest in the way they produce a profusion of plantlets. But for an eye-catching display of feathery foliage, plant a container with a mixture of asparagus.

—— *Asparagus densiflorus* ——
(syn. *A. sprengeri*)

Emerald Feather

Masses of trailing stems, densely packed with small green phyllocades (flattened stems serving as leaves). These toughen and become prickly as the plant develops. Modest green flowers followed by red berries may appear. Cultivars of *A. densiflorus* only are usually available with stems up to 15 in (37.5 cm) long. *A. setaceus* 'Nanus', the Lace Fern, has much finer, delicate foliage, with upright young stems which arch over as they mature, growing to 3 ft (90 cm) long.

Likes a well-lit spot out of direct sunlight.
Compost should be kept moist in the growing period, but water less frequently in winter so that compost is barely moist. Never allow it to dry out completely or the foliage will fall. If this should happen and the plant becomes totally bare, drastic action may rescue it. Cut off all stems at compost level and plunge the pot into a bucket of water to soak the compost thoroughly. With luck the plant will soon begin to throw out new shoots.
Feed every two weeks in spring and summer. Pot-on every spring in loam compost.
Propagate by division in spring.

—— *Browallia speciosa 'Major'* ——

Sapphire Flower

Bright, rich green, pointed oval leaves, on short stems. Tubular violet flowers with white centres appear from summer through to winter. Grows to 2 ft (60 cm). A white-flowered form,

B.s. 'Silver Bells', is also available. *B. viscosa* 'Sapphire' grows to 12 cm (30 cm) and its violet flowers are smaller than those of *B. speciosa* 'Major'. *B.v.* 'Alba' has white flowers. For a dazzling effect, plant different-coloured forms in the same container.

Likes bright light with some direct sunlight, but shade from the hottest sun, which can burn flowers.
Compost should be kept moist always, but reduce frequency of watering in winter.
Feed every two weeks after flower buds first appear until flowering is finished. Potting – on is not necessary since these plants are treated as annuals and discarded after flowering. Pinch out growing tips regularly for bushy plants and remove faded flowers.
Propagate from seed sown in late winter and early spring for summer flowering, and in late summer and early autumn for winter flowering.

Campanula isophylla

Bell Flower

Heart-shaped, pale, grey-green leaves on 12 in (30 cm) stems. Produces star-shaped flowers in profusion from late summer to early autumn – white in *C.i.* 'Alba'; blue in *C.i.* 'Mayi'. Mixing the two colours in the same container is very effective.

Likes bright light with some sun, but is best not exposed to scorching sun. Poor light means few flowers. Flowers will drop rapidly if plants are not in a well-ventilated and cool spot all the year. In warm weather provide humidity.
Compost should be moist during growing period, but when plant has died down water only every two weeks or so.
Feed every two weeks in spring and summer. Pot-on each year in spring in loam compost. When flowering is over, cut back stems to 2 in (5 cm).
Propagate from 3 in (7.5 cm) stem cuttings taken in late spring when new growth has started.

Chlorophytum comosum 'Vittatum'

Spider Plant

Thin, arching leaves up to 18 in (45 cm) long with a white to cream vertical stripe along the central rib. Plant several together for a really bushy effect. In spring and summer, stems bearing small white flowers emerge from the centre of the clumps, followed by plantlets which are replicas of the parent plant. These can be used to raise new plants, but look particularly attractive if they are left to grow hanging over the edge of the container.

Likes good light to maintain bright leaf colour, but keep out of hot midday sun, which may burn the leaves.
Compost should be kept moist in growing period, but in winter allow surface to dry out between waterings. If compost is too dry, leaf tips will turn brown.
Feed every two weeks in spring and summer. Pot-on each year in loam compost.
Propagate in spring and summer by detaching plantlets when they start to produce roots. Put into water for roots to develop properly and then plant into compost, or plant direct into compost. Alternatively, layer the runners by pinning the plantlets, still attached to the parent, into pots of compost. Sever from the parent plant when well established.

Pelargonium peltatum

Ivy-leaved Geranium

Ivy-shaped, fleshy leaves on 2 ft (60 cm) stems. From spring until late autumn, clusters of 1 in (2.5 cm) flowers, in shades of pink, lavender and red, appear on 6 in (15 cm) stalks. Some forms have attractively variegated leaves, with white to pink edges.

Likes a sunny spot with good light and ventilation.
Compost should always be moist in growing period, but barely moist when plant is resting; watering once every three weeks should be enough.
Feed every two weeks in spring and summer. Pot-on in spring in either loam or peat compost. Cut back stems to 6 in (15 cm) in early spring. Pinch out growing tips when new growth is established.
Propagate from 4 in (10 cm) stem cuttings taken in summer.

Saxifraga stolonifera

Mother of Thousands

Rosettes of somewhat hairy, rounded, dark green leaves up to 3 in (7.5 cm) across. Network of silvery veins on upper surface and red undersides. Runners carrying small replicas of the parent are thrown out from the centre of the rosette. Clusters of white flowers in summer. *S.s.* 'Tricolor' has leaves with cream edges, tinted pink. Plant grows no more than 8 in (20 cm) high, but runners may be up to 2 ft (60 cm).

Likes bright light with some direct sunlight, as long as there is shade from scorching sun. Provide extra humidity in warm weather.
Compost should be kept moist during growing period, but barely moist during winter rest; water probably every seven to ten days.
Feed every two weeks in spring and summer. Pot-on in spring each year in loam compost.
Propagate by removing plantlets when they show roots and plant them in compost. Otherwise, layer the runners in compost, severing plantlet from the parent when it is established.

Tolmiea menziesii

Piggyback Plant

Heart-shaped, hairy, bright green leaves about 3 in (7.5 cm) wide. Small plantlets grow from points where the short stalks join the leaves. Inconspicuous greenish-brown flowers may appear in summer. Grows to 12 in (30 cm) with a similar spread.

Likes good light but out of direct sun; if too shaded, foliage will be pale. Provide a well-ventilated spot and humid atmosphere in hot weather.
Compost should be moist always in growing period but barely moist in

Climbers

winter. Too-dry compost makes leaves limp and shrivel.
Feed every two weeks in spring and summer. Pot-on in spring every year in peat compost.
Propagate in spring and summer by removing a leaf with its plantlet and 2 in (5 cm) of stalk. Plant in compost. Otherwise, a leaf with plantlet can be pinned down in compost at the point where stalk and leaf join. When roots have developed and plant is growing well, sever from the main plant.

—— *Tradescantia fluminensis* ——

Wandering Jew

Oval, bright green leaves with purple undersides. Other varieties and species sport different colours. *T.f.* 'Quicksilver' has green and white striped leaves, so has *T.f.* 'Variegata', but with broader stripes. *T. albiflora* 'Tricolor' has green, white and purple stripes. *T. blossfeldiana* 'Variegata' has green, cream and purple stripes. Produces insignificant pink or white flowers in spring and summer. Stems grow to 2 ft (60 cm) or more, but are best cut back to about 15 in (37.5 cm). Longer stems become straggly and untidy as older leaves die off.

Likes bright light with some direct sun to maintain good leaf colour. Shade from very hot sun.
Compost should be moist always in growing period, but allow surface to dry out between waterings in winter.
Feed every two weeks in spring and summer. Pot-on every second or third year in spring in loam or peat compost. Change compost for fresh in years between. Replace bedraggled plants with new cuttings. Pinch out growing tips for bushiness. Cut away stems with few leaves or with plain green leaves.
Propagate by taking 4 in (10 cm) stem cuttings in spring or summer, rooting them in water or compost.

In a cool lean-to conservatory, little occupied by the owners in winter, the best climbers to cover the back wall are those which flower in summer and autumn. Among those suggested are passiflora (Passion Flower), plumbago, and the two annuals ipomoea (Morning Glory) and thunbergia (Black-eyed Susan). The heavy fragrance of winter-flowering jasmine also makes an ample reward for your daily visits to see that nothing is amiss. For decorative foliage try the exuberant cissus and rhoicissus.

The perennial climbers all need cool winter conditions; without a winter rest the flowers of jasmine will refuse to open and the foliage will fall, while passiflora and plumbago will flower poorly. Climbers also need support of some kind, either strong canes or netting. Those which throw out tendrils, such as cissus, ipomoea and rhoicissus, are better trained against netting, over which they spread quickly to form a blanket of greenery.

—— *Cissus antarctica* ——

Kangaroo Vine

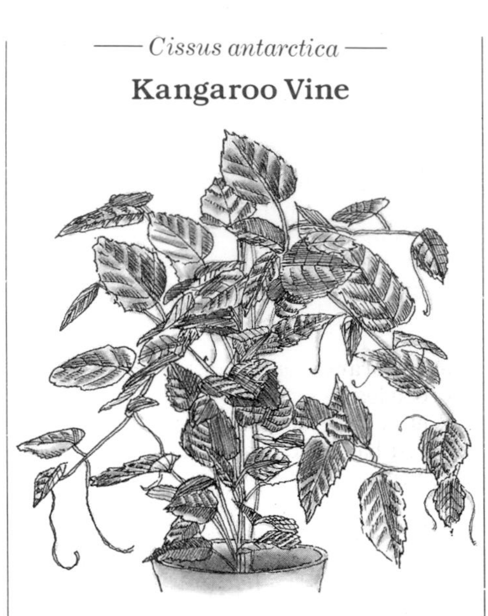

Shiny, leathery leaves, oval and pointed with serrated edges. The light green of the leaves darkens with age. Grows to 10 ft (3 m) and needs support for the tendrils to cling to. The leaves of *C. striata* are carried on red stems and divided into five tooth-edged leaflets, dark green on top and pink underneath. This plant is much smaller than *C. antarctica* and more suitable for a hanging container. *C. rhombifolia* has groups of three rhomboid-shaped leaves with a metallic sheen.

Likes good light, but shade from direct sun, which browns the leaves.
Temperature in winter should be 50°F (10°C) minimum.
Compost must be kept moist during growing period and barely moist in winter.
Feed every fortnight in spring and summer. Pinch out growing tips regularly for bushy growth. Straggly stems should be cut back to 4 in (10 cm). Pot-on every spring in a mixture of loam, peat, leaf mould and sand.
Propagate by taking stem cuttings in spring and summer.

—— *Ipomoea tricolor* ——

Morning Glory

Twining, thin stems with heart-shaped leaves. Produces pale blue trumpet flowers with yellow throat from mid-summer to early autumn. Flowers open in the morning and fade by afternoon, to be replaced by more flowers the following morning. Half-hardy annual raised from seed. Grows to 8 ft (2.4 m).

Likes bright light with direct sun for good flowering.
Compost should always be moist.
Feed weekly once foliage is well established and until flowering is over, when the plant is discarded.
Sow seed in spring in temperature of 65°F (18°C).

—— *Jasminum polyanthum* ——

Jasmine

Many-branching climber, with dark green leaves divided into six leaflets. White, long-tubed flowers with five flared-back petals appear in winter months. Grows to 10 ft (3 m).

Likes bright light with direct sunlight, but out of the strongest sun. Needs good ventilation.
Compost should always be moist in spring and summer, but just moist for rest of year.
Feed every fortnight in spring and summer. Cut back stems to 6 in (15 cm) when flowering is over. Pot-on in summer every year in a loam compost.
Propagate by taking 4 in (10 cm) stem cuttings in summer.

—— *Passiflora caerulea* ——

Passion Flower

Five-lobed, shiny, dark green leaves. Fascinating, complex flowers with white petals and purple and white filaments produced from summer to early autumn. Grows to 10 ft (3 m) and needs firm support for the weak stems.

Likes bright light with direct sun.
Compost should be kept moist in growing period, but water in winter about once a fortnight.
Feed every two weeks in spring and summer. Cut back stems to 6 in (15 cm) in spring. Pot-on every second spring in loam compost, changing compost for fresh in the year between.
Propagate by taking 4 in (10 cm) cuttings in summer.

—— *Plumbago capensis* ——

Cape Leadwort

Oval green leaves on somewhat straggly 4 ft (1.2 m) stems. Clusters of five-petalled pale blue flowers appear from spring to autumn. *P.c.* 'Alba' is a white flowered cultivar; grow mixtures of the two for the best effect.

Likes bright light with direct sun.
Temperatures in winter should not fall below 50°F (10°C).
Compost should be kept moist during growing period, but just moist in winter.
Feed every fortnight in spring and summer. Prune back stems by two thirds of their length in spring. Pot-on in spring in a loam compost.
Propagate in summer from 4 in (10 cm) stem cuttings.

—— *Rhoicissus capensis* ——

Cape Grape

Round to heart-shaped glossy, bright green leaves with serrated edges produced on woody stems. Grows quickly to 6 ft (1.8 m)
Likes bright light but out of direct sun, which burns the leaves.
Compost should be moist in growing period and barely moist in winter.
Feed every two weeks in spring and summer. Pinch out growing tips for bushy growth and cut back stems hard in spring if you wish to check the exuberant growth. Pot-on every spring in loam compost.
Propagate from 4 in (10 cm) stem cuttings in summer.

—— *Thunbergia alata* ——

Black-Eyed Susan

Oval, mid-green leaves with toothed edges on 10 ft (3 m) twining stems. Tubular flowers flare out into five orange-yellow lobes with a dark brown eye. They appear from early summer to early autumn. Half hardy annual raised from seed.

Likes bright light with direct sun for successful flowering.
Compost should always be moist.
Feed every two weeks from the time growth is well established until flowering is over. Nip out fading flowers to encourage more. The plants are discarded after flowering.
Sow seed in spring in temperature of 65°F (18°C).

—— *Tropaeolum peregrinum* ——

Canary Creeper

A rapidly-growing annual for a fine splash of summer colour. Dark green, deeply dissected, five-lobed leaves. Bright yellow flowers with fringed petals. Grows to 8 ft (2.4 m) and needs support. Discard after flowering.

Likes bright light and direct sun.
Compost should always be moist.
Feed every two weeks when growth is well established.
Propagate by seed in late winter or early spring.

Bulbs

A whole range of bulbs, corms and tubers brings bursts of colour to the cool conservatory – not only the familiar tulips, daffodils, crocus, snowdrops and hyacinths, but the less widely grown and just as attractive chionodoxa, muscari and scilla. These are spring-flowering, but colchicums and zephyranthes give autumn colour, while winter is brightened by the brilliant pink flowers of veltheimia.

When grown indoors, bulbs and corms are planted with their tips just showing above the surface of the compost, but tubers should be planted about 1 in (2.5 cm) below the surface. After planting, some bulbs should spend a period in the dark; this is indicated under the individual entries. Many bulbs will be good for only a single season indoors, but can be replanted in the garden where they will develop and flower in later years. Single season indoor bulbs need no feeding.

Chionodoxa luciliae

Glory of the Snow

Short, strap-shaped bright green leaves. From late winter to early spring appear the mid-blue, six petalled flowers, about 1 in (2.5 cm) across with white centres. Cultivar *C.l.* 'Rosea' has pink flowers. *C. gigantea* has larger pale blue flowers and those of *C. sardensis* are deep blue. All grow no more than 6 in (15 cm) high.

Plant bulbs in autumn in peat compost and store in a cool, dry place until shoots appear.
Compost should be kept moist.
Dry off bulbs when leaves have withered after flowering and plant in the garden in autumn.

Colchicum autumnale

Naked Boys

Cup-shaped, rose-lilac flowers open almost flat in autumn, followed by the leaves. *C.a.* 'Album' has pure white flowers; *C. speciosum* produces deep purple flowers with a white centre; and *C.s.* 'Album' has white flowers. Grows to 6 in (15 cm).

Plant tubers in summer and early autumn in peat compost. Place in sun.
Compost should be kept moist.
Dry off tubers when leaves have withered after flowering and replant in garden in summer.

Crocus chrysanthus

Crocus

Grass-like leaves with white line along the centre. Oval, cup-shaped flowers from late winter to early spring. Many hybrids are available, in varying shades of yellow, pale to deep mauve, and white. Some are bi-coloured – white striped with purple – or have contrasting colours on the inside and outside of the petals. Grows to 4 in (10 cm).

Plant corms in autumn in bulb fibre or peat compost, just below the surface. Place in the dark or cover pot with black plastic until shoots appear.
Compost should be kept moist.
Dry off bulbs when leaves have withered after flowering and replant in garden in autumn.

Cyclamen neopolitanum

Cyclamen

Ivy-shaped leaves with silver markings. Shuttlecock-like pink or white flowers in autumn and winter. Grows no more than 5 in (12.5 cm).

Plant tubers, dented side upwards, in peat compost in summer. Keep in shaded place.
Compost should be moist always, but do not water directly on to corm or it may rot.
Feed once a fortnight when flower buds appear until foliage dies down. As foliage dies, stop watering and store tubers dry in a cool place until autumn. Then repot in fresh peat compost.

Galanthus nivalis

Snowdrop

Strap-shaped, narrow leaves. Small, pendant, white flowers with some petals tipped green appear from winter to early spring. Grows to 6 in (15 cm).

Plant bulbs in autumn in peat compost and keep in a cool, dark place until shoots appear.
Compost should be moist always.
Dry off bulbs when leaves have withered and replant in garden in autumn.

Iris reticulata

Dwarf Iris

Narrow, grass-like leaves. Deep blue to violet flowers, with yellow markings and flared-back petals, appear in late winter and early spring.

Plant bulbs in peat compost in autumn. Keep in cool, dark place until shoots show.
Compost should be kept moist.
Dry off bulbs when leaves have completely withered after flowering and replant in garden in autumn.

Hyacinthus orientalis

Hyacinth

Strap-shaped leaves. Dense clusters of waxy red, pink, purple, blue, yellow or white bell-like flowers are carried on 10 in (25 cm) stems in spring.

Plant bulbs in autumn in either bulb fibre or peat compost. Keep in cool, dark place until shoots appear.
Compost should be moist always.
Dry off bulbs when leaves have withered and plant out in garden in autumn.

Lilium longiflorum

White Trumpet Lily

Narrow, pointed, dark green leaves, about 5 in (12.5 cm) long, carried on 3 ft (90 cm) stems. Produces large, trumpet-shaped, white flowers with orange stamens, about 6 in (15 cm) across, from late spring to summer.

Plant bulbs in autumn in either loam or peat compost. Keep in cool but sunny spot.
Compost should be moist always, but not sodden, or the bulb will rot.
Dry off bulbs when leaves have withered and replant in garden in autumn.

Muscari armeniacum

Grape Hyacinth

Narrow, strap-shaped leaves. Clusters of very small, bell-like blue flowers in spring, on 6 in (15 cm) stems.

Plant bulbs in autumn in peat compost. Keep in cool, dark place until shoots appear.
Compost should be moist always.
Dry off bulbs after leaves have withered and replant in garden in autumn.

Narcissus bulbocodium

Dwarf Narcissus

Narrow, strap-shaped leaves, and the flower, in spring, is a yellow trumpet surrounded by small petals. The plant grows to only 6 in (15 cm).

Plant bulbs in autumn in bulb fibre or peat compost. Store in cool, dark place until shoots appear.
Compost should be kept moist.
Dry off bulbs after leaves have died down and replant in garden in autumn.

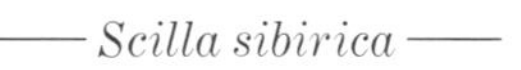

Scilla sibirica

Squill

Strap-shaped leaves, appearing along with the flowers. Dark blue or white, hanging, bell-like flowers in spring. Grows no more than 6 in (15 cm).

Plant bulbs in autumn in peat compost. Keep in cool, dark place until shoots appear.
Compost should always be moist.
Dry off bulbs when leaves and flowers wither and plant in garden in autumn.

Tulipa forsteriana

Water Lily Tulip

Lance-shaped, grey-green leaves. Bright scarlet, cup-shaped flowers, about 4 in (10 cm) long, appear in spring. Grows only 15 in (37.5 cm) high. Many cultivars are also available, with single and double flowers in shades of red, pink and orange.

Plant bulbs in autumn in bulb fibre or peat compost and put in a cool, dark place until shoots appear.
Compost should be moist always.
Dry off bulbs after leaves have died down and replant in garden in autumn.

Veltheimia viridifolia

Forest Lily

Rosette of wavy-edged, glossy, bright green leaves, about 10 in (25 cm) long. Clusters of pink tubular flowers bloom at the end of 18 in (45 cm) stems. The flowers appear in winter and last for several weeks.

Plant bulb in either loam or peat compost in autumn. Keep in a well-ventilated spot in bright light with direct sunlight, but shade when in flower.
Compost should be just moist until leaves appear, then water more frequently to ensure compost is thoroughly moist. In summer, when foliage wilts and begins to turn yellow, stop watering. Store the bulb dry in the compost, preferably in the sun, and repot in the autumn.
Feed every two weeks when foliage is established until flowering stops. Pot-on every other year in autumn and renew compost in the year between.
Propagate by removing offsets when repotting or potting-on.

Zantedeschia aethiopica

Calla Lily

Large, arrow-head leaves on long stems up to 3 ft (90 cm) high. Pure, white flower spathes with curved-back edges and yellow spadix on stems up to 4 ft (120 cm) long. A dramatic lily for spring flowering.

Likes bright light with full sun, requiring shade from only the fiercest sun.
Plant tubers in autumn in peat

Orchids

compost and keep just moist until leaves appear.
Compost should then be kept moist all the time during growing period. Water daily in very hot weather. After flowering, and when foliage starts to die down, stop watering and store tubers dry in the compost until they are repotted in autumn.
Feed every two weeks when foliage is established until flowering is over. Pot-on every year in autumn.
Propagate by dividing tubers or removing offsets when potting-on.

Zephyranthes grandiflora

Zephyr Lily

Narrow, grass-like leaves. Funnel-shaped pink flowers with six petals, gradually opening up in late summer and autumn. Grows to 10 in (25 cm).

Likes bright light but shade from direct sun.
Plant bulbs in early spring in peat compost.
Compost should be just moist to begin with, but water more often when shoots appear. After flowering, foliage begins to die down, but if it is reluctant to do so, reduce watering. Store bulbs dry in compost in a light spot until the following spring when they are repotted.
Feed once a fortnight from appearance of leaves until flowering is over. Pot-on every three years in early spring, changing compost for fresh in intervening years.
Propagate by removing bulblets when potting-on or repotting.

Of the orchids listed here, possibly the best for the absolute beginner are cymbidium, dendrobium and laelia. Not that the others – or indeed most orchids – are difficult, given the right temperatures and correct watering.

Plants in this group require cool winter conditions of no more than 55°F (13°C); closer to 50°F (10°C) is better. Careful watering is vital.

The compost should be just moist, never sodden, during the growing period; and when plants are resting it should be allowed to dry out before watering again. Water is certainly required if the pseudobulbs, in which orchids store food and water, begin to shrivel.

Coelogyne cristata

Round to egg-shaped pseudobulbs about 2 in (5 cm) tall, from which usually two strap-shaped leaves, up to 12 in (30 cm) long, appear. Beautiful white flowers with yellow markings on the lips are carried on 12 in (30 cm) stems from winter to spring.

Likes excellent light, but shade from direct sun.
Temperature needs to be kept cool in the weeks before flowering as well as during flowering; no more than 55°F (13°C) by day – and 50°F (10°C) is better – while night temperature should go down to 45°F (7°C).
Compost should be moist always except during the rest period when it should be allowed almost to dry out between waterings. If the plant is short of water the pseudobulbs will shrivel.
Feed every fortnight in spring and summer. Pot-on every three years in spring in an orchid compost. Change compost for fresh in years in between. Roots do not like being disturbed so treat with great care when repotting.
Propagate in spring by removing a piece of rhizome with at least three pseudobulbs to which roots are attached.

Cymbidium
'Peter Pan'

Pointed, bright green leaves. Flower stems bearing up to twelve greenish-yellow flowers with deep crimson lips appear in late spring and early summer; these are up to 3 in (7.5 cm) across. The plant grows to 15 in (37.5 cm).

Likes bright light but shade from

direct sun. Provide a humid atmosphere throughout the year.
Temperatures in winter should be no more than 55°F (13°C) by day, with night temperatures dropping to 45° (7°C).
Compost should be moist in growing period but in winter allow it almost to dry out between waterings.
Feed every two weeks in spring and summer. Pot-on every two years in spring in an orchid compost. Change compost for fresh in intervening years.
Propagate in spring by detaching two or three pseudobulbs with roots attached.

Dendrobium nobile

Stems up to 3 ft (90 cm) tall, rather like bamboo in appearance. Strap-shaped leaves, 5 in (12.5 in) long, appear near the top of stems in autumn. Leaves begin to fall in late winter, heralding the appearance of pink to purple flowers with pale yellow tips and central maroon blotch. Flowers are about 3 in (7.5 cm) across.

Likes bright light but shade from direct sun. In warm weather provide a humid atmosphere.
Temperatures should be warm in spring and summer, around 70°F (21°C), and cool in winter, around 50°F (10°C).
Compost should be watered thoroughly in growing period, but allowed almost to dry out between waterings. In winter, compost should be barely moist.
Feed once a month in spring and summer. Pot-on every third year, after flowering, in an orchid compost. Change compost for fresh in years in between.
Propagate by division when potting-on or repotting. Each piece should have at least five pseudobulbs, including some which have yet to flower.

Encyclia vitellania

Oval pseudobulbs from which pairs of blueish-green, pointed, strap-shaped leaves appear. A 12 in (30 cm) flower spike emerges from the leaves, bearing stunning deep orange to red flowers, lighter in shade on the lip. Flowers appear in autumn and in cool conditions will last for many weeks.

Likes good light, but keep away from direct sun.
Temperatures around 50°F (10°C) are required in winter if plant is to flower successfully the following year.
Compost should be moist in growing season, not over wet, and allow it almost to dry out between waterings. In winter, while the plant is resting, compost should be barely moist. Shrivelling of the pseudobulbs shows that the plant is short of water.
Feed every two weeks in spring and summer. Pot-on every other year in spring in an orchid compost. Change compost for fresh in years in between.
Propagate by division, taking a piece of rhizome with at least two or three pseudobulbs and adequate roots.

Laelia anceps

Slant-growing pseudobulbs, 4 in (10 cm) long, bear one or sometimes two strap-shaped leaves about 12 in (30 cm) long. Pink to purple flowers, with a darker tubular tip blotched yellow at its base, are carried on 18 in (45 cm) stems. They last for several weeks in autumn and early winter. This is a good orchid for beginners.

Likes good strong light, but shade from direct sun. In warm weather provide humidity.
Temperature in winter of 50°F (10°C) needed.
Compost should be thoroughly watered; allow surface to dry out before watering again during growing season. During the winter rest, keep compost barely moist.
Feed once a month in spring and summer. Pot-on in spring every third year in an orchid compost. Renew compost in years in between.
Propagate by division in spring. Each piece of rhizome should have at least four pseudobulbs and plenty of roots.

Oncidium ornithorhyncham

Small pseudobulbs of only 1 in (2.5 cm) bear narrow 8 in (20 cm) strap-shaped leaves. Rose pink flowers about ¾ in (1.8 cm) long have a yellow crest at the base of the lip. They are carried on a gracefully arching stem, 2 ft (60 cm) long, from autumn to winter. Large number of flowers on each stem compensate for their small size and last for many weeks.

Likes bright light and even a little sun, but shade from scorching rays.
Temperatures between 50° – 55°F (10° – 13°C) during the rest period after flowering.
Compost should be watered thoroughly but allowed almost to dry out before watering again. Never allow it to become sodden; this is the sure way to choke the fine roots and kill the plant.
Feed once a month in spring and summer. Pot-on in an orchid compost in spring each year.
Propagate by division when potting-on, making sure that each piece of rhizome has several pseudobulbs and enough roots to support them.

Vanda cristata

Pairs of bright green, strap-shaped leaves about 6 in (15 cm) long are arranged in layers, with aerial roots growing from the stem. Yellow-green flowers with a white lip, striped and blotched with maroon, appear in early summer. The 2 in (5 cm) flowers last many weeks. Grows to 12 in (30 cm).

Likes bright light with direct sunlight, but shade from hot sun. Provide humidity on warm days.
Temperatures between 50° – 55°F (10° – 13°C) are necessary during winter for successful flowering the following year.
Compost should be moist always in the growing period but in winter allow it almost to dry out before watering again.
Feed once a month in spring and summer. Pot-on every two years in spring in a special orchid compost and change the compost for fresh in the years in between.
Propagate by removing offsets when potting-on or repotting.

Cacti

Cacti add variety to the cool conservatory, and there is a wide choice of plants. Non-addicts will probably prefer flowering kinds, which produce often dramatic blooms. The following descriptions include a gymnocalycium lobivia, parodia, mammillaria and rebutia, which will flower while still young, and an astrophytum and echinocereus, which flower only after several years. Eminently suitable for hanging containers is the Rat's Tail Cactus *(Aporocactus flagelliformis).*

All cacti require a cool winter rest, especially those which flower freely. If it is too warm, plants may flower poorly or not at all.

Aporocactus flagelliformis

Rat's Tail Cactus

Twelve-ribbed green stems about ½ in (1.75 cm) in diameter covered in brown spines. Tubular deep pink flowers emerge at points along the stems in spring and early summer. Stems may trail to 3 ft (90 cm) so this is an excellent cactus for a hanging container.

Likes bright light with direct sun for successful flowering.
Compost should be kept moist in growing period, but barely moist in winter. Too much water causes stem rot.
Feed monthly in spring and summer. Pot-on every spring in peat compost or loam compost with added sand.
Propagate from 6 in (15 cm) stem cuttings taken in summer.

Astrophytum myriostigma

Bishop's Cap

Globular cactus with four or five prominent ribs covered in white scales and fluffy grey hairs. Funnel-shaped yellow flowers with red throats appear in summer.
A. ornatum has up to eight ribs covered in silvery scales and stout, yellow-brown spines about 1 in (2.5 cm) long. Yellow flowers, but only on mature plants – about ten years old. These cacti grow to around 8 in (20 cm) in height and diameter.

Likes good light with direct sun.
Compost should be watered thoroughly in growing period, but allow almost to dry out before watering again. Water about once a month in winter.
Feed every two months in spring and summer. Pot-on each spring in a mixture of loam compost, grit and sand.
Propagate by sowing seed in spring.

Cephalocereus senilis

Old Man Cactus

Columnar cactus covered in fine white hairs, up to 5 in (12.5 cm) long, which conceal short spines. Hairs darken as plant matures and progressively fall from the base of the column.

Likes bright light with direct sun.
Compost should remain moist in growing period; water once a month in winter.
Feed every fortnight in spring and summer. Gently brush hairs regularly, using a soft brush, to keep them clean. Pot-on every spring in a mixture of two thirds loam or peat compost to one third of sand.
Propagate by sowing seed in spring.

Cereus peruvianus

Tree Cactus

Blue-green, five- to eight-ribbed, columnar cactus covered in brown spines. Grows quickly to 6 ft (1.8 m) but can be kept more manageable if confined to a 6 in (15 cm) pot.

Likes bright light with direct sun.
Compost should be moist in growing season, but almost dry in winter.
Feed every two months in spring and summer. Pot-on every spring for a large plant, otherwise pot-on only every two or three years, replacing the compost in the other years. To discourage growth, leave in a 6 in (15 cm) pot, merely refreshing compost regularly.
Propagate by sowing seed in spring, but early growth will be slow.

Echinocereus pectinatus

Hedgehog Cactus

Many-ribbed, green columnar cactus, densely covered with white spines. Grows slowly to 8 in (20 cm). When stem has reached about 4 in (10 cm), the cactus may throw out new stems from the base. Produces bell-shaped pink flowers in summer.

Likes excellent light with direct sun in

a well-ventilated position.
Feed monthly in spring and summer.
Compost should be just moist in growing season. Do not water in winter. Pot-on in spring if the roots have filled the pot, using a loam compost with added sand or grit.
Propagate from seed in spring.

—— *Epiphyllum 'Ackermanii'* ——

Orchid Cactus

Clumps of flattened stems, thrown up from compost level, can grow to 2 ft (60 cm). Stems are notched with small bristles growing from the areoles. Large, cup-shaped red flowers about 3 in (7.5 cm) across appear in late spring. *E.* 'Cooperi' has white to yellow flowers.

Likes bright light but shade from direct sun.
Compost should be thoroughly moist in growing period, but barely moist in winter. Buds are likely to drop if compost is too dry.
Feed monthly in spring and summer. Until a 6 in (15 cm) pot is reached, pot-on each spring, in a loam compost with added sand. After that merely repot in fresh compost each spring.
Propagate by taking 5 in (12.5 cm) stem cuttings in summer.

—— *Ferocactus latispinus* ——

Devil's Tongue

Globular shape with many ribs. Groups of four red spines surrounded by shorter white spines protrude from rib edges. Mature plants produce red flowers in summer. Grows slowly to height of 10 in (25 cm) with 8 in (20 cm) spread.

Likes bright light; direct sun essential for good spine colour and successful flowering.
Compost should be kept moist in growing period and barely moist in winter, when watering about once a month should be enough.
Feed once a fortnight in spring and summer. Pot-on each spring in a mixture of three parts peat compost to one part sand.
Propagate by sowing seed in spring.

—— *Gymnocalycium baldianum* ——

Globular green stem with 10 to 12 ribs, sprouting groups of white or yellow spines. In spring and summer, red daisy-like flowers appear. Grows to 3 in (7.5 cm). *G. bruchii* forms a clump of smaller globes; its flowers are pink.

Likes bright light with direct sun for good flowering.
Compost should be kept moist in growing period; water about once a month in winter.
Feed monthly in spring and summer. Pot-on each year in spring in mixture of two thirds loam compost and one third sand. When cactus is fully grown, stop potting-on but repot each year in fresh compost.
Propagate by removing offsets in spring.

—— *Lobivia hertrichiana* ——

Clumps of globular, ribbed stems with brown spines which often turn yellow in good light. During summer produces scarlet flowers which close at night. Grows to 4 in (10 cm) in height, with similar diameter.

Likes excellent light with direct sun for good flowering and spine colour.
Compost should be kept moist in growing period; water about once a month in winter.
Feed once a fortnight in spring and summer. Pot-on every two or three years in spring in loam compost with added sand, changing compost for fresh in intervening years.
Propagate by removing offsets or sowing seed in spring.

—— *Mammillaria bocasana* ——

Powder Puff

Clusters of small, green globes about 2 in (5 cm) across covered in small mounds (known as tubercles) from which silky white hairs and spines grow. Bell-shaped cream to yellow flowers produced in spring, followed by purple-red seed pods. *M. elegans* is cylindrical, covered with short white spines. Mature plants produce red flowers in spring. *M. zeilmanniana* eventually covers surface of the compost with its globes, from which groups of white and hooked brown spines protrude. Produces red flowers in summer. Grows to 4 in (10 cm).

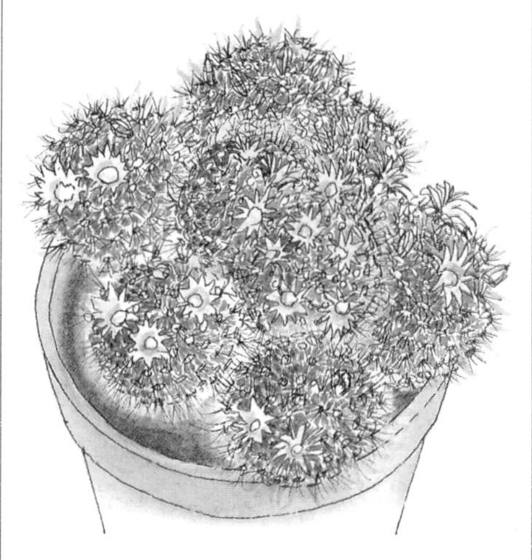

Likes bright light and direct sunlight for good flower and spine colour.
Compost should be watered thoroughly during growing period, but allow it almost to dry out between waterings. Water about once a month in winter.
Feed once a month in spring and summer. Pot-on every spring in two thirds loam compost and one third grit or sand.
Propagate by removing offsets or sowing seed in spring.

—— *Myrtillocactus geometrizans* ——

Lime green, six-ribbed columns covered in short black spines. This branching cactus grows to 3 ft (90 cm), but slowly. Occasionally small cream flowers may appear in summer.

Likes good light with direct sun.
Temperatures of 50°F (10°C) minimum required in winter, otherwise brown patches appear on the columns.
Compost should be watered thoroughly in growing period, but allow it almost to dry out between waterings. Water about once a month in winter.

Succulents

Succulents may not be most people's first choice for a conservatory, but they are an unusual group, interesting if only for their oddly assorted shapes and textures. There are small plants, such as the star-shaped faucaria and the pebble-like lithops, and large specimen plants, such as the fierce agave and the bloated bulbous beaucarnea. Among the hanging succulents the trails of tiny hearts of ceropagia, the hairy cyanotis, the bead-like senecio and the donkey-tailed sedum offer a remarkable variety of foliage.

Some succulents are shy to flower indoors, but those that flower readily will do so only if they have a rest period in winter at temperatures between 40° – 55°F (4° – 13°C).

Feed once a fortnight in spring and summer. Pot-on every spring in three parts loam compost to one part sand.
Propagate from seed sown in spring.

— *Rebutia miniscula* —

Red Crown

Clumps of globular stems, about 2 in (5 cm) across, covered with white spines. Trumpet-shaped, bright red flowers appear in late spring and summer.

Likes bright light with direct sun. Good ventilation necessary.
Compost should be thoroughly watered in growing period and allowed almost to dry out before watering again. Water about once a month in winter.
Feed every two weeks in spring and summer. Pot-on every spring in mixture of two parts loam compost to one part sand.
Propagate by division or by sowing seed in spring.

— *Opuntia microdasys* —

Prickly Pear

Branching flattened oval stems (also called pads) about 3 in (7.5 cm) long, joined to each other. Stems covered in areoles from which small yellow bristles sprout. May produce yellow flowers. Grows slowly to 12 in (30 cm).

Likes bright light with direct sun.
Temperature of 50°F (10°C) minimum required in winter, otherwise reddish-brown patches appear on stems.
Compost should be kept moist in growing period and just moist in winter. If compost is too dry the pads may shrivel and fall.
Feed every two weeks in spring and summer. Pot-on every spring in mixture of two parts loam compost and one part sand.
Propagate by removing a complete pad in summer and planting it in compost.

— *Parodia chrysacanthion* —

Pale-green, globular cactus covered in golden yellow spines. Yellow, funnel-shaped flowers produced in late spring and early summer. Grows to diameter of 5 in (12.5 cm) and height of 3 in (7.5 cm). *P. sanguiniflora* is globular, becoming cylindrical with age, covered with groups of white and brown spines. Bright red flowers appear in summer. Grows to height of 5 in (12.5 cm).

Likes excellent light with direct sun for good spine colour and flowering.
Compost should be watered thoroughly in growing period, but allow it to dry out between waterings. Water no more than once a month in winter.
Feed monthly in spring and summer. Pot-on every spring, in mixture of half loam compost and half grit, until the plant has reached maximum size. After that change compost for fresh each year.
Propagate from offsets or seed sown in spring.

Aeonium tabulaeforme

Saucer-shaped rosette, up to 12 in (30 cm) across, of close-packed green leaves, carried on a short stem. Mature plants bear yellow flowers on 2 ft (60 cm) stems. *A. haworthii* has branching stems up to 2 ft (60 cm) high, with rosettes of blue-green leaves, edged red. Pink-tinged yellow flowers appear in late spring.

Likes good light with direct sun. Water about once a week in spring and summer; once a month for the rest of year. Shrivelling leaves indicate lack of water.
Feed once a fortnight in spring and summer. Pot-on each year in spring in loam compost
Propagate from seed in spring, or take leaf cuttings of *A. tabulaeforme*, or stem cuttings of *A. haworthii.*

Agave americana

Century Plant

Rosette of leathery, grey-green leaves up to 3 ft (90 cm) long, sharply pointed and edged with spines. Suitable only for a large conservatory since it has a spread of about 5 ft (1.5 m). There are variegated forms: *A.a.* 'Marginata' has yellow edges on its leaves, *A.a.* 'Mediopicta' has a yellow band running the length of each leaf.

Likes bright light with direct sun. Water weekly in spring and summer and monthly the rest of the year.
Feed once a month in spring and summer. Pot-on each year in spring in two parts loam compost to one part sand.
Propagate from seed in spring or by detaching offsets when potting-on.

Aloe variegata

Partridge Breasted Aloe

Ranks of green triangular leaves banded with white, in rosette formation. Tubular pink flowers on 12 in (30 cm) stems appear in spring and summer. Grows to 12 in (30 cm). *A. aborescens* has woody stems up to 10 ft (3 m) long, bearing loose rosettes of narrow, tooth-edged leaves about 9 in (22.5 cm) long.

Likes bright light, but with filtered sun for *A. variegata* and direct sun for *A. aborescens.*

Compost should be moist always in active growth period, but when plant is resting in winter months, water about once a month.
Feed once a month in spring and summer. Pot-on *A. aborescens* every spring until it grows too big to move, using a loam compost. *A. variegata* will need potting-on only every two or three yers, changing compost for fresh in intervening years.
Propagate by removing offsets when potting-on or repotting. Make sure the offsets have plenty of roots to support them.

Beaucarnea recurvata

Pony Tail

Woody stem growing from a swollen bulbous root on the surface of the compost. The leaves, in rosette formation, are about 3 ft (90 cm) long, narrow and drooping. The plant grows slowly to 3 ft (90 cm).

Likes a well-lit spot with direct sunlight, but out of scorching sun.
Compost should be moist always, except in winter months when watering once a month is enough. The bulbous root acts as a reservoir for water; if it begins to shrivel, the plant needs water.
Feed once a month in spring and summer. Pot-on every two or three years in a mixture of peat, loam and sharp sand, changing the compost for fresh in intervening years.
Propagate by sowing seed in spring or by removing offsets when potting-on or repotting.

Ceropagia woodii

String of Hearts

Purple, trailing stems about 3 ft (90 cm) long, carrying pairs of fleshy, heart-shaped, grey-green leaves, marked silvery grey on the top surface and purple on the underside. Small lantern-shaped purple flowers appear in summer. Looks best in a hanging container.

Likes bright light with direct sun to maintain leaf colour, but shade from very hot sun.
Compost should be just moist throughout the year.
Feed monthly in spring and summer. Pot-on in spring each year in a mixture of two parts loam compost to one part sand.
Propagate in spring by removing a piece of stem to which small tubers are attached; place them on the surface of compost. Roots take several weeks to develop.

Crassula aborescens

Silver Dollar Plant

Woody branching stems carry groups of almost circular leaves, about 2 in (5 cm) in diameter, grey-green and tipped with red.
C. argentea is very similar, but has oval leaves. Both grow to 3 ft (90 cm). Other species include: *C. falcata*, with sickle-shaped, grey-green leaves about 4 in (10 cm) long, carried almost the length of 2 ft (60 cm) stems; *C. lycopodioides*, with thin, branching fingers of overlapping, close-packed leaves and growing to 8 in (20 cm); and the creeping *C. rupestris*, with blue-grey fleshy leaves on thin stems.

Likes good light with direct sunlight, but shade from fierce sun.
Compost should be moist, but not sodden, in growing period and barely moist in winter months; shrivelling leaves indicate need for water.
Feed once a month in spring and summer. Pot-on every two years in two parts loam compost to one part sand. Change compost in intervening years.
Propagate by taking leaf cuttings in spring and summer.

—— *Cyanotis kewensis* ——

Teddy Bear Vine

Short trailing stems of oval, fleshy leaves, green on the upper surface and purple underneath, and covered with reddy-brown hair. Purple flowers may sometimes appear in spring and summer. Stems grow to about 8 in (20 cm). *C. somaliensis* has oval, pointed, 2 in (5 cm) leaves, glossy green and edged with white hairs. Indoors, even in a conservatory, it will seldom produce its purple-blue flowers.

Likes excellent light with direct sun.
Compost should be kept moist throughout the growing period, but barely moist in winter months. Avoid wetting the leaves as they mark easily.
Feed every two weeks in spring and summer. Pot-on every two or three years in spring in a mixture of two thirds loam compost to one third sand. Change compost in years in between.
Propagate by taking stem tip cuttings, about 4 in (10 cm) long, in spring and summer.

—— *Echeveria derenbergii* ——

Painted Lady

Short stems carry rosettes of close-packed, spoon-shaped, grey-green leaves, tipped red. Orange-red flowers on 3 in (7.5 cm) stems in early summer. Hybrid *E.* 'Doris Taylor' is worth looking out for; its rosettes are about 3 in (7.5 cm) across. *E. harmsii* has rosettes of lance-shaped hairy leaves on long stems. Its red, bell-shaped flowers, tipped yellow, appear in early summer. Grows to 12 in (30 cm). *E. gibbiflora* has a solitary stem bearing mauve-pink, spoon-shaped leaves covered with warts. Red, bell-shaped flowers may appear in winter. Grows to 18 in (45 cm).

Likes bright light with direct sun, unless it is fierce. Compost should be just moist in growing period, but during the winter rest, watering once a month is enough. Lower leaves shrivel naturally during winter, not through lack of water. Remove them.
Feed once a month in spring and summer. Pot-on each spring in loam compost with added sand.
Propagate from stem cuttings taken in summer or remove offsets when potting on.

—— *Faucaria tigrina* ——

Tiger's Jaws

Layered rosette formed by opposite pairs of 2 in (5 cm) pointed leaves, grey-green with white spots and edged with sharp teeth. Yellow, daisy-like flowers about 2 in (5 cm) across are produced in autumn.

Likes bright light with direct sun if plant is to flower. Compost should be kept moist in the growing season, but barely moist in winter months.
Feed once a month in spring and summer. Pot-on every third year in spring in loam compost with added sand. Change compost for fresh in intervening years.
Propagate by division when potting-on.

—— *Gasteria verrucosa* ——

Ox Tongue

Opposite pairs of fleshy, pointed, dark green leaves about 6 in (15 cm) long, arranged on top of each other. Leaves are covered with small white warts. Grows to a height of about 6 in (15 cm). From spring to early autumn, red tubular flowers appear on long stems.

Likes bright light but out of direct sun, which can turn leaves brown.
Compost should always be moist in growing season. Water about once a month in winter.
Feed monthly in spring and summer. Pot-on every two or three years in spring, in loam compost with added sand. Renew compost in between.
Propagate by removing offsets when potting-on or repotting.

—— *Haworthia margaritifera* ——

Pearl Plant

Rosette of fleshy, dark green leaves, covered with pearly warts. Leaves are pointed and oval, about 3 in (7.5 cm) long. White flowers appear on a slim stem in summer and early autumn. Grows to 4 in (10 cm).

Likes bright light but shade from direct sun; too much sun turns leaves red.
Compost should be kept moist in growing period. Water once a month in winter.

Feed once a month in spring and summer. Pot-on each year in spring in mixture of two thirds loam compost and one third sand.
Propagate by removing offsets when potting-on or sow seed in spring.

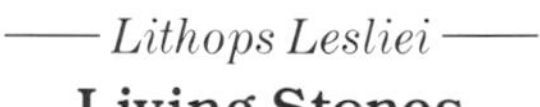

—— *Lithops Lesliei* ——

Living Stones

Pairs of fleshy, flat-topped leaves split along the centre, grey-green in colour with reddish brown spots. They protrude only 1 in (2.5 cm) or so above the surface of the compost and do indeed look like stones. Yellow flowers emerge from the leaf splits in late summer and autumn.

Likes excellent light with direct sun for good leaf colour and successful flowering.
Compost should be just moist in growing period. When leaves begin to shrivel after flowering, stop watering until new leaves appear, which may not be until the following spring. Never water into the split.

Alpines

Feed once a month in spring and summer. Pot-on every two or three years in spring in half loam compost and half sand. Repot in fresh compost in years between.
Propagate by division in spring.

— *Sedum morganianum* —

Burro's Tail

Pointed, cylindrical, overlapping, pale green leaves on 3 ft (90 cm) trailing stems make this a plant for a hanging container. Pink flowers sometimes show in summer. *S. sieboldii* 'Mediovariegatum' has round, green leaves, edged with red and marked with yellow, on 8 in (20 cm) trailing stems.

Likes bright light with direct sun in a well-ventilated spot.
Compost should be just moist during growth; water once a month in winter. Leaves will soften if watered too frequently.
Feed once a month in spring and summer. Pot-on every spring in loam compost.
Propagate by taking 4 in (10 cm) stem cuttings in summer.

— *Senecio rowleyanus* —

String of Beads

Trailing stems, 2 – 3 ft (60 – 90 cm) long, and leaves like green beads with a pointed tip. Sweet-smelling purple and white flowers appear in early autumn. An excellent plant for a hanging container.

Likes bright light with some sunlight, but not hot midday sun.
Temperature should not drop below 50°F (10°C) or leaves may fall.
Compost should be kept moist in growing period. Water once a month in winter.
Feed once a month in spring and summer. Pot-on every spring in a mixture of two thirds loam compost and one third sand.
Propagate from stem cuttings taken in summer.

The true alpine addict would buy an alpine house – with no artificial heat and endless fresh air – and think nothing of spending freezing days in it. Conditions for alpines in a cool conservatory are not ideal, but if the winter temperature is at the lower end of the scale – 45°F (7°C) – you could find room for some; they are certainly not demanding of space. Growing alpines in a group on a table or waist-high staging makes them easy to look after, and to admire.

In cultivation, the two vital requirements are a free-draining compost and good ventilation, winter and summer. Spending summer outdoors in the sun will do alpines a power of good, but bring them indoors in the autumn – it is damp that they cannot stand.

— *Androsace pyrenaica* —

Rock Jasmine

Small mound of narrow, slightly hairy leaves up to 3 in (7.5 cm) across. Tiny white flowers, similar to those of a primrose, bloom from early to late spring.

Likes bright light with direct sun.
Compost should be thoroughly watered and allowed almost to dry out between waterings. In winter water about once a month. Do not water from above. Immerse the pot in water to about half way up the side and leave until all the compost is moist. Then remove and let excess water drain away.
Feed once a month in spring and summer. Pot-on every two or three years, after flowering, in a mixture of three parts loam compost and one part coarse sand or grit. Change compost for fresh in years in between.
Propagate by division after flowering or from seed sown in spring.

— *Campanula cochlearifolia* —

Bellflower

Small, almost round, leaves. Blue or white bell-shaped flowers are carried on slender, wiry stems in late spring and early summer. Grows to 4 in (10 cm).

Likes good light with direct sun.
Compost should be allowed almost to dry out between waterings in growing period. In winter watering once a month should be enough.
Feed once a month in spring and summer. Pot-on every two or three years, after flowering, in a mixture of three parts loam compost and one part grit or coarse sand.
Propagate by division or by sowing seed in spring.

— *Cassiope* x 'Bearsden' —

Narrow, somewhat scaly leaves. Pure white hanging bell flowers appear in late spring and early summer. Grows to 6 in (15 cm).

Likes bright light with direct sun.
Compost should be just moist in growing period. During winter keep on the dry side; watering about once a month should be enough.
Feed monthly in spring and summer. Pot-on every two or three years after

flowering in a mixture of three parts acidic peat compost and one part grit or sand.
Propagate from cuttings taken in summer.

Convolvulus mauritanicus

Convolvulus

Small, narrow, bright green leaves. Trumpet-shaped, pale violet-blue flowers produced over a long period from early summer to early autumn. Grows to 8 in (20 cm).

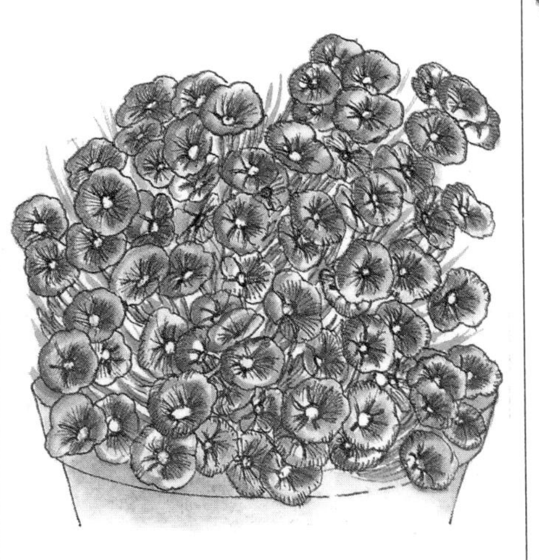

Likes excellent light with direct sun.
Compost should be kept watered in growing period, but in winter allow compost almost to dry out between waterings; once a month should then be enough.
Feed monthly in spring and summer. Pot-on every two or three years in a mixture of three parts loam compost to one part sand. Change compost for fresh in years in between.
Propagate by taking cuttings in late summer.

Dianthus alpinus

Pinks

Mat of short, narrow, bright green leaves. Flat, five-petalled pink flowers flecked with crimson appear in summer. Grows to 6 in (15 cm).

Likes good light with direct sun.
Compost should always be moist in growing period, but allow it almost to dry out between waterings in winter.
Feed monthly in spring and summer. Remove dead flower heads to encourage fresh blooms. Pot-on every two or three years in spring in mixture of three parts loam compost to one part limestone grit. Change compost for fresh in years between.
Propagate from cuttings in summer or sow seed in spring.

Gentiana verna

Spring Gentian

Tufts of lance-shaped leaves. Royal blue, trumpet flowers with five flattened lobes appear in spring. Grows to 4 in (10 cm).

Likes to grow in full sun.
Compost should be moist in growing period but in winter allow it almost to dry out between waterings.
Feed monthly in spring and summer. Pot-on every two or three years, after flowering, in three parts loam compost to one part coarse sand or grit. Change compost for fresh in other years.
Propagate from seed sown in spring.

Geranium napuligerum

Cranesbill

Tufts of deeply incised leaves. Lilac pink, five-petalled flowers produced in spring and early summer. Grows to 6 in (15 cm).

Likes bright light with direct sun.
Compost should be kept well watered but not sodden in growing season. In winter allow it almost to dry out between waterings.
Feed monthly in spring and summer. Pot-on every two or three years, after flowering, in a mixture of three parts loam compost to one part grit or sand. Change compost for fresh in years in between.
Propagate by sowing seed in spring or by division when potting-on or repotting.

Oxalis laciniata

Small leaves divided into leaflets. Cup-shaped pink to deep purple flowers, with darker markings on veins, produced in late spring and early summer. Dies down in late summer after flowering. Grows to 3 in (7.5 cm).

Likes to grow in full sun.
Compost should be moist in growing period, but barely moist after foliage dies down until it starts into growth again.
Feed monthly in spring and summer. Pot-on every third year in mixture of three parts loam compost to one part coarse sand or grit. Change compost for fresh in years between.
Propagate from seed sown in spring.

Phlox nana

Narrow, grey-green leaves about 2 in (5 cm) long. Five-petalled, star-like pink flowers with a white eye produced in late spring and early summer. Grows to 6 in (15 cm).

Likes bright light with direct sun.
Compost should be kept moist in growing period but barely moist in winter.
Feed monthly in spring and summer. Pot-on after flowering every third year in a mixture of three parts loam compost to one part coarse sand or grit. Change compost for fresh in years between.
Propagate from cuttings taken in summer.

Primula allionii

Primula

Hummocks of broad, lance-shaped leaves, slightly sticky to the touch, up to 2 in (5 cm) long. Masses of almost flattened flowers in various shades of pink with a white centre appear in spring. Grows to 6 in (15 cm).

Likes to grow in full sun. Compost should be kept well watered in growing period but barely moist in winter.
Feed monthly in spring and summer. Pot-on every third year after flowering

in three parts loam compost to one part grit. Renew compost in years between.
Propagate from cuttings taken in summer.

—— *Ranunculus amplexicaulis* ——

Oval to lance-shaped leaves. Stems bear two or more buttercup-shaped white flowers with a yellow centre in late spring and early summer. Grows to 12 in (30 cm).

Likes bright light with direct sun.
Compost should be moist in growing season but barely moist in winter.
Feed monthly in spring and summer.
Pot-on every other year after flowering in mixture of three parts loam compost to one part of grit or coarse sand, changing compost in alternate years.
Propagate by division when repotting or potting-on, or sow seed in spring.

—— *Saxifraga* x *jenkinsae* ——

Saxifrage

Rosettes of silvery, grey-green leaves forming a tussocky mat. Covered with masses of pale pink flowers in spring. Grows to 6 in (15 cm).

Likes bright light with direct sun.
Compost should be kept well watered when in growth, but barely moist in winter.
Feed monthly in spring and summer.
Pot-on every third year after flowering in three parts loam compost and one part coarse sand or grit, changing compost in years between.
Propagate by division when repotting or potting-on.

—— *Soldanella montana* ——

Snowbell

Clump of round to heart-shaped dark green leaves on short stems. Funnel-shaped, downward hanging, pale to deep violet flowers on long stems produced in spring. Grows to 6 in (15 cm).

Likes bright light, but shade from direct sun.
Compost should be well watered in growing period but barely moist in winter.

Feed monthly in spring and summer.
Pot-on every other year after flowering in mixture of three parts loam compost to one part of grit or coarse sand.
Propagate from seed in spring.

—— *Viola papillonacea* ——

Violet

Dark green, shiny leaves. White violet flowers in spring and early summer. Grows to 6 in (15 cm).

Likes to grow in full sun.
Compost should be moist in growing season, but barely moist in winter.
Feed monthly in spring and summer.
Pot-on every other year after flowering in three parts loam compost and one part of coarse sand or grit, renewing in year between.
Propagate from seed sown in spring.

The Temperate Conservatory

Winter temperatures: 55–65°F (13–18°C)

In the temperate conservatory, people can spend more time comfortably alongside their plants than is possible in the cool conservatory. Another advantage is that some of the less common and more demanding plants can be grown here; more than 60 species are recommended. They include a number of very graceful foliage plants and an interesting collection of ferns. The choice can be extended with some plants from the cool section, with the proviso that you should be able to move them to a cooler place for their winter rest.

1 *Philodendron scandens* (Foliage) 2 *Impatiens wallerana* (Flowering) 3 *Schefflera actinophylla* (Foliage) 4 *Pachystachys lutea* (Flowering) 5 *Odontoglossum grande* (Orchid) 6 *Guzmania lingulata* (Bromeliad) 7 *Dizygotheca elegantissima* (Foliage) 8 *Phoenix canariensis* (Palm) 9 *Hoya bella* (Hanging) 10 *Streptocarpus* hybrid (Flowering) 11 *Neoregelia carolinae* 'Tricolor' (Bromeliad) 12 *Manettia bicolor* (Climber)

Foliage plants

Several extremely attractive foliage plants can be combined for display in the temperate conservatory. For splendour of colour and intricacy of marking there is no rival to the calathea known as the Peacock Plant. For gracefulness the dizygotheca has no equal. And the ever-popular philodendrons offer a whole host of varieties to choose from.

Some plants of this group, in particular calathea, coffea, dizygotheca and jacaranda, need a minimum winter temperature of 60°F (16°C) if they are to stay in good condition. Others will tolerate lower winter heat, down to 55°F (13°C). If plants from the two groups are growing together it is best to keep the temperature at the higher level – and take advantage of the fact that some parts of the conservatory may be cooler than others. Plants kept at the higher end of the temperature range in winter months will require more frequent watering, however, since having only a brief resting period, they may continue to grow.

—— *Calathea makoyana* ——

Peacock Plant

Broad, oval green leaves about 10 in (25 cm) long carried on stems of similar length, embossed with a pattern of darker green, narrow, oval shapes which look like small leaflets. In between are fine silvery lines. Leaves are shaded purple underneath. *C. insignis* (syn *C. lancifolia*) has erect, lance-shaped, light green leaves with olive markings and purple undersides; it grows to 2 ft (60 cm). *C. zebrina* has emerald green, oval leaves with paler shading of central rib and veins and purple undersides; it grows to 18 in (45 cm).

Likes good light but away from direct sun.
Temperature of 60°F (16°C) minimum required in winter if leaves are not to brown and curl. Requires humidity otherwise leaf tips turn brown.
Compost should be moist always in growing period but barely moist in winter. Use soft water only.
Feed every two weeks in spring and summer. Pot-on in early summer in peat compost.
Propagate by division in spring.

—— *Coffea arabica* ——

Coffee Plant

Dark green, glossy, elliptical leaves with crinkly edges. Produces white, fragrant, starry flowers in summer followed by green berries ripening to red, but only on plants three to four years old.

Likes good light but in slightly shaded position. Keep out of direct sun.
Temperature of 60°F (16°C) minimum required in winter. Requires humidity otherwise leaf tips turn brown.
Compost should be moist always in growing period, but barely moist in winter.
Feed every two weeks in spring and summer. Pot-on every other spring in peat compost with added sharp sand. Change compost for fresh in year between. Pinch out growing tips for bushy growth.
Propagate from seed in spring with bottom heat of 75°F (24°C).

—— *Coleus blumei* ——

Flame Nettle

Heart-shaped, green, brown, yellow, red or orange leaves, but more often in two or more combinations of these colours. Grows to 18 in (45 cm). Though perennial, the plant is best treated as an annual.

Likes bright light with direct sunlight to maintain leaf colour, but shade from scorching sun. Benefits from humidity.
Compost should always be moist in growing period but just moist in winter. If it becomes too dry, leaves will fall.
Feed every two weeks in spring and summer. When roots have filled the pot, pot-on in lime-free loam or peat compost. You may need to do this every two to three months in growing period. Pinch out growing tips for bushy growth. Remove flower buds.
Propagate from stem cuttings taken in summer. They will root in water.

Cyperus alternifolius

Umbrella Plant

Rosettes of up to a dozen arching, thin, sword-shaped leaves carried on 4 ft (1.2 m) stems. Undistinguished brown-green flowers appear at centre of rosette in summer. *C.a.* 'Gracilis' is a dwarf form, growing to 18 in (45 cm). Leaves of *C.a.* 'Variegatus' have white stripes.

Likes bright light with some sun, but shade from fierce heat.
Compost should be moist throughout the year; stand the pot in a container with water 1 in (2.5 cm) deep and keep it topped up. If compost dries out, leaves yellow and wither. Should this happen the plant may be rescued (assuming roots have not been killed) by cutting down all the stems and soaking compost thoroughly. New growth will appear.
Feed every two weeks in spring and summer. Pot-on in spring in loam compost.
Propagate by division when potting-on.

Dizygotheca elegantissima

False Aralia

Woody stem bearing leaves on short stalks, which are divided into several glossy, narrow leaflets with toothed edges. Leaves are coppery green when young, changing to dark green as they mature. Grows to 5 ft (1.5 m). *D. veitchii* is similarly formed but with broader leaflets and red undersides.

Likes bright light but shade from direct sun.
Temperature minimum of 60°F (16°C) required in winter, otherwise leaves

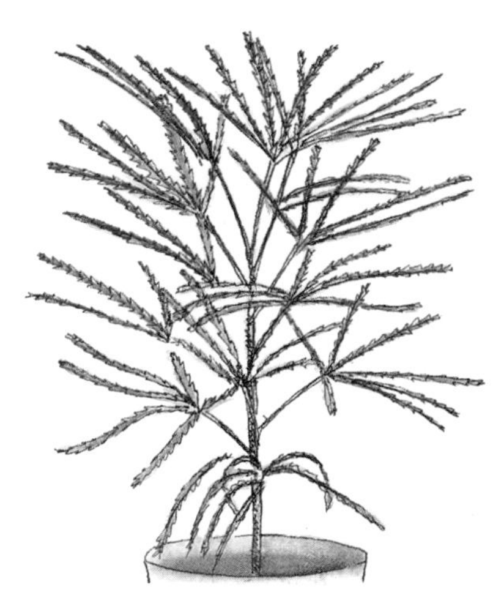

fall. Requires humidity.
Compost should be moist always in growing period, but just moist in winter.
Feed every two weeks in spring and summer. Pot-on every other spring in peat compost, changing compost for fresh in years between. Bare, leggy stems can be cut back to about 6 in (15 cm) in spring.
Propagate by sowing seed in spring.

Gynura aurantiaca

Velvet Plant

Dark green, oval leaves with toothed edges. Both stems and leaves are covered with short, purple hairs, giving a velvety look. Grows to 3 ft (90 cm). *G. sarmentosa* has smaller, more deeply-toothed leaves, also covered in purple hairs. This climbing plant needs support but looks best when growth is checked for display in a hanging container. In spring produces small orange flowers with unpleasant smell.

Likes excellent light with some direct sun to maintain rich colour. Benefits from humidity.
Compost should be moist always in growing period and barely moist in winter.
Feed monthly in spring and summer. Potting-on is not necessary since it is better to raise new plants each year. Pinch out growing tips for bushy growth.
Propagate by taking stem cuttings in spring or summer. Grow in a loam or peat compost.

Jacaranda mimosifolia

Branching shrub with fern-like leaves up to 18 in (45 cm) long. Each leaf is divided into many opposite pairs of branches covered in small, bright green leaflets. Grows to 6 ft (1.8 m) long.

Likes bright light with some direct sun, but shade from scorching rays.
Temperature of 60°F (16°C) minimum required in winter.
Compost should be moist always in growing period, but barely moist in winter.
Feed every two weeks in spring and summer. Pot-on in spring in loam compost.
Propagate from seed sown in spring with bottom heat of 75°F (24°C).

Pandanus veitchii

Screw Pine

Narrow, dark green, sword-shaped leaves, striped creamy white to yellow along their length, carried in rosette formation. The edges of the leaves are fearsomely toothed, so the plant should be kept out of the reach of children, and handled with the greatest care by adults. As it matures it develops a short woody stem. Leaves grow to 3 ft (90 cm). The plant spreads to 5 ft (1.5 m), so is suitable for only a large conservatory.

Likes bright light with direct sun for good leaf colour. Benefits from a humid atmosphere; in dry air, leaf tips are likely to turn brown.
Compost should always be moist in growing period but barely moist in winter.
Feed every two weeks in spring and summer. Pot-on in loam compost.
Propagate by removing suckers at the base of the plant in spring.

Philodendron erubescens

Blushing Philodendron

Dark green, coppery, arrowhead leaves with red undersides. *P. scandens* has dark green, glossy, heart-shaped leaves about 6 in (15 cm) long. A climber, it can be supported or displayed in a hanging container. Pinch out growing tips for bushy growth and to keep in check. Other climbers needing support include *P. andreanum* (syn. *P. melanochryson*) with young heart-shaped leaves, dark green on top and purple underneath, elongating to 24 in (60 cm) as they mature. *P.* 'Burgundy' has lance-shaped 12 in (30 cm) leaves carried on 10 in (25 cm) stalks. Young leaves are red, gradually turning green but deep red underneath. The leaves of *P. panduraeforme* develop from a heart-shape to fiddle-shape, 12 in (30 cm) in length, as they mature. All will grow to 6 ft (1.8 m) or more. *P. bipinnatifidum* grows erect to 5 ft (1.5 m) and the leaves have deeply divided lobes. *P. selloum* is similar, with leaves up to 2 ft (60 cm) long. Both need plenty of room. *P. wendlandii* has a rosette of dark green, glossy, lance-shaped leaves about 12 in (30 cm) long.

Likes bright light but keep away from direct sun.
Compost should be kept well-watered in growing period, and barely moist in winter, but do not allow it to dry out completely.
Feed every two weeks in spring and summer. Pot-on in spring in a peat compost.
Propagate climbers from stem cuttings taken in summer. For erect types, sow seed in spring.

Pilea cadieri

Aluminium Plant

Oval, dark green leaves with raised patches shaded silvery white. Grows to 10 in (25 cm). *P.c.* 'Nana' has smaller leaves and grows to 6 in (15 cm).

Likes bright light for good leaf colour but shade from direct sun.
Compost should be moist always in growing period but allow it to almost dry out between waterings in winter.
Feed every two weeks in spring and summer. Pinch out growing tips for bushy growth. Potting-on is not necessary; plants become straggly and are best replaced each year.
Propagate by taking stem tip cuttings in spring and summer. Grow in a loam or peat compost.

Rhoeo spathacea

Boat Lily

Rosette of erect, lance-shaped, olive green leaves with purple undersides. Boat-shaped purple bracts at base of leaves from which clusters of white flowers appear from late spring to summer. Grows to 12 in (30 cm). *R. s.* 'Vittata' has green leaves striped with yellow and purple undersides.

Likes good light but shade from direct sun. Requires humidity.
Compost should be moist always in growing period but barely moist in winter.
Feed every two weeks in spring and summer. Pot-on every other spring in a loam or peat compost. Change compost for fresh in year between.
Propagate by removing offsets when potting-on.

Schefflera actinophylla
(syn. *Brassaia actinophylla)*

Queensland Umbrella Tree

Eight or more oval, glossy leaflets about 10 in (25 cm) long in umbrella-spoke formation and carried on short, arching stalks from a central stem. *S. digitata* (syn. *S. arboricola*) has less coarse-looking leaflets about 6 in (15 cm) long. Both grow to 6 ft (1.8 m).

Likes bright light but shade from direct sun. Benefits from humidity in temperatures above 65°F (18°C).
Compost should be moist always in growing period, but just moist in winter.
Feed every two weeks in spring and summer. Pot-on in spring in loam compost.
Propagate from seed sown in summer.

Scirpus cernus

Club Rush

Clumps of wiry, dark green, grass-like, cylindrical leaves, up to 10 in (25 cm) long, erect at first but arching over later. Small, white flowers appear at the tips of the leaves in summer. Larger plants are best displayed in a hanging container.

Likes good light but away from direct sun; will tolerate light shade. Benefits from humidity.
Compost should be moist all year, otherwise leaf tips are likely to brown.
Feed every two weeks in spring and summer. Pot-on in spring in loam compost until maximum pot size of 6 in (15 cm) is reached. Plants should then be replaced.
Propagate by division when potting-on.

Setcreasea purpurea

Purple Heart

Narrow, lance-shaped, purple leaves up to 6 in (15 cm) long and carried on trailing purple stems. Clusters of small, deep pink flowers emerge from bracts at leaf axils in summer.

Likes bright light to maintain rich colouring, and a little sun, but shade from fierce heat.
Compost should be thoroughly watered all year round, allowing it almost to dry out before watering again.
Feed once a month in spring and summer. Plants will probably require potting-on only once in spring in loam compost. After that, stems become straggly and it is better to start with new plants.
Propagate by taking stem cuttings in spring and summer.

Flowering plants

Suggested flowering plants for the temperate conservatory range from the compact but beautiful members of the large gesneriad family – sinningia, smithiantha and streptocarpus – to the dramatic strelitzia with its tall clumps of spear-shaped leaves and exotic orange and blue flowers looking like birds in flight. Most of the plants require a winter rest period if they are to flower well the following year, but temperatures should not fall below 60°F (16°C). Two exceptions are sinningia and smithiantha, which die down after flowering. The tubers of one and the rhizomes of the other should be stored in compost, completely dry, at a temperature of 55°F (13°C).

Aphelandra squarrosa 'Louisae'

Shiny, bright green elliptical leaves with white veins. Flower spike of overlapping layers of yellow bracts from which yellow flowers appear in summer. Bracts turn green after flowering. Grows to 18 in (45 cm). The more compact form is *A.s.* 'Brockfeld', which grows to 12 in (30 cm).

Likes bright light but shade from direct sun. Requires humidity to prevent leaf edges turning brown.
Compost should be kept moist in growing period, otherwise leaves fall, but just moist during winter rest.
Feed every two weeks in spring and summer. Cut back stems by a quarter when bracts have turned green to produce new growth the following year. Pot-on in spring in a peat compost. Plants are usually worth keeping only for a second year.
Propagate from 4 in (10 cm) stem cuttings taken in late spring.

Chrysanthemum indicum hybrids

Chrysanthemum

Dark green, deeply cut, lobed leaves 2–3 in (5–7.5 cm) long. The red, yellow, white, pink and orange flowers consist of close-packed circles of petals with yellow centres. Normal flowering time is from late summer to autumn but pot chrysanthemums are usually available in flower all year round. Grows to 12 in (30 cm).

Likes good light with some direct sunlight but not fierce sun. Plants will do better in a humid atmosphere.
Compost should be thoroughly moist always.
Feeding and potting-on is not necessary since the plants are normally thrown away after flowering.

Gardenia jasminoides

Gardenia

Dark green, shiny, oval leaves carried in opposite pairs. White, waxy, strongly-scented, semi-double and double rose-like flowers grow about 3 in (7.5 cm) across and bloom through summer into autumn. Plant grows to about 2 ft (60 cm).

Likes bright light but shade from direct sun.
Temperature should be between 60° and 65°F (16 to 18°C) when plant is in bud, otherwise they are likely to fall.
Compost should be kept moist in growing season, but allow surface to dry out between waterings, and just moist in winter. Use rainwater in preference to tap water since gardenias are lime-haters.
Feed every two weeks with a weak solution of fertilizer. Cut back stems by about a half in spring for bushy plants, and pinch out growing tips. Pot-on in spring in a loam or peat compost which should be lime-free.
Propagate from 4 in (10 cm) stem tip cuttings taken in early spring. Temperature of 65°F (18°C) required.

Hibiscus rosa-sinensis

Rose of China

Glossy, oval, dark green leaves with

serrated edges. Single or double yellow, orange, red or pink, funnel-shaped flowers have prominent stamens and grow up to 5 in (12.5 cm) across. They appear from early summer to autumn. Cultivar *H. r-s.* 'Cooperi' has red and cream markings on the leaves. Grows to 6 ft (1.8 m), but can be controlled by pruning.

Likes bright light with some direct sun for good flowering but protect from scorching sunlight. Benefits from humidity.
Compost should always be kept moist in growing period but barely moist in winter.
Feed every two weeks in spring and summer. Pot-on in spring in a loam compost. Cut back stems to 6 in (15 cm) in early spring.
Propagate by taking 4 in (10 cm) cuttings in summer.

— *Impatiens wallerana* —

Busy Lizzie

Fleshy, branching stems bear bright green, rubbery, elliptical leaves. Red, orange, pink and white flowers, single or double, with flattened petals, produced from spring until autumn. Hybrids grow to 15 in (37.5 cm). 'New Guinea' hybrids grow to 2 ft (60 cm) with larger flowers and their leaves have cream to yellow markings.

Likes bright light for good flowering but shade from direct sun.
Temperature in winter should be no lower than 60°F (16°C). Benefits from humidity.
Compost should be always moist in growing period; daily watering may be

necessary in hot weather. In winter, compost should be just moist.
Feed monthly in spring and summer. Pot-on in spring in a peat compost. Cut back unsightly bare stems to 6 in (15 cm) about four weeks after potting-on. Pinch out growing tips for bushy growth.
Propagate by taking 4 in (10 cm) cuttings in summer. They will root in water. Sow seed in spring.

— *Ixora coccinea* —

Flame of the Woods

Leathery, dark green, oval, pointed leaves. Clusters of tubular scarlet flowers open to four spreading petals in summer. Grows slowly to 4 ft (1.2 m).

Likes bright light with direct sun but shade from fierce sun.
Temperature should not fall below 60°F (16°C) in winter. Requires a humid atmosphere.
Compost should be kept moist in growing period but allowed almost to dry out between waterings in winter.
Feed every two weeks in spring and summer. Pot-on in spring in either a peat or loam compost.
Propagate from 4 in (10 cm) stem cuttings taken in spring. Bottom heat of 70°F (21°C) required.

— *Jacobinia carnea* —

King's Crown

Glossy, oval, pointed, dark green leaves up to 6 in (15 cm) long. Feathery plumes of pink or red flowers appear in late summer. Grows to 5 ft (1.5 m).
J. pauciflora has 1 in (2.5 cm) long leaves and tubular red flowers with yellow tips in late autumn.

Likes bright light with some direct sun but shade from fierce sunlight.
Compost should be well watered in growing period but barely moist in winter.
Feed every two weeks in spring and summer. Pot-on in spring in peat compost or, better still, raise new plants every year. Pinch out growing tips for bushy growth.
Propagate by taking 4 in (10 cm) stem cuttings in spring.

— *Lantana camara* —

Yellow Sage

Bright green, oval, somewhat coarse leaves. Heads of small tubular flowers, which change from yellow to orange and then red, produced from late spring to autumn. Each head may have flowers in all three stages of colour. Grows to 4 ft (1.2 m) but can be kept in check by regular pruning.

Likes bright light with direct sun and good ventilation. Benefits from humidity in warm weather.
Compost should be always moist in growing period but barely moist in winter.
Feed every two weeks in spring and summer. Pot-on every spring in a loam compost. Cut back stems to 6 in (15 cm) in early spring. Pinch out growing tips for bushy growth.
Propagate from stem cuttings taken in summer or sow seed in spring.

— *Nerium oleander* —

Oleander

Narrow, lance-shaped, leathery leaves up to 10 in (25 cm) long. In summer, clusters of five-petalled flowers appear. These are usually pink, but some forms have white, orange, yellow or red flowers. *N.o.* 'Variegata' has yellow striped leaves. Grows to 6 ft (1.8 m), but can be kept smaller by regular pruning.

Likes bright light with full sun all year round, and a well ventilated position.
Compost should be kept moist in growing period but barely moist in winter. Do not allow it to dry out completely.
Feed every two weeks in spring and summer. Pot-on in spring in a loam

compost. When flowering is over, cut back stems by a half. Watch for scale insects.
Propagate by taking stem cuttings in summer. They can be rooted in water.

Pachystachys lutea

Lollipop Plant

Opposite pairs of dark green, lance-shaped leaves carried on erect stems. Cones of overlapping yellow bracts from which white-lipped flowers emerge during late spring to early autumn. Flowers are short-lived, but bracts last for about three months. Grows to 18 in (45 cm).

Likes good light but shade from direct sun. Requires a humid atmosphere.
Compost should be moist always in growing period and just moist in winter.
Feed every two weeks in spring and summer. Pot-on in spring in a loam or peat compost. Prune stems to 6 in (15 cm) in spring to encourage bushiness.
Propagate from 4 in (10 cm) stem cuttings taken in spring.

Plumeria rubra

Frangipani

Shiny, oval, tapering leaves, carried on short stalks, make this quite a handsome foliage plant before it flowers. However, the leaves usually fall in winter. Clusters of extremely fragrant, waxy, five-petalled flowers bloom mainly in summer but they may appear off and on at other times. The colours are pink, rosy red or purple. The variety *P.r. acutifolia* has creamy white flowers with a yellow throat. The plants grow to 4 ft (1.2 m) and more.

Likes good light with sun throughout the year.
Compost should be moist always in spring and summer, but in winter should be barely moist.
Feed every two weeks in spring and summer. Pot-on in spring in a loam compost.
Propagate by sowing seed in spring.

Sinningia speciosa hybrids

Gloxinia

Rosette of velvety, mid-green, oval leaves up to 8 in (20 cm) long. Velvety, trumpet-shaped, white, pink, red and violet flowers about 3 in (7.5 cm) across appear from spring to autumn. Grows to 12 in (30 cm).

Likes good light but shade from direct sun. Requires humidity.
Compost should be moist always in growing period. After flowering, when leaves die down, reduce watering, cut off dead leaves and store tuber in pot completely dry at 55°F (13°C). In late winter, start tuber into growth by beginning to water compost and maintaining temperature at 65°F (18°C).
Feed every two weeks in spring and summer. Pot-on in late winter every three to four years in peat compost. Change compost for fresh in years between.
Propagate from stem cuttings in summer or sow seed in spring.

Smithiantha zebrina hybrids

Temple Bells

Dark green, velvety, nearly circular leaves with reddish-brown veins. Long flower stalks bearing tubular yellow, orange, pink or white flowers produced from early summer to autumn. Grows to 12 in (30 cm).

Likes excellent light for good flowering but shade from direct sun. Requires humidity.
Compost should be moist always in growing period. Reduce watering when leaves start to die after flowering. Remove dead leaves and store rhizome, completely dry, in a temperature of 55°F (13°C).
Temperature when starting into growth in late winter should be 65°F (18°C). Keep compost barely moist until growth is well established.
Feed every two weeks in spring and summer. Repot rhizome in late winter in peat compost.
Propagate by dividing rhizome when repotting.

Spathiphyllum wallisii

Peace Lily

Glossy, bright green, lance-shaped leaves. Flowers are carried on 10 in (25 cm) stems and consist of an oval white spathe (which turns pale green after a few days) surrounding a yellow spadix. They appear in spring and summer and last for several weeks. Grows to 12 in (30 cm). *Spathiphyllum* 'Mauna Loa' has larger spathes and grows to 2 ft (60 cm).

Likes good light but protect from direct sun.
Temperature in winter should not fall below 60°F (16°C); if it does, the plant may refuse to flower. Requires humidity.
Compost should be moist always in growing period but barely moist in winter.
Feed every two weeks in spring and summer. Pot-on in spring in a peat or loam compost.
Propagate by dividing the rhizome in spring. Each piece should have three or more leaves and a good root system.

Strelitzia reginae

Bird of Paradise

Green, spear-shaped, leathery leaves borne on long stems. Dramatic blue and orange petals appear from a red-edged green bract carried on 3 ft (90 cm) stems in spring and early summer. Grows to 4 ft (1.2 m).

Likes bright light with some direct sun but shade from fierce sunlight.
Compost should be watered thoroughly in growing period but allow surface to dry out between waterings. In winter compost should be just moist.
Feed every two weeks in spring and summer. Pot-on in spring in peat compost.
Propagate by division in spring or sow seed with bottom heat of 70°F (21°C). It will be several years before flowers appear from seed-sown plants.

— *Streptocarpus hybrids* —

Cape Primrose

Rosette of bright green, wrinkled, strap-shaped leaves up to 12 in (30 cm) long. From late spring to autumn, groups of funnel-shaped white, pink, red or purple flowers with flaring petals appear on 6 in (15 cm) stalks.

Likes bright light but shade from direct sun.
Temperature of 60°F (16°C) minimum needed in winter. Requires good ventilation at all times and humidity in warm weather. Surface of compost should be allowed to dry out between waterings in growing period. In winter, compost should be barely moist.
Feed every two weeks in spring and summer. Pot-on every other year in early spring, or when roots fill the container, in a loam or peat compost. Change compost for fresh in years between.
Propagate from leaf cuttings in summer. Cut a leaf along the central vein and insert the cut edge in damp sand. Tiny plantlets will grow from the cut edge and can be potted in compost.

Palms and ferns

The three palms described here – chamaedorea, cycas and phoenix – will grow to between 4 and 6 ft (1.2 and 1.8 m), but only slowly. Eventually they become specimen plants, needing room both to spread and to be shown off to best advantage. A humid atmosphere and a not too dry compost help to prevent the leaf tips from turning brown.

The great variety of fern fronds is particularly well illustrated in this group. Polystichum, polypodium and asplenium with their lace-like foliage provide the conventional idea of what we expect ferns to be. Pteris has well-defined groups of strap-shaped pinnae to its fronds, while cyrtomium has glossy leaflets rather like holly leaves. Platycerium is in a class of its own, with bold, fleshy fronds resembling stags' horns.

All ferns require humidity throughout the year and good ventilation if they are to stay in tip-top condition.

— *Chamaedorea elegans* —

Parlour Palm

Almost opposite pairs of tapering narrow leaflets about 6 in (15 cm) long carried on arching, 2 ft (60 cm), yellow-green stems. Yellow, mimosa-like sprays of flowers may be followed by berries. Grows slowly to 4 ft (1.2 m).

Likes a slightly shaded spot out of direct sunlight. Benefits from humid atmosphere which helps to prevent leaf tips from turning brown.
Compost should always be moist in growing period and barely moist in winter.
Feed monthly in spring and summer. Pot-on every other year in a mixture of two parts peat compost to one part sand. Change compost for fresh in intervening years.
Propagate by sowing seed in spring in bottom heat of 75°F (24°C).

— *Cycas revoluta* —

Sago Palm

Erect-growing, 3 ft (90 cm) fronds which arch about halfway along their length and carry close-packed opposite pairs of narrow leaflets, giving a fern effect. As old fronds die, a circular base emerges. Grows slowly over many years to 6 ft (1.8 m).

Likes bright light with some direct sun but shade from scorching sun.
Compost should be kept moist in growing period and barely moist in winter. The circular base holds a reserve of water which is used by the plant if the compost becomes too dry.
Feed every two weeks in spring and

summer. Pot-on every two or three years in spring in two parts loam compost to one part sand.
Propagate from seed sown in spring with bottom heat of 75°F (24°C).

Phoenix canariensis

Canary Date Palm

Opposite pairs of narrow, oval, sharply-pointed leaflets carried on stiffly erect fronds. Grows to 6 ft (1.8 m) at the rate of about 6 in (15 cm) a year. *P. roebelenii* has softer, gracefully arching fronds. Grows to 5 ft (1.5 m) with a 4 ft (1.2 m) spread.

Likes bright light with direct sun but *P. roebelenii* requires some shade. Poor light causes leaves to turn yellow.
Compost should be evenly moist in growing period and just moist in winter. Leaf tips will turn brown if plant is short of water. Pot-on in spring in a mixture of two parts loam compost and one part sand.
Propagate from seed sown in spring; a slow process. Remove the suckers of *P. roebelenii* when potting-on.

Asplenium bulbiferum

Hen and Chicken Fern

Gracefully arching, narrow, bright green fronds, similar to carrot tops, up to 2 ft (60 cm) long. On the fronds grow small bulbils, from which new asplenium plants emerge. These can be removed and potted up.

Likes good light but away from direct sun; will tolerate some shade. Benefits from humidity.
Compost should always be moist in growing period but barely moist in winter.
Feed every two weeks in spring and summer. Pot-on every spring in a peat compost or a mixture of loam, peat and sand.
Propagate by removing the small bulbils, which should have several small fronds.

Cyrtomium falcatum

Holly Fern

Pairs of dark green, glossy leaflets, resembling holly leaves, carried on erect stems up to 18 in (45 cm) long. *C.f.* 'Rochfordianum' has larger leaflets, but stems of only 12 in (30 cm). New fronds are covered in a white scale which wears off; the bases of the stems bear a furry silvery scale which remains.

Likes good light but away from direct sun. Requires humidity, especially in warm weather.
Compost should always be moist in growing period and just moist in winter.
Feed every two weeks in spring and summer. Pot-on in spring in peat compost or a mixture of loam, peat and sand.
Propagate by dividing rhizome in spring. Each piece should have several fronds and enough roots to support them.

Platycerium bifurcatum

Staghorn Fern

Sterile, round fronds from the centre of which emerge fertile, forked fronds resembling stags' horns. Fronds grow 2 ft to 3 ft (60 to 90 cm) long with a similar spread. *P. grande* has dark green fronds similar in shape but they grow to 5 ft (1.5 m). These ferns look most impressive in half pots attached to the wall like hunting trophy displays.

Likes bright light but shade from direct sun.
Temperature in winter should be at least 60°F (16°C). Requires humidity.
Compost should be thoroughly watered all year round, but allowed almost to dry out before watering again.
Feed monthly in spring and summer. Pot-on every third year in a mixture of peat and sphagnum moss. Change compost for fresh in intervening years.
Propagate from offsets produced at base when potting-on.

Polypodium aureum

Hare's Foot Fern

Leathery fronds consisting of opposite pairs of pinnae, up to 18 in (45 cm) across and 4 ft (1.2 m) long, thrown up from a rust-brown, furry rhizome. Undersides are coated with golden spore cases. *P.a.* 'Mandaianum' has blue-green fronds with crinkly-edged pinnae.

Likes good light but do not expose to direct sun; will tolerate somewhat shady position. Requires humidity especially in warm weather.
Compost should always be moist in growing period, but barely moist in winter. Do not allow the compost to dry out completely.
Feed every two weeks in spring and summer. Pot-on in spring in a mixture of loam, peat and sand or peat compost.
Propagate by dividing the rhizome when potting-on. Make sure each piece has several fronds and enough roots to support them.

Polystichum tsus-simense

Shield Fern

Fronds consisting of almost opposite pairs of dark green, lance-shaped pinnae up to 18 in (45 cm) long. Each pinna has several pairs of tiny leaflets, or pinnules, giving an overall lacy effect.

Likes good light but away from direct sun; tolerates half shady position. Requires humidity, especially in warm weather.
Compost should always be moist in growing period but just moist in winter. Do not allow compost to dry out completely otherwise leaves will fall.
Feed monthly in spring and summer. Pot-on every third spring in peat compost or a mixture of loam, peat and sand. Change compost for fresh in intervening years.
Propagate by dividing the rhizome in spring.

Pteris cretica 'Albolineata'

Ribbon Brake

Black stalks carrying up to four bright green, strap-shaped pinnae with a white-green stripe along the length of each one. Grows to 18 in (45 cm). *P. ensiformis* 'Victoriae' has darker

Hanging plants

green fronds with several pairs of more delicate pinnae, striped silver-white on the ribs. This species is more compact, growing to 12 in (30 cm).

Likes good light to maintain leaf colour but shade from direct sun. Requires humidity, especially in warm weather.
Compost should be kept moist throughout the year, but not sodden. If it dries out completely, leaves will shrivel and die. Should this happen, cut down all fronds at compost level and spray the surface of the pot daily. New growth should soon appear.
Feed every two weeks in spring and summer. Pot-on in spring in peat compost or a mixture of loam, peat and sand.
Propagate by dividing the rhizome in spring. Each piece should have several fronds and good root structure.

Pellionia and zebrina provide year-round interest with their striking coloured foliage. The purple undersides of their leaves are seen to best advantage in a hanging container. On the other hand, the beauty of *Hoya bella* is in its clusters of white, fragrant flowers. They fill the conservatory with delicious perfume from late spring to early autumn.

—— *Hoya Bella* ——

Miniature Wax Plant

Oval, dark green leaves about 1 in (2.5 cm) long are carried on erect stems which begin to trail when they reach 1 ft (30 cm) long. Clusters of sweet-smelling, white flowers with a red to purple star centre bloom from late spring to early autumn.

Likes bright light with direct sun but shade from fierce midday sun.
Temperatures for the winter rest should be between 55° – 60°F (13° – 16°C).
Compost should be thoroughly watered in growing period, but allowed almost to dry out between waterings. It should be just moist in winter.
Feed every two weeks in spring and summer. Allow spent flowers to drop of their own accord. Do not prune spurs since new flower growth appears from there. Pot-on every other spring in loam or peat compost. Change compost for fresh in intervening years.
Propagate from stem cuttings in summer; bottom heat of 70°F (21°C) is required.

—— *Mikania apiifolia* ——

Groups of up to five small, lobed leaves carried on short stalks from the main trailing stems. Leaf colour is dark green but if the plant is kept in a well-lit position the leaves will become tinged with purple. Regularly pinch out growing tips to promote bushy growth. The trailing stems will grow to 18 in (45 cm) in length, but can be cut back.

Likes good light but should not be exposed to direct sun. It does best in a humid atmosphere and with a hanging plant this is best achieved by daily mist spraying.
Compost should be thoroughly watered in spring and summer. In the winter rest period, allow the surface to dry out between waterings.
Feed monthly in spring and summer. Pot-on in spring in a peat compost. Replace straggly plants after three years.
Propagate by taking cuttings in spring – several to a pot for bushy growth.

Climbers

The choice of climbers for the temperate conservatory includes four beautiful flowering plants – hoya and stephanotis, with their clusters of small, white, fragrant flowers; the bright red and yellow flowers of manettia; and the large pink blooms of dipladenia. By contrast, the rather coarse leaves of *Tetrastigma voinieriana* can be of practical use too, possibly in a new lean-to conservatory to cover up the brick wall quickly. But this plant will need more than normal support – stout staking, in fact.

—— *Pellionia pulchra* ——

Light green, oval leaves with purple veins on top and purple shading underneath, carried on purple stems. Grows to 18 in (45 cm). *P. daveauana* grows to 2 ft (60 cm) with round to oval leaves edged with bronze green.

Likes good light to maintain leaf colour, but shade from direct sun.
Compost should be moist in growing period; barely moist in winter.
Feed every two weeks in spring and summer. Pot-on in spring in peat compost if roots have filled the pot. Otherwise change the compost.
Propagate from 3 in (7.5 cm) stem cuttings taken in spring.

—— *Zebrina pendula 'Quadricolor'* ——

Wandering Jew

Oval, green leaves, striped cream, pink and silver with purple undersides, about 2 in (5 cm) long. Small pink flowers produced in spring and summer. Trailing stems about 15 in (37.5 cm) long.

Likes bright light with direct sun for good leaf colour. Shade from scorching sun which can burn leaves.
Compost should be watered thoroughly throughout the year but allowed almost to dry out before watering again.
Feed every two weeks in spring and summer. Pinch out growing tips for bushy growth. Pot-on in second spring in peat compost with added sand. After that it is best to raise new plants.
Propagate by taking 4 in (10 cm) stem cuttings in spring and summer. They will root in water as well as compost.

—— *Dipladenia splendens* ——

Glossy, broad, oval leaves up to 2 in (5 cm) long. Clusters of trumpet-shaped, rose pink flowers with orange throats up to 3 in (7.5 cm) across bloom in summer. Grows to 12 ft (3.6 m), but begins to flower when about 1 ft (30 cm).

Likes bright light but shade from direct sun. In warm weather benefits from humid atmosphere.
Compost should be moist always in growing period but barely moist during winter rest.
Feed every two weeks in spring and summer. Pot-on in spring in loam compost. Cut back stems to 1 ft (30 cm) after flowering.
Propagate by taking stem cuttings in spring with bottom heat of 75°F (24°C).

—— *Gloriosa rothschildiana* ——

Glory Lily

Lance-shaped, bright green leaves on thin stems. Stunning yellow and red flowers with swept-back petals appear from early to late summer. Grows to 6 ft (1.8 m) and must have support.

Likes bright light with direct but not fierce sunlight, and humid atmosphere.
Temperature around 55°F (13°C) needed when tuber is stored.
Compost should be kept moist in growing period. When leaves yellow after flowering, water less often. When they are dead, store tuber dry. Start into growth again in spring.
Feed every two weeks after growth is well established until flowering is over. Pot-on in spring when roots have filled the pot, using loam compost.
Propagate by dividing the tuber.

Hoya carnosa

Wax Plant

Glossy, elliptical, dark green leaves about 3 in (7.5 cm) long. In summer clusters of fragrant white to pink waxy flowers with a red star centre appear. Grows to 9 ft (2.7 m) or more at the rate of about 18 in (45 cm) a year. *H.c.* 'Variegata' has leaf edges flushed pink.

Likes good light with some direct sun, but shade from scorching heat.
Temperatures between 55° – 60°F (13° – 16°C) required in winter. Good ventilation and humidity also required.
Compost should be watered thoroughly in growing period but allow compost almost to dry out between waterings. Compost should be barely moist in winter.
Feed every two weeks in spring and summer. Allow dead flowers to drop of their own accord. Flowering spurs should not be pruned since new flower growth appears from there. Pot-on every other spring in a loam or peat compost. Change compost for fresh in years between.
Propagate by taking stem cuttings in summer in bottom heat of 70°F (21°C).

Lapageria rosea

Chilean Bell Flower

Dark green, leathery, elongated oval leaves. Waxy, rose-crimson, pendant bell-shaped flowers bloom from summer to late autumn. Grows to 15 ft (4.5 m); needs good support.

Likes good light with non-fierce sun.
Compost should be moist in growing period; just moist during winter rest.
Feed every two weeks in spring and summer. Pot-on each spring in loam compost.
Propagate by layering stems in spring.

Manettia bicolor

Firecracker Plant

Oval, pointed, dark green leaves, about 2 in (5 cm) long, on short stalks. Small, hairy, tubular orange flowers with yellow tips appear from early summer to late autumn. Grows to 6 ft (1.8 m) and more, but can be controlled.

Likes good light but shade from direct sun. Rest plants in winter between 55° – 60°F (13° – 16°C).
Compost should be moist always in growing period, but barely moist in winter.
Feed every two weeks in spring and summer. Pot-on every spring in loam compost. Prune plants by about a third when flowering is over.
Propagate by taking stem cuttings in summer.

Stephanotis floribunda

Madagascar Jasmine

Oval, leathery, evergreen leaves about 3 in (7.5 cm) long, arranged in opposite pairs on twining stems. Clusters of fragrant white wax flowers produced from late spring to early summer. Grows to 10 ft (3 m) and more.

Likes good light, but away from direct sun. Benefits from humidity.
Temperature in winter should be around 55°F (13°C).
Compost should be moist always in growing period, but barely moist in winter.
Feed every two weeks in spring and summer. Pot-on each spring in loam or peat compost.
Propagate by taking stem cuttings in spring, but avoid those with developing flower buds. Bottom heat of 70°F (21°C) required.

Tetrastigma voinieriana

Chestnut Vine

Large, chestnut-like leaves consisting of five dark green, glossy toothed leaflets up to 8 in (20 cm) long. Stems and leaf undersides are covered in reddish hairs. Rapidly grows to 12 ft (3 m) and more at a rate of about 5 ft (1.5 m) a year. Needs plenty of room.

Likes good light but shade from direct sun.
Compost should be moist always in growing period and barely moist in winter.
Feed every two weeks in spring and summer. Pot-on every spring in loam compost.
Propagate by taking 6 in (15 cm) stem cuttings in summer.

Bulbs

Two bulbs only would be enough to provide beautiful flowers for the conservatory from mid-summer through to early autumn: first vallota and then amaryllis. (This amaryllis should not be confused with hippeastrum, which is often sold under that name, wrongly, although the two plants are botanically related.)

The leaves of *Amaryllis belladonna* die down and the bulb has a dormant period when it is kept completely dry. *Vallota speciosa* produces leaves all year round, but still requires a rest period at temperatures between 55° and 60°F (13 – 16°C).

Amaryllis belladonna

Belladonna Lily

Strap-shaped, green leaves appear after the rose-pink, trumpet-shaped, six-petalled flowers. The flowers, up to 5 in (12.5 cm) across, are carried in a cluster on 2 ft (60 cm) long stalks from late summer to early autumn.

Likes bright light but shade from direct sun. Bulbs are started into growth in late summer. Requires good ventilation.
Compost should be kept moist until the foliage begins to turn yellow and die down, when watering should be stopped.
Feed every two weeks from appearance of first leaves until they start to die down. Cut off dead flower heads but leave flower stalks and leaves to shrivel before removing them. Pot-on every third year in late summer in a loam compost. Leave the shoulder of the bulb showing above the compost surface. Change compost for fresh in years between.
Propagate by removing offsets when potting-on.

Haemanthus katharinae

Blood Flower

Lance-shaped, green, leathery leaves with wavy edges, up to 18 in (45 cm) long. In summer a stout flower stalk carries a mop head of dark red, spidery flowers tipped with contrasting yellow. The leaves may die down, but more often remain all year. *Haemanthus multiflorus* (Salmon Blood Lily) has similar leaves, but without the wavy edges. They die down in early autumn. In late spring a circular head of salmon pink flowers appears.

Likes bright light, with direct sun. Dormant bulbs do not need light.
Compost must be thoroughly watered in growing period, but let surface dry out between waterings. If leaves die down, water less often, and during dormancy only once a month or so. Bulbs which keep their leaves need water more often, say every two to three weeks.
Feed every two weeks in spring and summer. Pot-on in loam compost every three or four years when roots show above surface.

Nerine bowderii

Nerine

Strap-shaped, bright green leaves which grow after the 20 in (50 cm) flower stalks. Clusters – 6 in (15 cm) across – of pink flowers with flared-back petals bloom in autumn.

Likes bright light with direct sun.
Temperature 55° – 60° F (13° – 16° C) in winter.
Compost should be always moist from appearance of flower stalks until leaves die down. As leaves yellow, stop watering and keep dry from early to late summer.
Feed every two weeks after flower stalks appear until leaves die. Pot-on every three years in loam compost.
Propagate from bulb offsets.

Vallota speciosa

Scarborough Lily

Bright green, strap-shaped leaves up to 2 ft (60 cm) long. Clusters of scarlet, funnel-shaped flowers carried on 2 ft (60 cm) long hollow stems.

Likes excellent light with some direct sun but shade from fierce sun. Start the bulbs into growth in spring.
Compost should always be moist in growing period, but barely moist during winter rest.
Feed every two weeks when growth is well established until end of summer. Cut off dead flower heads but leave flower stalks to wither naturally. Pot-on every third spring in a loam compost. Tips of the bulbs should just show above compost surface. Change compost for fresh in years between.
Propagate by removing offsets.

Orchids

By growing the selected group of orchids described here, the conservatory should have something in bloom from the spring of one year to the late winter of the next. Orchids need humidity and good ventilation when growing, but during the rest period which all these plants must have, humidity should be reduced. Night temperatures should fall by between 5° and 10°F (3° – 6°C) – an essential requirement for most orchids if they are to flower well.

—— *Calanthe vestita* ——

Large pseudobulb, about 6 in (15 cm) long, from which ribbed leaves appear. In winter the arching flower spike, up to 3 ft (90 cm) long, bears many white flowers with deep pink lips. This orchid is started into growth in spring. Leaves die down in autumn and are followed by the flower spike. After flowering, pseudobulbs are stored dry until the following spring.

Likes bright light with direct sun. In winter, pseudobulbs should be kept in a sunny, warm spot around 65°F (18°C). Start tuber into growth in spring.
Compost should be kept moist until leaves begin to yellow in autumn. Reduce watering and stop when leaves are completely dead. Flowering plants should not require water.
Feed monthly in spring and summer. Repot pseudobulbs each spring in an orchid compost.
Propagate by division when repotting.

—— *Epipendrum radicans* ——
(syn. *E. ibaguense*)

Cone-like stems up to 5 ft (1.5 m) long with fleshy, pale green oval leaves ranged alternately along their length. The flower spike, a cluster of orange, red or pink flowers with deeply fringed lips, appears from the top of the stem in late summer or autumn. Train against a wall or trellis.

Likes bright light and some direct sun but shade from fierce midday sun. Requires humidity.
Temperature in winter should be minimum of 60° – 65°F (16° – 18°C).
Compost should be thoroughly watered all year round and allowed almost to dry out before watering again.
Feed monthly in spring and summer. Pot-on every two to three years in spring in an orchid compost. Change compost for fresh in years between.
Propagate by division when potting-on or take cuttings after flowering.

—— *Lycaste deppei* ——

Flattened, oval pseudobulbs about 4 in (10 cm) long, usually producing a group of three leaves up to 12 in (30 cm) long. Flowers have pale green sepals spotted reddish brown, white petals and a yellow lip with red spots. They appear in spring, carried singly on 6 in (15 cm) stems.

Likes good light but shade from direct sun. Requires humid atmosphere.
Compost should be watered thoroughly in growing period and allowed to dry out before watering again. In autumn, when foliage begins to die down, gradually decrease watering and stop altogether when leaves are completely dead. During rest period atmosphere should be drier. Commence watering again when new growth appears.
Feed monthly in spring and summer. Repot each spring in orchid compost.
Propagate by dividing the rhizome when repotting. Each piece should have two or three pseudobulbs.

—— *Miltonia vexillaria* ——

Pansy Orchid

Short pseudobulbs bearing strap-shaped leaves 10 in (25 cm) long. Deep pink to red pansy-like flowers about 3 in (7.5 cm) across and with yellow markings carried on 2 ft (60 cm) stalks in spring and summer.

Likes light but shade from direct sun.
Temperature in winter should be at least 60° F (16° C). Good ventilation and humidity required.
Compost should be watered thoroughly in growing period and allowed to dry out before watering again. In winter compost should be just moist.
Feed monthly in spring and summer. Pot-on in summer, after flowering, in an orchid compost.
Propagate by dividing the rhizome.

—— *Odontoglossum grande* ——

Tiger Orchid

Short, egg-shaped pseudobulb, producing two strap-shaped, bright

Succulents

green leaves about 10 in (25 cm) long. In autumn 12 in (30 cm) flower stems appear bearing several large, bright yellow flowers striped reddish-brown and about 6 in (15 cm) across.

Likes good light but shade from direct sun. Requires humid atmosphere.
Compost should always be moist in growing period but allow almost to dry out between waterings in winter.
Feed monthly in spring and summer. Pot-on after flowering in an orchid compost.
Propagate by dividing the rhizome when potting-on. Each piece should have at least three pseudobulbs.

— *Paphiopedilum callosum* —

Slipper Orchid

Overlapping, opposite pairs of strap-shaped, dark green leaves about 2 in (5 cm) long, mottled with lighter green. White flowers with maroon and green stripes and light purple lips are produced on 12 in (30 cm) stems in spring. *P. insigne* has 10 in (25 cm) strap-shaped leaves and yellow-green flowers with purple-brown spots which appear in late winter.

Likes light but shade from direct sun.
Temperature in winter should not be less than 60°F (16°C). Requires humidity, especially in warm weather.
Compost should be kept moist in growing period, but not sodden. After flowering, allow almost to dry out between waterings for about two and a half months.
Feed monthly in spring and summer. Pot-on every second or third year in an orchid compost. Change compost for fresh in years between.
Propagate by division when potting-on.

Most succulents are more suited to the lower temperatures found in the cool conservatory in winter, but a few will do well at higher temperatures. The four suggested here are a mixed lot: the spiny shrub *Euphorbia milii* (Crown of Thorns); the virtually indestructible sansevierias; a small variegated stapelia (Starfish Plant) with its curiously beautiful though malodorous flowers; and the popular winter-flowering *Kalanchoe blossfeldiana*. The kalanchoe is a short-day plant, so to bring it into bud it must have a period with restricted hours of daylight.

All these succulents require a rest period when they should not be watered more than about once a month.

— *Euphorbia milii* —

Crown of Thorns

Stout, brown, branching stems, covered in sharp spines, bearing groups of bright green, oval leaves towards their tips. Bright red or yellow bracts about ½ in (1.75 cm) across surround tiny flowers from spring to summer. Flower stems are slightly sticky. Grows to 3 ft (90 cm).

Likes excellent light with direct sun all year round for prolonged flowering.
Compost should always be moist in growing period. Water about once a month in winter, but do not allow compost to dry out completely.
Feed every two weeks in spring and summer. Pot-on in spring in a mixture of two parts loam compost to one part sand.
Propagate by taking cuttings in spring and summer or sow seed in spring.

— *Kalanchoe blossfeldiana* —

Dark green, fleshy, circular leaves about 2 in (5 cm) long, flushed red at their edges. Short stalks bear clusters of small, four-petalled red, orange or yellow flowers in winter and spring. Though often discarded after flowering, the plant can be induced to flower in subsequent years. *K. pumila* has pink-grey, oval leaves with serrated edges covered in white powder and pink flowers. Both grow to 12 in (30 cm). *K. tomentosa* has rosettes of fleshy, oval leaves edged brown and covered in white down. It seldom blooms. Grows to 18 in (45 cm).

Likes good light with direct sun. To bring *K. blossfeldiana* into flower

again the following year, the plant should have ten hours of daylight and fourteen hours of total darkness for a period of two months from mid autumn.
Compost should be watered thoroughly all year round, allowing it almost to dry out before watering again. Leaves bloat and rot if over-watered.
Feed monthly in spring and summer. Pot-on in spring in a loam compost.
Propagate from 3 in (7.5 cm) stem cuttings or sow seed in spring.

Sansevieria trifasciata 'Laurentii'

Mother-in-law's Tongue

Narrow, mid-green, sword-shaped leaves with darker green horizontal wavy bands and yellow edges. Leaves grow from compost level and can reach height of 18 in (45 cm).
S. 'Hahnii' has a rosette of triangular-shaped mid-green leaves with darker green horizontal banding. Grows to 6 in (15 cm). *S.* 'Golden Hahnii' has leaves edged and striped with yellow.

Likes bright light with direct sun for good leaf colour.
Temperature in winter should be at least 60°F (16°C).
Compost should be watered once a week in growing period and once a month in winter. Too much water causes root rot and leaf collapse. Rosette-forming plants should not be watered in the centre of the rosette.
Feed monthly in spring and summer. Pot-on in spring every two to three years in a loam compost. Change compost for fresh in intervening years.
Propagate from offsets removed when potting-on or from leaf cuttings taken in summer. Cut the leaf into 2 in (5 cm) sections and plant bottom end down in compost. Small plants will appear but they will be plain green.

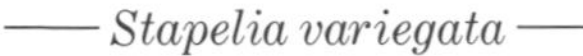

Stapelia variegata

Starfish Plant

Cluster of bright green, upright, finger stems with brown markings and four rows of notches running their length. Greenish-yellow, starfish-shaped flowers with brown and purple markings appear at the base of the stems in summer. They have an unpleasant smell but their beauty and unusual formation compensates for this disadvantage.

Likes good light with direct sun all year round.
Temperature in winter should be at least 60°F (16°C).
Compost should be watered thoroughly in growing period, allowing top half to dry out before watering again. In winter it should be barely moist; watering once a month should be enough. If kept too wet, the plants will rot at compost level.
Feed monthly in spring and summer. Pot-on every other year in spring in a mixture of two parts loam compost to one part sand.
Propagate by sowing seed in spring, or take cuttings in summer. These should be dried off for a day or two before potting.

Bromeliads

These bromeliads provide long-lasting colour; the guzmania and tillandsia with their bracts, and the neoregelia and nidularium with the leaves at the centre of their rosettes which turn bright red and yellow at the time of flowering. The guzmania and neoregelia die down after flowering but leave offsets to start new growth, though it will be some years before they come into flower.

Guzmania lingulata

Scarlet Star

Narrow, bright green, sword-shaped leaves up to 18 in (45 cm) long grow in rosette formation. The flower stalk appears from the centre of the rosette and consists of short, orange to red, leaf-like bracts surrounding yellow flowers. The bracts remain colourful for many weeks in autumn and winter. Leaves of *G.l.* 'Minor' grow to 12 in (30 cm). *G. zahnii* has leaves about 20 in (50 cm) long, striped red on both top and bottom surfaces. It has deep red bracts and white flowers. After flowering the main plant will eventually die down, but not before producing offsets.

Likes bright light but shade from fierce direct sun. Requires humidity.
Compost should be kept moist in growing period, when the centre of the rosette should be topped up with water regularly. In winter, compost should be just moist and the rosette centre should then be kept dry.
Feed monthly in spring and summer. Pot-on every other spring in a peat compost. Change compost for fresh in intervening years.
Propagate by removing offsets when potting-on.

Neoregelia carolinae 'Tricolor'

Blushing Bromeliad

Rosette of shiny green leaves with yellow stripes and toothed edges growing to 12 in (30 cm) long. Leaves flush pink as they mature. With the onset of flowering, which can be at any time of the year, leaves at the centre of the rosette turn bright red and remain colourful for many months. Small white flowers appear from the centre of the rosette. Although the main plant dies down eventually, it leaves behind offsets.

Likes excellent light for good leaf colour, but away from direct sun. Benefits from humidity, especially in warm weather.
Compost should always be moist in growing period and centre of rosette should be topped up with water. In winter, compost should be just moist and centre of rosette kept dry.
Feed monthly in spring and summer. Pot-on every other spring in peat compost. Change compost for fresh in intervening years.
Propagate by removing offsets when potting-on.

Nidularium innocentii

Bird's Nest

Narrow, strap-shaped, finely-toothed leaves in rosette formation, metallic purple-green on the top surface and deep red underneath. Before flowering, the leaves at the centre of the rosette turn orange-brown. The white flowers usually appear in autumn. Rosette grows up to 2 ft (60 cm) across. *N.i.* 'Nana' stays a compact 12 in (30 cm). *N. fulgens* is similar to *N. innocentii* but the leaves are spotted darker green. The centre of the rosette turns bright red before blue flowers appear.

Likes good light but out of direct sun.
Temperature of 60°F (16°C) minimum needed in winter. Also requires humidity.
Compost should be thoroughly watered all year round and the surface allowed to dry out before watering again. Centre of rosette should be topped up with water regularly, except in winter when it should be kept dry.
Feed monthly in spring and summer. Pot-on every other spring in peat compost. Change compost for fresh in years between.
Propagate by removing offsets when potting-on.

Tillandsia lindeniana

Blue-flowered Torch

Rosette of narrow, grey-green leaves about 15 in (37.5 cm) long with undersides flushed purple. The showy flower spike consists of pink overlapping bracts in a fan shape, from which blue flowers with white throats emerge in summer. *T. cyanea* is similar, but the undersides of the leaves are striped reddish brown. *T. usneoides*, Spanish Moss, has wiry, intertwining, grey-green stems. Yellow flowers may appear in summer. This plant is not grown in compost but attached to a piece of cork or bark with fine wire.

Likes bright light but shade from direct sun.
Temperature in winter should be at least of 60°F (16°C). Good ventilation and humidity are essential.
Compost should be barely moist at all times as tillandsias have very little root structure. A constant humid atmosphere will give them all the moisture they need. Otherwise plants should be sprayed daily.
Feed monthly in spring and summer apart from *T. usneoides* which does not require feeding. Potting-on is not usually necessary but compost can be freshened each year in spring. Use two parts compost to one part sand.
Propagate by removing offsets of *T. lindeniana* and *T. cyanea* in spring. For *T. usneoides*, remove a few stems and attach them to a piece of cork or bark.

The Warm Conservatory

Winter temperatures: 65–75°F (18–24°C)

The fortunate owner of a warm conservatory can enjoy it in comfort all year. Although many warmth-loving plants are unsuitable because they demand more humidity than people can tolerate, the 50 or so plants in this section provide choice enough for even a large conservatory. The most dramatic year-round effects come more from the spectacular colours and shapes of leaves than from flowers. But bromeliads and orchids, and a score of flowering plants, add long-lasting seasonal colour. And for a summer burst of bloom there are the numerous annuals.

1 *Ficus lyrata* (see Garden Room: Foliage) 2 *Vriesea splendens* (Bromeliad) 3 *Ananas comosus* 'Variegatus' (Bromeliad) 4 *Chrysalidocarpus lutescens* (Palm) 5 *Caladium hortulanum* (Foliage) 6 *Sanchezia speciosa* (Flowering) 7 *Persea gratissima* (Foliage) 8 *Mimosa pudica* (Foliage) 9 *Asplenium nidus* (Fern) 10 *Anthurium scherzeranum* (Flowering) 11 *Aeschynanthus speciosus* (Hanging) 12 *Codiaeum variegatum pictum* (Foliage) 13 *Crossandra infundibuliformis* (Flowering) 14 *Allamanda cathartica* (Climber)

Foliage plants

Among plants needing the warmth of a heated conservatory there are some with strikingly variegated leaves – not just different shades of green, but of reds, purples and yellows. The codiaeums and iresines are especially notable, and so is the caladium, but unfortunately this dies down totally each winter. One of the few plain green-leaved plants is the large and ubiquitous monstera, or Swiss Cheese Plant. There is no need to give this a dominating position; instead, use its large slashed leaves as a background to display other plants, especially those with variegated leaves.

With few exceptions, the foliage plants described here need humid conditions. Some may survive in a dry atmosphere but the leaf tips will turn brown, leaving a dejected-looking plant. Others will die.

Aglaonema crispum 'Silver Queen'

Chinese Evergreen

Oval, leathery leaves up to 10 in (25 cm) long, carried on short stems, with silvery markings against a dark green background. The plant grows no more than 15 in (37.5 cm) high.
A. commutatum 'Pseudobracteatum' has lance-shaped, glossy, leathery leaves up to 12 in (30 cm) long; its cream to yellow and grey-green markings show against a green background.
A. nitidum (syn. *A. oblongifolium*) 'Curtisii' has lance-shaped, mid-green leaves, with veins picked out in silver, growing up to 20 in (50 cm) long.

Likes a humid atmosphere; shade plant from direct sun all year round.
Compost should always be kept moist.
Feed every two weeks in spring and summer. Pot-on every other spring in peat compost, changing compost in the years between.
Propagate by division in spring or from stem tip cuttings in summer.

Caladium hortulanum

Angel Wings

Arrow-head leaves, up to 12 in (30 cm) long, growing on individual stems from compost level. The striking leaf colour depends on the cultivar: white with veins and mid-rib picked out in green; red with green margins; mottled green and white leaves with bright red veins – in groups they are a real feast for the eyes. After the foliage dies down in autumn, the tubers are stored nearly dry in warmth, until started into growth again in early spring. The plant grows to 2 ft (60 cm).

Likes bright light, which is essential to maintain strong leaf colour, but shade from direct sun. During growing period it needs a humid atmosphere and freedom from draughts.
Compost should be kept moist until foliage begins to die down. Then reduce watering, cutting it down finally to no more than once a month so that the tuber is almost dry.
Feed every two weeks while the plant is growing vigorously, stopping as the leaves die. In early spring, remove tuber from the old compost, cut away any dead roots and pot-on into fresh peat compost.
Propagate by removing offsets when potting-on.

Codiaeum variegatum pictum

Croton

Leaves of varying size, shape and colour according to the cultivar. They may be oval, lance-shaped, lobed, thin-fingered or oblong. The colour may be orange, black, brown, yellow, green or pink, in combinations of two or more colours. Veins are sometimes picked out in a different colour or the leaves may be covered with spots or blotches of colour. Cultivars grouped together make a startling impact. The plants grow up to 3 ft (90 cm). Consistently warm temperatures and a draught-free spot are vital if the leaves are not to fall.

Likes excellent light all year, with direct sun except when it may scorch. Leaves lose their brilliant colouring in poor light. Also requires a humid atmosphere.
Compost should always be moist.
Feed every two weeks in spring and summer. Straggly plants may be cut back to 6 in (15 cm) in spring. Pot-on each spring in a peat compost.
Propagate by taking 4 in (10 cm) stem cuttings in summer.

— *Ctenanthe oppenheimiana* —

Never Never Plant

Lance-shaped, pointed, dark green leaves, up to 12 in (30 cm), banded with silvery-grey on the surface and purple undersides. Bushy plant, throwing up offsets from compost level. The most popular form is *C.o.* 'Tricolor', the leaves of which are splashed with cream to pink markings. Grows to 20 in (50 cm). Must have consistently high temperatures and high humidity for good results.

Likes bright light, but shade from direct sun, which may cause leaf curl. If the light is poor the colour of the foliage will fade.
Compost should be kept moist, but reduce watering during the winter rest period.
Feed every two weeks in spring and summer. Pot-on each year in a peat compost.
Propagate by removing an offset when potting-on, or take stem cuttings in early summer.

— *Fittonia verschaffeltii* —

Red Net Leaf

Dark green, oval leaves, about 3 in (7.5 cm) long, with prominent carmine veins. The whole plant is no more than 6 in (15 cm) tall, but the creeping stems reach 12 in (30 cm). *F. argyroneura* has similar shaped leaves, but the veins are silvery white. *F. a.* 'Nana' has smaller leaves about 1 in (2.5 cm). If fittonias do not have warmth and humidity their foliage falls, leaving unsightly bare stems.

Likes a slightly shaded spot, certainly out of direct sunlight, which can damage the leaves.
Compost should be kept moist, but reduce frequency of watering during rest period. Sodden compost will cause stem and root rot.
Feed every two weeks in spring and summer. Pot-on each year in spring in a shallow pot, using a peat compost, with added sand for good drainage.
Propagate from 3 in (7.5 cm) cuttings taken in early summer. The creeping stems may also be layered.

— *Geogenanthus undatus* —

Seersucker Plant

Broad, oval, dark green leaves, about 4 in (10 cm) long, with lighter green stripes running their length. Their top surface has a metallic sheen and quilted effect; undersides are purplish red. In summer there are short-lived blue flowers which last no more than a day. Grows to 12 in (30 cm).

Likes good light, but no direct sun. Too much shade will make leaves lose their colour. Humid atmosphere essential; red spider mite and mealy bugs may attack if plant becomes too dry.
Compost should be kept moist always, but water less frequently in winter.
Feed every two weeks in spring and summer. Pot-on each spring in a loam or peat compost.
Propagate by taking 3 in (7.5 cm) stem cuttings in spring when potting on.

— *Hypoestes sanguinolenta* —

Freckle Face

Dark green, oval leaves, about 2 in (5 cm) long, spotted or splashed with pink. When stems have grown to 12 in (30 cm), cut back to within 4 in (10 cm) of compost level. Stems allowed to grow longer become straggly; cutting promotes thicker growth at the base.

Likes bright light with some direct sun (to preserve the high colouring) but shade from scorching sun.
Compost should be kept moist always; lower leaves fall if it becomes too dry.
Feed every two weeks in spring and summer. Pinch out growing tips to make a bushy plant. Pot-on each spring in a peat compost and cut back straggly stems when growth is under way.
Propagate by taking 4 in (10 cm) stem cuttings, rooting them in a heated propagator at 70°F (21°C).

— *Iresine herbstii* —

Beefsteak Plant

Wine-red, heart-shaped leaves, about 3 in (7.5 cm) long, with paler coloured mid-rib and veins, carried on fleshy stems. Requires regular pinching out of growing tips to encourage bushy growth. *I.h.* 'Aureoreticulata' is equally colourful: the red stems carry bright green leaves with veins picked out in yellow. The insignificant flowers rarely appear on plants indoors. Grows to 2 ft (60 cm).

Likes bright light with direct sun all year round to preserve the plant's high colour, but even so there must be shade from fierce summer sun which will scorch the leaves. A humid atmosphere is needed.
Compost should always be kept moist, but water less frequently in winter rest period.
Feed every two weeks in spring and summer. Pinch out growing tips every three or four months. Pot-on each year in spring in a loam or peat compost. Plants that have reached their maximum height of about 2 ft (60 cm) are past their best and should be replaced.
Propagate by taking 3 in (7.5 cm) stem cuttings in spring and summer, rooted either in compost or water and then moved to compost.

—— *Monstera deliciosa* ——

Swiss Cheese Plant

Distinctive shiny, dark green leaves, deeply incised and perforated, about 18 in (45 cm) long and 16 in (40 cm) wide, borne on long stiff stems. The monstera needs firm support as it grows and a moss pole is often used for this purpose. The moss is kept damp and provides an additional source of moisture if the ends of the plant's aerial roots are inserted into it. It is not advisable to insert these aerial roots into the compost itself since they will quickly fill the pot and impede development of the main roots.

Mature plants may produce cream-coloured spathes followed by edible fruit with a pineapple flavour. They are more likely to appear when the monstera is grown under glass than in a living room, but they cannot be counted on. The plant grows to 6 ft (1.8 m) or more and has a similar spread. If there is room, look for a group planting – two or three together in a pot – to give a bushier effect. *M.d.* 'Variegata' is the form to go for; its green leaves are splashed with cream or white.

Likes bright light, but shade from direct sun. *M.d.* 'Variegata' must have good light all year to maintain leaf colour. A humid atmosphere benefits monsteras, but is less essential than for many plants in this section.
Compost should be watered thoroughly, but allow the surface to dry out before watering again. Never allow plant to dry out completely since leaf tips will turn brown.
Feed every two weeks in spring and summer. Pot-on each spring in a loam compost. Potting-on is no longer practicable after a 12 in (30 cm) pot has been reached and the plant is several feet tall. Then each year remove the top 2 in (5 cm) of compost and replace with fresh. Over a period of years a monstera may grow too big. It cannot be pruned, but can be cut down to size by air layering (done in summer) although this is not always successful.
Propagate by a stem tip cutting in spring.

—— *Persea gratissima* ——

Avocado Pear

A plant which you have to raise yourself from the pit of an avocado, since it is ignored by nurseries. The larger the pit, the better the specimen, but there is no guarantee that every pit will grow because it may not be fertile. Start pits into growth in spring and summer so that plants become established in warmer, brighter months. Plants have to be cut back when young or they will not develop a bushy habit. They produce bright green, elliptical leaves up to 12 in (30 cm) and will grow to 6 ft (1.8 m) or more.

Likes bright light with some direct sun, but protect from scorching. Leaf tips will turn brown without adequate humidity.
Compost should always be kept moist, but water less frequently in winter.
Feed every two weeks in spring and summer. Pot-on each spring in a mixture of loam, peat and sharp sand.
Propagate by standing the pit blunt end down in water, but only so that the water is just touching the base of the pit. A hyacinth bulb glass is ideal for this, but other containers with a narrow neck will serve. Keep the container topped up with water so that the base of the pit is wet. Place in warmth – 70° – 75°F (21° – 4°C) – and in the dark. It may take weeks to germinate, showing a white root growing from the base into the water. When more roots appear, plant in a mixture of peat, loam and sharp sand with the tip of the pit just showing above the compost. Alternatively, germinate the pit in peat compost, with the tip just showing. Place the pot in a plastic bag and put it in a warm, dark place until signs of growth are seen. Bring into the light, let it become established and then repot it in a loam, peat and sand mixture. When the stem is 8 in (20 cm) high cut it back to 5 in (12.5 cm). This means losing all the leaves, but new and bushier growth will soon appear. Failure to cut back will leave a single stem growing taller and taller with a few leaves at the top – a ridiculous sight. Pinch out growing tips occasionally to encourage bushiness.

—— *Polyscia balfouriana* ——

Balfour Aralia

Ornamental shrub with interesting variegated, round leaves which in mature plants are carried in groups of three on stalks from the central stem. Leaves are dark green, with cream to white wavy edges, or with veins picked out in yellow. The stalks are also an attractive green, striped with grey and darker green. The plant grows slowly, usually to 3 ft (90 cm), but to 6 ft (1.8 m) or more in ideal conditions. As the plant matures, some shedding of the lower leaves is to be expected but serious leaf loss is caused by lack of warmth, humidity and light.

Likes good light to preserve variegations, but shade from direct sun. Requires high humidity at all times, which also helps to keep red spider mite at bay.
Compost should be moist always, but allow surface to dry out between waterings.
Feed every two weeks in spring and summer. Pot-on each spring in loam compost. To keep plant a reasonable size, stop potting-on after reaching an 8 in (20 cm) pot. Each year after that remove the top 2 in (5 cm) of compost and replace with fresh. To grow a tall specimen, keep potting-on into larger pots, eventually transferring the plant to a tub.
Propagate from 4 in (10 cm) stem cuttings, with bottom heat of at least 70°F (21°C).

Flowering plants

Not all these dozen or so plants depend for their colour on flowers alone. Some are included more for their highly-coloured bracts (which last longer than the flowers) notably the euphorbia known as Poinsettia. Others also have richly marked leaves, such as bertolonia, episcia, siderasis and sonerila.

On the whole they are not easy plants to grow; all come from tropical regions of the world where they have consistent warmth and, often, steamy humidity. You may have no wish to match such extreme conditions in your conservatory, but will have to go some way to meeting the plants' needs if they are to flower well and the leaves be prevented from curling and browning.

Acalypha hispida

Chenille Plant

Hairy, bright green, oval, pointed leaves about 6 in (15 cm) long. Tassels of red flowers up to 15 in (37.5 cm) long appear in summer. The plant soon grows to 6 ft (1.8 m). *A. wilkesiana* has oval leaves, 6 in (15 cm) long, with copper, red and pink markings. It produces insignificant flowers. Grows to 6 ft (1.8 cm).

Likes bright light with direct sun all year round for good flowering, and to maintain rich leaf colouring of *A. wilkesiana*, but shade from fierce sun. Requires humid atmosphere, otherwise leaves will curl and red spider mite may attack.
Compost should be moist always.
Feed every two weeks in spring and summer. Pot-on every spring in a peat compost. To keep plants a reasonable size, cut back to 12 in (30 cm) at the same time.
Propagate in spring from stem tip cuttings of about 4 in (10 cm). Temperature of 75°F (24°C) is needed for cuttings to strike.

Anthurium scherzerianum

Flamingo Flower

Lance-shaped, leathery, dark green leaves, 6 in (15 cm) long, carried on stalks of about the same length. A thin, orange-red, fleshy, curling flower spike appears from the centre of a similarly coloured spathe, from early spring to summer. *A. andreanum* has dark green, leathery, heart-shaped leaves, about 8 in (20 cm) long on similar length stalks. The yellow flower spike emerges from heart-shaped pink or red spathes.

Likes good light, but shade from direct sun all year round. Unless the atmosphere is humid leaves will curl, becoming thin and papery. Dry air also encourages red spider mite.
Compost should be kept moist always. Pot-on in spring each year, using a peat compost mixed with sphagnum moss.
Propagate by division in spring when potting-on.

Bertolonia marmorata

Jewel Plant

Velvety, heart-shaped, bright green leaves are streaked silvery-white on top with purple undersides. Small pink to purple flowers may appear at any time during the year, but the plants are grown more for their distinctively marked leaves. Bertolonias are not particularly long lived, but new plants can be raised from cuttings. Plants are of creeping habit, growing no more than 6 in (15 cm) high.

Likes shade from direct sun all year round. Provide a humid atmosphere.
Compost should be kept evenly moist in spring and summer, but barely moist in winter. Avoid wetting the leaves, which are easily marked.
Feed every two weeks in spring and summer. As long as the plant survives, pot-on every other year in late spring or early summer in peat compost, using shallow pots or pans. Change compost in years between.
Propagate from stem cuttings taken in summer or by sowing seed with bottom heat in spring.

—— *Espicia cupreata* ——

Flame Violet

Attractive plant grown for both beautifully marked leaves and brilliantly coloured flowers. Oval, puckered leaves up to 5 in (12.5 cm) long are bright to copper green with silvery or green markings, depending on the cultivar. Groups of orange to red tubular flowers, opening to five circular lobes, appear from spring through to autumn. Plant has a creeping habit, forming a mat of foliage no more than 6 in (16 cm) high.

Likes bright light, but shade from direct sun, for good flowering and to maintain leaf colour. Needs a humid atmosphere.
Compost should be kept moist.
Feed every two weeks in spring and summer. When flowering is over, cut back stems to encourage new growth. Pot-on each year in spring, using a shallow container, in a peat compost with added sphagnum moss.
Propagate by division or take cuttings from rooted runners in spring and summer. Watch for aphids.

—— *Crossandra infundibuliformis* ——

Firecracker Flower

Bright green, glossy, lance-shaped leaves with wavy edges, up to 5 in (12.5 cm) long. Clusters of tubular, orange to salmon-pink flowers produced on 6 in (15 cm) spikes which appear from leaf axils in spring and summer. Grows to 3 ft (90 cm). Hybrid *C. i.* 'Mona Walhed' has larger orange flowers and remains a compact 15 in (37.5 cm).

Likes to be shaded from direct sun for most of the year, but weak winter sun will do no harm. Requires humid atmosphere to prevent leaves from curling and for continued flowering. Dry air will also attract red spider mites.
Compost should be kept moist in growing period, but only barely moist for rest of the year.
Feed every two weeks in spring and summer. Pinch out growing tips in spring to make plants bushy and cut back to 6 in (15 cm) any plant getting out of hand. Pot-on each spring in a peat compost.
Propagate by taking 4 in (10 cm) stem tip cuttings or from seed sown.

—— *Euphorbia pulcherrima* ——

Poinsettia

Toothed, oval, bright and mid-green leaves provide the background for brilliant red and pink bracts or more subtle white ones. Tiny yellow flowers emerge from the bracts. The plant remains colourful for many weeks in winter until bracts begin to fall. The bracts will not appear unless a strict regime of light and darkness is imposed on the plant. Grows to 18 in (45 cm).

Likes bright light but out of direct sun. For two months in autumn the plant must have a period of ten hours of daylight and 14 hours of darkness each day. Total darkness is vital. At the end of this period bring into normal light, but away from direct sun. Bracts should soon appear. When bracts have fallen in spring, cut back stems to 6 in (15 cm).
Compost should be kept just moist after the spring cutting-back until new growth appears, followed by frequent watering for the rest of the year. If plants are kept too dry, leaves will drop.
Feed every two weeks in spring and summer. Pot-on each year in late spring in either a peat or loam compost, but before potting-on allow the plants to recover from the pruning.
Propagate from 4 in (10 cm) stem cuttings taken in early summer.

—— *Gerbera jamesonii* ——

Barberton Daisy

Bright green, gently lobed leaves. Red, pink, yellow or orange daisy flowers, about 5 in (12.5 cm) produced from spring to autumn. Grows to 2 ft (60 cm).

Likes bright light with full sun.
Compost should be always moist in growing season; barely moist when resting.
Feed every two weeks in spring and summer. Pot-on each spring in peat compost.
Propagate by sowing seed in winter or early spring.

—— *Medinilla magnifica* ——

Rose Grape

A true – and expensive – exotic which requires consistently high temperatures and humidity for best results. Broad, oval, dark green, shiny leaves up to 10 in (25 cm) long are carried on opposite pairs of long stems. Plants can grow to 5 ft (1.5 m), with a similar spread. The pendulous drooping clusters of pink flowers, surrounded by pink bracts, are carried on 12 in (30 cm) stems which appear from the branch tips. Flowering period is from spring to late summer.

Likes bright light all year round, but shade from direct sun. Needs a high degree of humidity to produce flowers.
Compost should be kept moist always during growth period, but barely moist in winter rest period.
Feed every two weeks from spring to autumn. Pot-on every other spring in a peat or loam compost, changing the compost in the years between. When flowering is over plants may be pruned by cutting back stems by half.
Propagate from cuttings taken in spring. Considerable heat will be necessary and success is not certain.

Mimosa pudica

Sensitive Plant

Touch the delicate leaves of this plant and they immediately fold along the central rib, but in half an hour or so they will have recovered from the assault and the plant will be back to its former glory. It is usually treated as an annual because the lower leaves fall and the plant looks woody. Freely branching stems carry feathery leaves consisting of opposite pairs of tiny leaflets. Puffball clusters of pink flowers appear on stems from the leaf axils during the summer months. Grows to 20 in (50 cm).

Likes good light and direct sun to flower well, but shade from fierce sun. Needs a humid atmosphere.
Compost should be kept moist; never allow the plant to dry out completely.
Feed every two weeks in spring and summer. Potting-on is not normally necessary as the plant is treated as an annual, but if kept for a second year use a loam compost.
Propagate from seed sown in early spring.

Rechsteineria cardinalis

Cardinal Flower

Mid-green, oval to heart-shaped velvety leaves up to 6 in (15 cm) long carried on 12 in (30 cm) stems. In fully grown plants the leaves are covered with white hairs. Groups of tubular scarlet flowers, 2 in (5 cm) long, on short stems, appear from leaf axils near the stem ends during the summer months. Foliage dies down after flowering and tubers are stored dry until started into growth in late winter.

Likes bright light during growing period but should be shaded from direct sun. Must also have a humid atmosphere, but if mist-spraying, avoid wetting leaves and flowers for they are easily marked. Remove dead flower heads to encourage prolonged flowering.
Compost should be kept moist, but reduce frequency of watering when foliage dies down.
Feed every two weeks during spring and summer. After the foliage has died, store the tuber completely dry until late winter. Then remove the tuber from the old compost, cut away any dead roots and plant in fresh peat compost with added sphagnum moss.
Propagate by dividing tubers when repotting, or by taking stem cuttings or sowing seed in spring.

Sanchezia speciosa

Zebra Plant

Attractively marked, oval, dark green leaves, up to 10 in (25 cm) long, with veins and mid-rib picked out in yellow or white. The toothed leaves are carried in opposite pairs on woody, freely-branching stems. Clusters of tubular yellow flowers surrounded by a pair of red bracts appear during the summer and autumn. Grows to 3 ft (90 cm), but a mature plant of this size has ceased to look attractive and it is best to raise new plants from cuttings.

Likes good light, but shade from fierce sun. Needs humidity to flower well.
Compost should be always moist in the growing period, with less frequent watering during the winter rest.
Feed every two weeks in spring and summer. Plants may be pruned in spring if necessary. Pot-on each spring in loam or peat compost.
Propagate by taking 4 in (10 cm) stem cuttings in summer.

Siderasis fuscata

Brown Spiderwort

Difficult plant to keep in tip-top condition but worth trying for the striking foliage and flowers. Rosette of oval leaves, each up to 8 in (20 cm) long, olive green with white streak along the mid-rib, covered with browny red hairs; undersides of leaves are red. Short flower stalks emerge from centre of the rosette in summer, with small red to purple flowers.

Likes a slightly shaded spot, never exposed to direct sunlight. Humid atmosphere is vital at all times.
Compost should be always moist, but not sodden, or the plant may rot.
Feed every three to four weeks in spring and summer. Pot-on each spring in loam or peat compost with added sand for good drainage. A siderasis does not grow quickly and the maximum pot size is likely to be only 6 in (15 cm).
Propagate by removing offsets.

Sonerila margaritacea

Frosted Sonerila

An exotic plant requiring heat and humidity to be grown successfully. Oval, pointed, dark green leaves up to 4 in (10 cm), marked with silver white spots, are carried in opposite pairs on creeping red stems. Short red leaf stalks bear clusters of three-petalled, rosy pink flowers during late spring and summer.

Likes bright light, but shade from direct sun. Requires high humidity, otherwise leaf tips turn brown and leaves will fall if the temperature is not consistently high.
Compost should be moist all year round, but not sodden.
Feed every two weeks in spring and summer. Pot-on each spring in shallow pots or pans, using peat compost.
Propagate from 3 in (7.5 cm) stem cuttings taken in early summer, or from seed sown in spring.

Tacca chantieri

Bat Plant

Cluster of lance-shaped leaves with a ripple effect on the surface. Most unusual flowers in summer: dark maroon, almost black, surrounded by deep purple bracts which trail long thin whisker-like strands, about 12 in (30 cm) long. Grows to 2 ft (60 cm).

Likes bright light with direct – but not fierce – sun all year round.
Compost should be moist in spring and summer; barely moist in winter.
Feed every two weeks in spring and summer. Pot-on every other spring in peat compost.
Propagate by division in spring.

Palms and ferns

If space in the conservatory is limited, *Microcoelum weddellianum* is the best palm to choose since it is sold when small and grows quite slowly, retaining a compact shape. *Chrysalidocarpus lutescens* is usually on sale as a specimen plant; large and expensive, it needs plenty of room. Both palms demand warmth and humidity to keep them looking healthy without unsightly brown tips to the leaves.

Two ferns at home in the warm conservatory are the epiphytic (air-nourished) *Asplenium nidus* and the terrestrial (earth-nourished) *Blechnum gibbum*. Most aspleniums on sale are small plants which remain a manageable size for many years, and are thus suitable for display on benches or tables. *Blechnum gibbum*, on the other hand, is usually sold as a large specimen, demanding space and deserving a prominent position, possibly in a tub on the floor.

— *Chrysalidocarpus lutescens* —

Areca Palm

Elegant palm with arching, delicate fronds. Each yellow stem carries nearly opposite pairs of yellowish-green leaves, about 8 in (20 cm) long. Overall length of stem and frond is some 6 ft (1.8 cm). Grows only slowly, a few inches a year, but eventually will reach 10 ft (3 m), with a wide spread. Recommended only for a large conservatory where warmth and humidity are constant, to prevent the tips from turning brown.

Likes bright light with some direct sunlight, but shade from fierce sun. Requires high humidity throughout the year.
Compost should be kept moist.
Feed once a month in spring and summer. Pot-on each spring in a mixture of peat and loam until a 12 in (30 cm) pot is reached. Thereafter each spring remove top 3 in (7.5 cm) of compost and replace with fresh.
Propagate by sowing seed in spring, but growth will be exasperatingly slow. Suckers may be thrown up about the base of the plant and these can be removed for propagation, but will need a good root system to establish themselves.

— *Microcoelum weddellianum* —

Coconut Palm

This palm, like the chrysalidocarpus, has delicate fronds, but being a much more manageable size is suitable for smaller conservatories. It will eventually reach 5 ft (1.5 m), but with a spread of only 30 in (75 cm) as the fronds are held erect. Young plants have fronds about 10 in (25 cm) long with almost opposite pairs of narrow pinnae. As they develop they will grow up to 3 ft (90 cm).

Likes bright light, with shade from direct sun. Needs a humid atmosphere if the palm is to stay in prime condition.
Compost should be kept moist in growing period. In winter rest period, the surface of the compost should be allowed to dry out, but total drying out of the compost will make the leaves turn brown. Use soft water if possible, as hard water is another cause of leaf browning.
Feed every two weeks in spring and summer. Pot-on every two years in spring in loam based compost.
Propagate from seed sown in spring, but it takes time to germinate and there is a further long wait while the plants develop to a reasonable size.

— *Asplenium nidus* —

Bird's Nest Fern

Glossy, bright green, lance-shaped fronds can in the fullness of time reach 4 ft (1.2 m) long and 8 in (20 cm) wide, but for many years are much smaller. The fronds grow in erect rosette formation, rather like a shuttlecock. The central base of the rosette is a brown, hairy tuft from which new fronds emerge. It looks very striking.

Likes good light but out of direct sun; will tolerate a somewhat shady spot. Requires high humidity if the frond edges and, eventually, whole fronds are not to turn brown and papery.
Compost should be kept moist at all

Hanging plants

times, but never sodden. Water into centre of rosette.
Feed every two weeks in spring and summer. Pot-on in spring in either a peat or loam compost. If the fern deteriorates into a generally poor shape, cut all fronds down to compost level in spring. New growth will soon appear.
Propagation is by means of spores on the underside of the fronds, an operation requiring great skill and infinite patience. The fern cannot be divided.

Blechnum gibbum

As this fern matures, its lower leaves fall and a scaly trunk develops. Light green, shiny fronds, divided into gently-tapering leaflets, are carried in rosette formation. Each frond may grow to 3 ft (90 cm) and the overall spread of the plant is 5 ft (1.5 m). It will require plenty of room and looks impressive as a centrepiece.

Likes bright light, but not direct sun, and a humid atmosphere. Good ventilation is essential in warm summer months.
Compost should be kept moist; if it dries out fronds will shrivel.
Feed every two weeks in spring and summer. Pot-on each spring in peat compost, or a mixture of peat, loam and sand.
Propagation is by spores, by no means an easy operation.

Three hanging plants – hemigraphis, oplismenus and plectranthrus – are remarkable for their variegated coloured foliage. Aeschynanthus and columnea are outstanding for their tubular, orange-red flowers in spring and summer, while the ruellia has both coloured, velvety leaves and carmine flowers from autumn into winter.

All the plants demand high humidity, in particular the flowering varieties, which will not bloom well without it.

Aeschynanthus speciosus

Basket Plant

Pairs of mid-green, sharply-pointed, oval leaves 4 in (10 cm) long, carried on stems up to 2 ft (60 cm). Clusters of tubular flowers, yellow at the base and merging to bright orange at the tip, appear at stem ends in late spring and summer. Very colourful, it makes a decorative plant.

Likes good light, but in a slightly shaded spot. Requires a humid atmosphere, especially when in flower.
Compost must be kept moist all year round.
Feed every two weeks in spring and summer. Pot-on each spring in peat compost with added sphagnum moss. Pinch out growing tips in spring to encourage bushiness.
Propagate by taking 4 in (10 cm) stem cuttings in summer.

Columnea microphylla

Goldfish Vine

Trailing stems, growing to 3 ft (90 cm) or more, densely packed with small, rounded, dark green leaves about ½ in (1.75 cm) across. Both stems and leaves are covered with short, red hairs. In spring, masses of tubular orange to red flowers with yellow throats appear and last about a month. The leaves of *C. gloriosa* have purplish hairs and those of *C. banksii* are fleshier, but otherwise the two species are much the same.

Likes bright light to flower well, but shade from direct sun. High humidity is essential.

Compost should be moist during growing period but not sodden or the stems will rot. During winter rest period, compost should be barely moist in the build-up to flowering.
Feed every two weeks in spring and summer. Pot-on every other year in peat compost when flowering has finished. Change compost in intervening years.
Propagate from 4 in (10 cm) stem cuttings in summer, after flowering.

Hemigraphis alternata

Red Ivy

Heart-shaped, puckered leaves about 3 in (7.5 cm) long, carried on red stems which grow to 12 in (30 cm). Leaves are softly notched round the edges, with purple metallic sheen on the top surface and deep red on the underside. Small white flowers appear in summer. This plant is a compact trailer.

Likes good light to maintain leaf colour and to prevent plants from becoming straggly. Requires high humidity.
Compost should be moist in growing period, but barely so in winter.
Feed every two weeks in spring and summer. Pot-on each spring in peat compost and cut back straggly stems.
Propagate by taking 4 in (10 cm) stem cuttings in summer. They can be rooted in water and then planted in compost.

Oplismenus hirtellus 'Variegatus'

Basket Grass

Many-branching stems, up to 12 in (30 cm), with 2 in (5 cm) lance-shaped, bright green leaves striped vertically with white and pink. Some leaves may take on a pink to purple tinge if the light is bright. Take cuttings each year to replace plants.

Likes bright light with direct sun all the year, but protect from scorching rays. Humid atmosphere is beneficial.
Compost should be kept moist in growing period, but barely moist at other times.
Feed once a month in spring and summer. Replace plants from cuttings rather than pot-on.
Propagate with 3 in (7.5 cm) stem cuttings taken in spring and summer. Plant in peat compost, at least 20 to a pot for a good display.

Plectranthus coleoides 'Marginatus'

Swedish Ivy

Dark green, heart-shaped, hairy leaves about 2 in (5 cm) long with scalloped, creamy-white edges. Trails to 2 ft (30 cm). White to pale violet flowers are carried on upright stems in autumn. *P. oertendahlii* has almost circular, bronze-green leaves about 1 in (2.5 cm) long with veins picked out in silver, and purple undersides. Clusters of tubular pink flowers on upright stems are produced in autumn. In both species the flowers are not noteworthy and can be removed as they emerge.

Likes bright light, but lightly shade from direct sun: if too shady they will lose their fine colouring. In temperatures above 70°F (21°C) they do better with a humid atmosphere.
Compost should be always moist; if too dry, leaves quickly drop.
Feed every two weeks in spring and summer. Potting-on is not necessary; raise fresh plants each year instead.
Propagate by taking 3 in (7.5 cm) stem cuttings in spring. Plant several to a pot for the best effect.

Ruellia makoyana

Velvet Plant

Attractive flowering trailer produces carmine, trumpet-shaped, five-petalled flowers about 2 in (5 cm) long. Opposite pairs of oval, olive-green, velvety leaves, with silver veins and purple undersides, are borne on stems 2 ft (60 cm) long.

Likes bright light, but shade from direct sun. Good light is especially important in winter months to prolong flowering. Requires humidity.
Compost should be kept moist, but water less frequently when flowering ends to induce plants to rest for a few weeks.
Feed every two weeks from spring until flowering is over. After their first flowering, pot-on in spring in one part loam compost and one part sphagnum moss. After two years it is better to replace plants from cuttings.
Propagate by taking 4 in (10 cm) stem cuttings in early summer. Plant several to a pot and pinch out growing tips of young plants to encourage bushiness.

Climbers

Two climbers – *Allamanda cathartica* and *Clerodendrum thomsoniae* – have been chosen for their outstanding flowers, which with luck will continue through the summer and into autumn. *Cissus discolor* and *Syngonium podophyllum* are noted for their beautiful foliage. *C. discolor* needs extra attention to keep it in prime condition, but at its best gives such a stunning display that the effect is worthwhile. To prevent the conservatory from being taken over by climbers – and it can easily happen – they can be kept under control by regular pruning. Instructions are given in the following entries on when to cut back and by how much.

Allamanda cathartica

Golden Trumpet

Tropical vine which needs a minimum temperature of 60°F (16°C) throughout the year, including winter nights. Dark green, glossy, oval, pointed leaves grow up to 6 in (15 cm) long. Produces striking bright yellow, tubular flowers, 3 in (7.5 cm) across, with five petals flaring outwards. Flowers from summer to autumn. Two popular varieties are *A. c.* 'Hendersoni' and *A. c.* 'Grandiflora'. Grows to 15 ft (4.5 m) and will need strong framework for support. Plants look more effective and flower more freely if the leading stems are pinched out when young.

Likes bright light with direct sun for prolonged flowering, but shade when very hot. It needs a humid atmosphere.
Compost should always be kept moist, but reduce frequency of watering after plants have been pruned back when flowering is over.
Feed every two weeks from spring until flowering finishes. Pot on each spring in loam compost.
Propagate by taking 4 in (10 cm) stem cuttings and provide bottom heat of 70°F (21°C) to get them to root. Pinch out growing shoots of young plants regularly in spring to encourage bushiness. When flowering is over, prune back to a third of the plant's size.

Clerodendrum thomsoniae

Bleeding Heart Vine

Clusters of red, star-shaped flowers, each one surrounded by a snowy-white calyx, show to superb effect against glossy leaves. Flowering period lasts from early summer to early autumn. Heart-shaped leaves up to 4 in (10 cm) long are carried on twining stems, which need support. Plants can be allowed to go on the rampage, reaching a height of 10 ft (3 m), or can be pruned back and pinched out to keep to a smaller size.

Likes good light for the plants to flower, but supply light shade from direct sun. Needs a humid atmosphere, which will also help flowering.
Compost should be kept moist at all times.
Feed every two weeks from spring until flowering is finished. Pot-on each spring in either a loam or peat compost. At the same time, cut back stems by three-quarters and begin to pinch out the growing tips for a bushy effect.
Propagate from 4 in (10 cm) stem cuttings taken in spring, or by sowing seed. Plants will do better if they have a winter rest around 60°F (16°C).

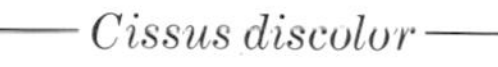

Cissus discolor

Rex Begonia Vine

One of the most beautiful climbers, it is also among the most difficult to keep looking at its best. High humidity, warmth and bright light are all essential. It has narrow, heart-shaped, olive-green leaves up to 6 in (15 cm) long, with silver and purple markings on the upper surface and red undersides. Young plants also have red stems. With the right conditions it will grow to 6 ft (1.8 m) or higher, putting out tendrils for support.

Likes good light throughout the year but shade from direct sun; excessive sun makes leaves shrivel and turn brown. High humidity at all times is especially important.
Compost should be moist but not sodden, and its surface allowed to dry out between waterings. Too much water causes the leaves to yellow and fall.
Feed every two weeks in spring and summer. Pot-on each spring in a mixture of loam, peat, leaf mould and sand. Pinch out growing tips in spring to induce bushy growth. Cut back straggly stems to 4 in (10 cm).
Propagate by taking 4 in (10 cm) stem cuttings in spring and summer and provide bottom heat of 75°F (24°C). Plants may also be raised from seed sown in spring.

Syngonium podophyllum

Goosefoot Plant

Climbing vine which may also be grown as a trailing plant. As the plant matures, its leaves change from an arrowhead shape to deeply divided lobes, with a more prominent central lobe. Usually there are three lobes to a plant, but there may be as many as eight. *S. p.* 'Emerald Green' has dark green, 8 in (20 cm) leaves with lighter shading on the veins. Other varieties have more pronounced variegated leaves, with large areas marked white or cream. Aerial roots are produced from the main stem and these can be inserted in a moss stick kept permanently damp. This provides the plant with an additional source of moisture. Grows to 6 ft (1.8 cm) and more.

Likes good light, especially the variegated forms, but no direct sun. Green plants will tolerate a slightly shaded spot. Needs humidity throughout the year.
Compost should be kept moist during the active growing season but allow the surface to dry out a little between waterings in the winter rest period.
Feed every two weeks in spring and summer. Pot-on each spring in a mixture of two parts loam compost and one part peat. If plants become straggly, cut back to 9 in (22.5 cm) in spring.
Propagate from stem cuttings, 4 in (10 cm) long, taken in summer.

Orchids

These warmth-loving orchids include a brassia, the Spider Orchid, and one of the most popular cattleyas, the Cluster Cattleya. The brassia flowers in early summer and the cattleya in late autumn over many weeks (for the rest of the year it is best kept out of sight).

Success with these orchids depends on consistently warm day temperatures (falling at night to 60°F (16°C) plus humidity and care in watering to keep the compost just moist.

Cluster Cattleya

Brassia verrucosa

Spider Orchid

Epiphytic (air-nourished) orchid with unusual, delicate, spidery-looking flowers. Oval pseudobulbs about 3 in (7.5 cm) high, each of which produces two strap-shaped leaves up to 14 in (35 cm) long. Flowers have five long, narrow sepals flared backwards and short, but prominent, petals. Both sepals and petals are light green, with dark green or reddish spots. Each flower spike grows about 2 ft (60 cm) and in early summer produces a dozen or more very fragrant flowers.

Likes bright light but prefers a somewhat shady spot; avoid exposing the plant to direct sun. Requires a humid atmosphere.
Temperatures at night for this orchid should be about 60°F (16°C).
Compost should be kept moist, but allow the surface to dry out between waterings. In winter, compost should be barely moist.
Feed once a month in spring and summer. Pot-on every two or three years in spring in an orchid compost. In intervening years replace the old compost with fresh.
Propagate by division in spring. Each piece of rhizome should have at least two pseudobulbs and enough roots to support them.

Cattleya bowringiana

Cluster Cattleya

With the right care this orchid produces a mass of purple flowers, about 3 in (7.5 cm) across, each with a darker shaded lip. Flowers appear in late autumn and last for many weeks. Unfortunately, the plant looks pretty abject for the rest of the year. The pseudobulbs are some 8 in (20 cm) long, topped with one or two 5 in (12.5 in) leathery strap-shaped leaves.

Likes good light but not direct sunlight, especially when the plant is in bloom, since the flowers will fade rapidly. Needs high humidity, but also good ventilation on warm days.
Temperatures at night should be around 60°F (16°C).
Compost should be kept moist until flowering is over. During winter months allow it to dry out a little between waterings, but not so much that the pseudobulbs start to shrivel.
Feed once a month in spring and summer. Pot-on every two or three years in late spring in an orchid compost, renewing the compost in intervening years.
Propagate by dividing the rhizome when potting-on or repotting. Each piece of rhizome should have at least two pseudobulbs, with plenty of roots.

Doritis pulcherrima

An epiphytic orchid with pairs of sword-shaped, grey-green leaves with brownish spots. Pale to dark rose purple flowers with darker lip grow on 2 ft (60 cm) stems. Each may have 20 flowers in succession over some months. The orchid may flower at any time, even twice a year.

Likes good light but no direct sun. A constantly humid atmosphere is essential, with good ventilation but no draughts.
Compost should be moist all year round.
Feed every fortnight in spring and summer. Pot-on every two or three years in spring in an orchid compost. In years between, replace the compost.
Propagate from new growth which may appear from the end of cut-back flower spikes. Wait until roots have fully developed before removing them.

Vanda rothschildiana

One of the few blue orchids, this plant blooms in winter, producing spikes of pale blue flowers with veins of darker blue. Each spike may have ten flowers, which are about 6 in (15 cm) across. Overlapping pairs of bright green, strap-shaped leaves 10 in (25 cm) long. Grows to 2 ft (60 cm).

Likes bright light with direct sun as long as it is not fierce.
Temperature in winter should be around 65°F (18°C). Humid air and good ventilation, free from draughts, are essential.
Compost should always be moist in growing period. During short rest period after flowering, watering should be reduced, but compost must not dry out.
Feed monthly in spring and summer. Pot-on every two years in an orchid compost, renewing compost in other years.
Propagate by removing offsets.

Bromeliads

Only three bromeliads have been selected for the warm conservatory: the dramatic *Vriesia splendens*, or Flaming Sword, with a towering red flower spike; the small cryptanthus, Starfish Plant, often planted in a bottle garden; and the familiar ananas, or Variegated Pineapple, which is really only suitable for a large conservatory.

Ananas comosus 'Variegatus'

Variegated Pineapple

Richly-coloured bromeliad, the leaves of which take on a pink hue if it has plenty of direct sunlight. Narrow, pointed leaves with sharp, serrated edges and grey-green with white, cream or yellow markings, which grow to 3 ft (90 cm) in rosette formation. Since the leaves arch, this plant is more suitable for a large conservatory. An ananas is often sold in fruit, with a miniature pink pineapple held on the end of a stem. Before the fruit appears, spikes of purple flowers emerge from the centre of the rosette. After the flowers and fruit die, so does the parent plant, but offsets at its base can be removed to start off new plants.

Likes direct sunlight all year round to maintain the plant's pink flush. Needs humid atmosphere to prevent leaf tips from turning brown and brittle.
Compost must be moist all year.
Feed every two to three weeks in spring and summer. Pot-on in spring in loam compost.
Propagate by potting-up offsets when leaves of parent have shrivelled.

Cryptanthus acaulis

Earth Star

This bromeliad and its related species are prized for their variegated foliage and compactness. The rosette of sharp-toothed, strap-shaped leaves, bright green on top with white scale on the undersides, is about 5 in (12.5 cm) in diameter. Insignificant white flowers appear at intervals throughout the year. *C. bromelioides* 'Tricolor', the Rainbow Star, has green, yellow and white striped leaves, edged with pink, in a rosette 12 in (30 cm) across. The leaves of *C. bivittatus* are deep green with salmon pink stripes.
C. forsterianum is one of the larger species, with a rosette up to 24 in (60 cm) in diameter. The leaves are horizontally banded with brown and grey, rather like pheasant feathers.
C. zonatus, the Zebra Plant, has a 15 in (37.5 cm) rosette of leaves banded with silver and browny grey.

Likes full sunlight throughout the year to bring out the full beauty of the colouring. Also needs a humid atmosphere, since the leaves become papery and shrivel if the air is too dry.
Compost should be kept just moist all the time; too heavy watering will make plants rot at the base. Keep the rosettes topped up with water, except in winter.
Feed once a month in spring and summer. Pot-on each spring in a peat compost.
Propagate by removing offsets.

Vriesea splendens

Flaming Sword

A combination of impressive foliage and dazzling flower spike. Strap-shaped, dark green leaves, about 12 in (30 cm) long, horizontally banded with reddish brown; forms a rosette some 20 in (50 cm) across. In summer, yellow flowers emerge from the overlapping bright red bracts carried on the end of a flower spike which is 15 in (37.5 cm) tall. After the flowers and bracts fade the whole plant dies, having first produced offsets at its base.

Likes bright light with direct sun to maintain variegations, but shade from scorching sun. High humidity needed.
Compost should be moist always and the central rosette kept filled with water, except in winter rest period when it must be dry.
Feed once a month in spring and summer. Pot-on every two or three years in spring in a mixture of sand, peat and sphagnum moss. Change the compost in intervening years.
Propagate by removing offsets, but wait until they are growing well, with leaves about 6 in (15 cm) long. Consistently high temperatures are vital if the bracts are to retain their high colour over a long period of time.

Fruit and Vegetables

The image of a conservatory festooned with huge branches of ripening grapes, or of walls hidden by a curtain of golden peaches or purple figs is an illusion. The conditions these fruits need – a spell with no artificial heat at all – are not those which would satisfy you, or even most of the plants you want to grow. Moreover, they take up an inordinate amount of room; a mature, fan-trained peach could swallow up 18 ft (4.5 m) of wall space, while a peach in a tub is a short-lived travesty of the real thing. There are other temptations, however, which need not be resisted – melons and cucumbers, especially in the warm conservatory, and early strawberries in the temperate. Growing tomatoes (in temperate or cool) is a good reason, or excuse, for imposing a no-smoking ban in the conservatory (because of the risk of tobacco virus). Sweet peppers and aubergines can be grown alongside the tomatoes, all of them attractive as well as rewarding. The cool conservatory can also profitably be used for forcing rhubarb, chicory and seakale and for providing a constant supply of winter lettuce.

Melons

In the warm conservatory
Although some melons can be grown in temperate or even cool conditions, the warm conservatory is the place for the best variety – the so-called English musk or netted melons. A day temperature of 70°F (21°C) is needed and though it can go somewhat higher, good ventilation is needed above 80°F (27°C). Night temperatures should be no lower than 65°F (18°C).

Suitable varieties Hero of Lockinge, white flesh and fine flavour; Blenheim Orange (or Superlative), scarlet fleshed of medium size; Emerald Gem, large fruit, succulent green flesh.

Sow in 3 in (7.5 cm) peat pots in late winter or early spring, one seed pushed in sideways to each pot. Germinate at 75°F (24°C). In a month or so transplant to growing bags, three plants to a bag, with top of the peat pot above the level of compost in the bag, to prevent the stems from rotting.
Training Melons can be grown against the wall of a lean-to conservatory. Fix horizontal wires, 1 ft (30 cm) apart, behind the spot where growing bags are to go and a little distance from the wall. Fix canes vertically to the wires, one for each plant. Tie the main stem to the cane as it grows and tie laterals and sub-laterals, which bear the fruit, to the wires. When about 6 ft (1.8 m) tall, pinch out growing point of main stem.
Pollination Male and female flowers are produced and female flowers, recognizable by the small melon-to-be behind the flower, have to be pollinated. To do this, push stamens of the male flower into the female flower. Wait until six or seven female flowers are fully developed and pollinate them all the same day. Pollinating at different times means that some fruits will stay huge and others shrivel.
After successful pollination, fruits start to swell. Remove all but four from each plant. Pinch out the growing point of each fruiting lateral or sub-lateral two leaves beyond the fruit, and non-fruiting laterals four leaves from the main stem. New shoots can be cut out completely. Feed every week. When fruits are about 3 in (7.5 cm) in diameter, support them by nets slung from the wires. Keep the compost in growing bags well watered until fruit begins to ripen (veins appear on skins) and water scarcely at all after that or fruits may split. Leaves wilt, there is a strong smell of melon in the conservatory, and when the base of the melon feels a little soft it is ripe – roughly four months after being sown.

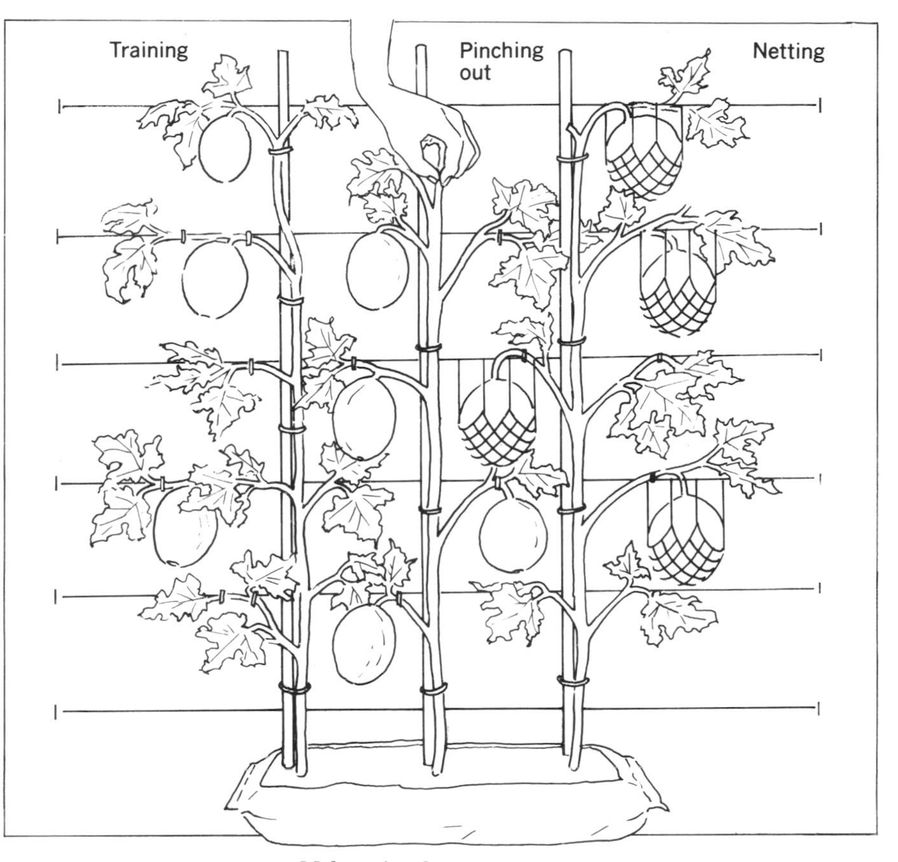

Melons in the conservatory

In the temperate conservatory
Cantaloupe melons are suitable for temperate conservatories, although early crops are not feasible. Sow seed in heat of 70° – 75°F (21° – 24°C) in spring or late spring, or buy young plants from early summer. When planted in growing bags, three to a bag, daytime temperatures should be around 65°F (18°C) and at night about 60°F (16°C). Growing instructions are the same as for the warm conservatory.

Suitable varieties Charentais, small, sweet, with orange-scarlet flesh; Ogen, sweet, yellow-green flesh; Early Sweet (F_1 hybrid) deep salmon flesh; Sweetheart (F_1 hybrid), quick maturing, light orange flesh; Romeo (F_1 hybrid), deep orange flesh, withstands cool temperatures better than most.

These melons crop a little more heavily than musk melons in a warm conservatory; perhaps six to a plant.

Strawberries

In the temperate conservatory
Although early strawberries grown under glass lack the full-bodied flavour of those ripening outdoors, there is a certain pleasure to be derived just from growing them. In early summer, root runners from first-season strawberries in 3 in (7.5 cm) pots of peat compost. Detach from the parent plant by end of summer and transplant to a 6 in (15 cm) pot in early autumn. Bring into the conservatory in winter with a minimum night temperature of 45°F (7°C). When growth starts, the temperature should be not less than 50°F (10°C), rising to 55°F (13°C) when flowering and fruiting. Pollinate flowers every day with child's soft paint brush. Thin trusses to six berries. Beware of powdery mildew; water with the fungicide Benomyl.

Tomatoes

In the temperate conservatory
The ideal conditions for an optimum crop of tomatoes cannot be produced in a conservatory. No matter, in a cool or temperate conservatory they will do well enough, and in a temperate conservatory they will grow along with aubergines and peppers and some melons and cucumbers.

Suitable varieties Alicante; Moneymaker; Eurocross BB (F_1); Shirley F_1; and Big Boy F_1, huge fruits with few seeds (restrict these to three trusses).

Sow seed in late winter and the plants will be ready for planting in growing bags, three plants to a bag, at the beginning of spring. Tomatoes will germinate at 65°F (18°C), but 68°F (20°C) is better. Germination takes a week or ten days. Prick out when the first true leaves appear and plant in 3 in (7.5 cm) peat pots.

Pinching out tomatoes

Temperatures while growing should be between 60° and 65°F (16° – 18°C) by day and 55°F (13°C) by night. They need good ventilation, especially with temperatures above 70°F (21°C), and above 80°F (26°C) adequate ventilation is vital to the survival of the plant.
Staking Tomatoes need support from the start. Fix two horizontal wires behind the spot where the growing bags are to go, a little distance from the back wall or side of the conservatory. The bottom wire should be near ground level and the top wire 7 ft (1.75 m) above it. Tie string between the wires behind each plant; the string is twisted round the stem as the plant grows. Remove the side shoots when still small, leaving the plant to grow as a single stem. When the plants are 5 ft (1.25 m) or so high, remove the leaves below the first truss of flowers, cutting cleanly with a sharp knife. When six trusses, at most, have set fruit, remove the growing point two leaves above the top truss. Water frequently to keep compost in the growing bag moist, but not sodden. In very hot sunny weather this may mean watering once, twice or even three times a day. When harvesting tomatoes, pick them with the calyx attached.

In the cool conservatory
Tomatoes can be grown in a cool conservatory by the same methods as in a temperate conservatory, but there will be no early crops. Seed is sown in heat in early spring for planting into growing bags up to eight weeks later. Alternatively, plants may be bought.

Sweet Peppers

In the temperate conservatory
Peppers can share similar conditions to tomatoes.

Suitable varieties Early Prolific F_1; New Ace F_1; and Gypsy F_1. Pepppers are germinated at temperatures between 65° – 68°F (18° – 20°C).

Sow seed in winter or late winter. Prick the seedlings into 3 in (7.5 cm) pots when a pair of true leaves has appeared; a few weeks later move them to 4 in (10 cm) pots. At eight or ten weeks from sowing they will be ready to go into the growing bags, three to a bag, or singly into 8 in (40 cm) pots. The slender pepper stems need staking. The plants crop most heavily if cut when green. It takes about three more weeks for the peppers to turn red.

In the cool conservatory
Planting should be delayed until well into late spring, from seed sown at the beginning of early spring.

Aubergines

In the temperate conservatory
Suitable varieties Slice-Rite No 23 F_1, large black fruits; Moneymaker F_1; and Dusky F_1.

Sow seed from early to late spring in a propagator at 65°F (18°C). Transplant the seedlings first into 3 in (7.5 cm) pots, then to 6 in (15 cm) pots and finally into 8 in (20 cm) pots where they can stay for fruiting. In pots they can be supported by canes. Alternatively, move the plants into growing bags. By pinching out when about 9 in (22.5 cm) tall, aubergines can be induced to put out more laterals and stay bushier. Allow five or six fruits to a plant and stop side shoots a couple of leaves beyond the fruit. Feed every week when flowers begin to set.

In the cool conservatory
Sow two to three weeks later than in the temperate conservatory, with planting and cropping correspondingly postponed. The variety Dusky F_1 is especially suitable.

Cucumbers

In the warm conservatory
Hothouse-type cucumbers ideally need a steamy heat, far more humid than liked by melons and tomatoes and more than humans can tolerate in a conservatory. However, even with conditions less than ideal they will yield acceptable fruits. One tedious trait of cucumbers is that, if fertilized, the fruits grow bitter and swollen. All male flowers must therefore be removed daily. Some F_1 hybrids produce female flowers only (but watch out for a few male rogues and remove them). A female flower has an incipient cucumber just behind it; the male does not.

Suitable varieties Telegraph and Butcher's Disease Resisting; F_1 female hybrids Femspot and Landora.

Sow in early spring, two seeds planted edge downwards in a 3 in (8 cm) peat pot. For rapid germination, especially of F_1 hybrids, a temperature of 80°F

(27°C) is needed, but when seedlings emerge reduce the temperature to 70°F (21°C) by day and 66°F (19°C) at night. Plants will be ready for moving to growing bags, three plants to a bag, in nearly a month. For two months after transplanting maintain similar temperatures; heat can then be lowered by a few degrees, both by day and night. Ventilate when around 75°F (24°C).

Training Grow the plants up wire or netting. When about 30 in (75 cm) high, pinch out the main growing tip. Pinch out the tips of all laterals after two leaves have formed and let only two fruits set on each lateral.

Keep the compost moist and shade plants from very hot sun. Cut cucumbers when they are still young and sweet. Red spider mite can be a menace.

In the temperate conservatory
Some cucumbers do well in a temperate conservatory, but unless seed can be germinated and raised in higher temperatures, plants will have to be bought in. Defer planting until spring or late spring, depending on climate.

Suitable varieties Sigmadew, pale skinned, produces male and female flowers; Petita, all female F_1 hybrid. Growing instructions are as for warm conservatories.

Lettuce

In the cool conservatory
Lettuce for eating in winter can be grown in the cool conservatory, given a minimum night temperature of 45°F (7°C) and a minimum day temperature of around 55°F (12°C). If the temperatures are constantly much above this the winter butterhead varieties will grow floppy, open heads. Above 70°F (21°C) they will not germinate at all.

Suitable varieties Kwiek is best for the earliest sowings in the cool conservatory; and Kloek for the later.

Sow a few seeds at fortnightly intervals, starting in late summer or early autumn and continuing until the end of autumn, to produce a succession of lettuces between autumn and early spring. The simplest method is to sow pelleted seed in 1 in (2.5 cm) peat blocks, one seed to a block, sowing only as many as you are likely to eat in two weeks or so, plus a few extra in case some seed does not germinate. When well grown, transplant into a growing bag (one which has been used for a previous tomato crop will do perfectly well with the addition of a little fertilizer). A bag can take 10 to 12 lettuces so two bags would probably accommodate all you need for the winter, planting new young lettuce as you cut the mature heads. Add a little liquid fertilizer when watering, which in a cool conservatory is unlikely to be frequently in winter.

In the temperate conservatory
A minimum night temperature of 55°F (12°C) produces good results, but if temperatures soar high during the day, good ventilation will be needed. Grow lettuce by the same method as in the cool conservatory, but it might be best to choose the quick-maturing variety Dandie. Sow in late summer to autumn for a succession from late autumn.

Forcing

Asparagus

In the warm conservatory
Asparagus out of season is a wasteful extravagance, but easy to indulge in if you have a large asparagus bed. Three- or four- year-old crowns are used. Dig up a few at times between autumn and late winter. Lay them on a 3 in (7.5 cm) bed of soil in a deep box and cover with 3 in (7.5 cm) of soil. Water well and make sure that the soil does not dry out. Cover with black polythene but let in a little light after the shoots emerge in order to green the tips. At a temperature of 70°F (21°C) shoots should be ready for cutting in two weeks or so; allow longer if the conservatory is cooler. The crowns are useless after forcing in this way whereas left outdoors they would have supplied 15 or more years of produce.

Rhubarb

In the cool conservatory
Lift a few two-year-old crowns in late autumn or early winter and leave them outdoors exposed to low temperatures for a week or two. Without a period of cold they cannot be forced. Then put the roots in a box at least 2 ft (60 cm) deep, cover lightly with soil and water well. Lay black polythene on top of the box to exclude all light. Water occasionally to keep the soil moist. With a temperature range of 50° – 55°F (10° – 13°C) the stalks should be ready in four to five weeks. 'Timperley Early' is a good variety and may be ready by Christmas. Forced crowns have no further use.

Chicory

In the cool conservatory
Lift Witloof chicory roots from the garden in autumn and store in sand in a cold place. As roots are needed to start being forced, say every two weeks, trim off the leaves to within 1 in (2.5 cm) of the crown and plant four or five in a 9 in (22.5 cm) pot in moist compost. Cover with another pot, blocking the drainage hole to exclude all light. A temperature of about 50°F (10°C) produces the sweetest chicons, in about three weeks.

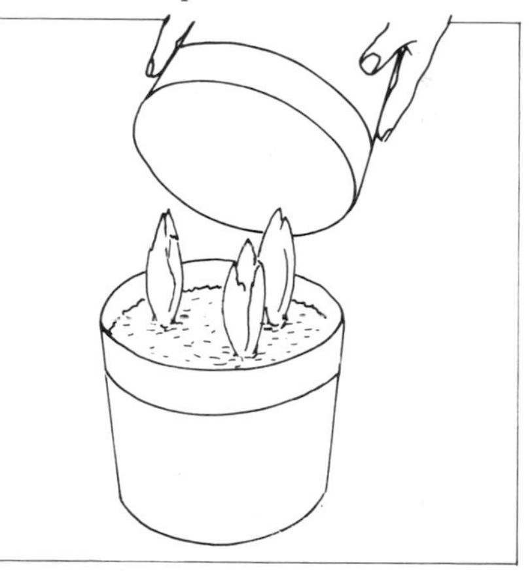

Forcing chicory

Seakale

In the cool conservatory
Lift seakale crowns from the garden in autumn and cut off the lateral roots, leaving only the main root with its bud. (Store the lateral roots in moist sand and plant out in the garden in early spring for that year's crop). The main roots can also be stored in moist sand to await their turn for forcing as required. To force, plant them in a pot of loam compost; a 9 in (22.5 cm) pot will hold three crowns. Water well and cover with another pot. In temperatures of 50° – 55°F (10° – 13°C) the leaf stalks will be ready in about a month. The spent roots are then thrown away.

The Garden Room

Winter temperatures: 60–70°F (16—21°C)

Garden room plants are basically houseplants, but given an environment with more light they thrive better than in an ordinary living room. The human occupants can use the garden room all year, as they would a warm conservatory, but in a softer light and on softer seating — designed for comfort rather than resistance to damp.

Many more plants than the 20 or so selected here will suit the garden room, but in making a choice, avoid those which need high humidity or a winter rest (unless you can move them to a cooler part of the house).

1 *Nephrolepis exaltata* (Fern) 2 *Callisia elegans* (Hanging) 3 *Billbergia nutans* (Bromeliad) 4 *Ficus benjamina* (Foliage) 5 *Begonia rex* (Foliage) 6 *Dieffenbachia picta* (Foliage) 7 *Begonia* 'Schwabenland' (Flowering) 8 *Achimenes longiflora* (Flowering) 9 *Beloperone guttata* (Flowering) 10 *Howea forsteriana* (Palm) 11 *Hoya carnosa* (Climber)

Foliage plants

Plants selected for the garden room are mainly those which are not excessively demanding; in other words, the general catalogue of houseplants which can be grown in a warm house. The choice can be widened by judicious selection among those recommended for the warm, or – more likely – the temperate conservatory, because many of the warm conservatory plants require almost constant humidity to keep them in peak condition. Conversely, of course, plants here recommended for the garden room can also be grown in temperate or warm conservatories.

All garden room plants will do better if given a winter rest period, when the temperature should be about 60°F (16°C).

— *Begonia rex* —

Painted Leaf Begonia

Hybrids with green, heart-shaped leaves marked silver, purple, red and pink in any number of combinations. Grows no more than 18 in (45 cm). *B. masoniana* has puckered, heart-shaped leaves bearing a brown-red cross. Grows to 9 in (22.5 cm).

Likes good light to maintain leaf colour but shade from direct sun.
Compost should always be kept moist.
Feed every two weeks in spring and summer. Nip out insignificant flowers to concentrate plant's energy on producing brightly-coloured leaves. Pot-on in spring in peat compost.
Propagate from leaf cuttings taken in summer.

— *Cordyline terminalis 'Red Edge'* —

Hawaiian Ti Plant

Bright green, lance-shaped leaves edged and sometimes streaked with red, carried in rosette formation. The green leaves of *C. t.* 'Lord Robertson' are marked with red and cream and those of *C. t.* 'Prince Albert' have red markings. All grow to 2 ft (60 cm).

Likes bright light but avoid direct sun which can mark leaves.
Compost should be moist always in growing period but barely moist during winter rest. Once a week watering should be enough.
Feed every two weeks in spring and summer. Pot-on every other spring in a peat compost, changing compost for fresh in year between.
Propagate by detaching suckers when potting-on.

— *Dieffenbachia picta* —

Dumb Cane

Lance-shaped green leaves up to 8 in (20 cm) long with cream to yellow markings, sometimes almost covering the whole leaf. Grows to 2 ft (60 cm). *D. amoena* has less prominent markings, but the oval leaves grow to 18 in (45 cm) with an overall plant height of 5 ft (1.5 m).

Likes bright light for good leaf colour but shade from direct sun.
Compost should be watered thoroughly all year round but allow top half of compost to dry out before watering again.
Feed every two weeks in spring and summer. Pot-on every spring in a loam compost. Cut down bare stems to 5 in (12.5 cm); new growth will soon appear.
Propagate from 4 in (10 cm) stem cuttings taken in early summer. Complete stems will also root in water. Cut the stem into sections, each with some roots, and plant bottom end down, in compost.

— *Dracaena marginata 'Tricolor'* —

Dragon Tree

Layers of arching, narrow, pointed leaves up to 18 in (45 cm) long, striped green, pink and cream grow in rosette formation from compost level. Mature plants start to lose their lower leaves, revealing a bare stem. Grows to 5 ft

(1.5 m). The sword-shaped 18 in (45 cm) leaves of *D. deremensis* 'Bausei' have a white stripe down the centre. Grows to 4 ft (1.2 m). *D. fragrans* 'Massangeana' has a rosette of sword- shaped leaves, striped yellow and carried on a stout trunk. Grows to 5 ft (1.5 m).
D. godseffiana, the gold dust plant, has oval, glossy, 3 in (7.5 cm) leaves, spotted white. Grows to 18 in (45 cm).

Likes good light to maintain leaf colour but shade from direct sun. All varieties benefit from some humidity.
Compost should be moist always in growing period, but barely moist in winter.
Feed every two weeks in spring and summer. Pot-on each spring in loam compost. *D. godseffiana* needs potting-on every two to three years only. Change compost for fresh in years between.
Propagate by taking stem tip cuttings in summer or from stem sections, with the exception of *D. godseffiana*.

Ficus benjamina

Weeping Fig

Elegant, arching stems carrying dark green, glossy, oval pointed leaves about 4 in (10 cm) long. Grows to 6 ft (1.8 m) and more. *F. diversifolia* (syn. *F. deltoidea*) has leathery, pear-shaped leaves and yellow berries on branching stems. Grows to 3 ft (90 cm). *F. elastica* 'Decora', the rubber plant, has glossy, dark green 12 in (30 cm) elliptical leaves. *F. e.* 'Tricolor' has pink and cream patches on its leaves while those of *F. e.* 'Schrijveriana' have pale green to yellow patches. All grow to 6 ft (1.8 m) and more. *F. lyrata* (syn. *F. pandurata*) the Fiddle Leaf Fig, has fiddle-shaped 18 in (45 cm) leaves. Grows to 6 ft (1.8 m) and more. *F. pumila*, Creeping Fig, has trailing stems of small, heart-shaped leaves. Stems grow to 4 ft (1.2 m).

Likes bright light but shade from direct sun. Good ventilation required.
Compost should be watered thoroughly all year round and the top half of compost allowed to dry out before watering again. *F. pumila* should be moist always, otherwise leaves will fall.
Feed every two weeks in spring and summer. Pot-on every other year in spring, in a mixture of loam, peat, leaf mould and sand. Change compost for fresh in years between. Bare stems of *F. pumila* can be pruned to 6 in (15 cm) to encourage bushy growth.
Propagate *F. elastica* and *F. lyrata* by air layering. The cut-back stem will also produce new growth. In summer take stem cuttings of *F. pumila*, *F. diversifolia* and *F. benjamina*.

Maranta leuconeura 'Erythrophylla'

Prayer Plant

Dark green, oval 4 in (10 cm) leaves with crimson veins, carried on short stems from compost level. Pairs of leaves fold together, erect, at night. The oval leaves of *M. l.* 'Kerchoveana' are blotched with dark brown, turning to dark green as they mature. Both grow to 9 in (22.5 cm).

Likes good light but keep away from direct sun which turns leaves brown and papery. Humidity prevents leaf tips from turning brown.
Compost should be moist always in growing period and barely moist in winter.
Feed every two weeks in spring and summer. Pot-on every spring in peat compost.
Propagate by division when potting-on.

Peperomia argyreia (syn. P. sandersii

Watermelon Plant

Dark green, fleshy, oval leaves about 3 in (7.5 cm) long with silver markings, carried on short stalks from compost level. *P. caperata* 'Emerald Ripple' has dark green, puckered, heart-shaped leaves with purple-grey markings on pink stalks. *P. hederifolia* has silver-grey, heart-shaped leaves with veins picked out in dark green. The mid-green leaves of *P. magnoliifolia* 'Variegata' are marked with yellow – green areas. They all produce insignificant white flowers in spring and summer. All grow to no more than 12 in (30 cm).

Likes good light with some direct sun, but shade from scorching sunlight. Benefits from humidity especially in warm weather.
Compost should be watered thoroughly all year round and allowed almost to dry out before watering again.
Feed monthly in spring and summer. Pot-on every two to three years in spring in a peat compost. Change compost for fresh in years between.
Propagate from stem cuttings taken in spring and early summer.

Scindapsus aureus

Devil's Ivy

Heart-shaped, green leaves with yellow markings carried on stems which can be trained to climb or left to hang. *S. a.* 'Marble Queen' has cream markings and *S. a.* 'Tricolor' has both white and yellow markings. Grows to 6 ft (1.8 m) but can be kept under control by cutting back.

Likes bright light for a good leaf colour but shade from direct sun. Benefits from humidity, especially in warm weather.
Compost should be kept moist always in growing period and just moist in winter.
Feed every two weeks in spring and summer. Pot-on every other year in spring in peat compost. Change compost for fresh in intervening years. Pinch out growing tips for bushy growth.
Propagate from stem cuttings taken in summer.

Flowering plants

—— *Achimenes longiflora* ——

Hot Water Plant

Dark green, hairy leaves with serrated edges on 20 in (50 cm) stems, which can either be supported or allowed to trail in a hanging container. Blue or purple, white-centred, tubular flowers with flaring petals appear from early summer to early autumn. Some cultivars have pink flowers. *A. l.* 'Alba' has white flowers with purple centres. Stems die down after flowering.

Likes good light but shade from direct sun. Start the rhizome into growth in spring.
Compost should be just moist until shoots appear, and then thoroughly moist at all times. After flowering, stop watering and allow stems to die down. Cut off dead foliage and store the rhizome at a temperature no lower than 50°F (10°C).
Feed every two weeks from appearance of new shoots until flowering is over. Pot-on in spring in peat compost.
Propagate by dividing the rhizome when potting-on or take stem cuttings in early summer.

—— *Begonia semperflorens* ——

Begonia

Green, red or purple, heart-shaped leaves. Masses of small white, pink or red flowers appear from late spring to autumn. Grows to 12 in (30 cm). Other fibrous-rooted begonia hybrids include 'Gloire de Lorraine', with rounded mid-green leaves and pink or red flowers from autumn to late winter. Grows to 12 in (30 cm). 'Schwabenland' hybrids have roughly heart-shaped leaves and orange, red or yellow flowers. They are available in flower throughout the year. Grows to 18 in (45 cm).

Likes bright light with some direct sun but shade from fierce midday sun.

Compost should be watered thoroughly all year round but allow top half to dry out between waterings. Flowers will fall if plants have too little water.
Feed every two weeks in spring and summer. If plants stop flowering cut back stems to 4 in (10 cm) and rest them at 60°F (16°C) for a few weeks. Pot-on each spring in peat compost.
Propagate by taking stem cuttings in spring and summer.

—— *Beloperone guttata* ——

Shrimp Plant

Shiny, oval, mid-green leaves about 2 in (5 cm) long. Layered pink-brown, shrimp-shaped bracts from which white flowers emerge from late spring to late autumn. Bracts last for many months. Grows to 2 ft (60 cm) but can be kept to a compact 12 in (30 cm) by annual pruning.

Likes bright light with direct sun for good bract colour but shade from scorching sun. Requires good ventilation.
Compost should be kept moist always in growing period but barely moist during winter rest.
Feed every two weeks in spring and summer. Pot-on in spring in a loam or peat compost. Prune back stems to 6 in (15 cm) in spring and pinch out growing tips for bushy growth.
Propagate by taking stem cuttings in spring.

—— *Brunfelsia calycina* 'Macrantha' ——

Yesterday, Today Tomorrow

Leathery, shiny, oval 4 in (10 cm) leaves. Fragrant, five-petalled 3 in (7.5 cm) flowers appear in summer and autumn; they change colour daily from purple, to lavender and finally white, before dying on the fourth day. Successions of flowers appear and can bloom throughout the year. Grows to 2 ft (60 cm).

Likes bright light with some direct sun but shade from scorching midday sun. Benefits from some humidity.
Compost should be moist always in growing period but barely moist in winter.
Feed every two weeks in spring and summer. Pot-on every two to three years in spring in peat compost with some leaf mould added. Change compost for fresh in years between. Mature plants should be pruned by half in spring. Pinch out growing tips to encourage bushiness.
Propagate by taking stem cuttings in spring. Bottom heat of 70°F (21°C) is required.

—— *Heliotropum hybrids* ——

Heliotrope

Bright green, oval leaves with a slightly puckered surface. Large heads of tiny white, lavender or purple flowers bloom from summer through the autumn. Grows to 2 ft (60 cm), but growing tips should be pinched out regularly. After two or three years the plants flower less prolifically, so it is then better to raise new ones from cuttings.

Likes bright light, with some direct sun, but not when fierce.
Temperature in the winter months should be kept close to 60°F (16°C).
Compost should be moist always in the growing period but barely moist when the plant is resting in winter.
Feed every two weeks in spring and summer. Pot-in each year in spring in a peat compost, until replaced.
Propagate by taking stem cuttings in summer. When well established, pinch out growing tips for bushiness.

Palms and ferns

Pentas lanceolata

Egyptian Star Cluster

Bright green, hairy, lance-shaped leaves. Clusters of small, star-shaped pink, red or white flowers appear in winter. Grows to 18 in (45 cm).

Likes bright light with direct sun. Keep close to 60°F (16°C) in winter months.
Compost should be well watered in growing period; just moist for about two months after flowering.
Feed every two weeks in spring and summer. Pot-on in spring in loam compost.
Propagate by stem cuttings in spring or summer.

Saintpaulia ionantha

African Violet

Heart-shaped, velvety, hairy leaves carried on short stems. Masses of single and double purple, red, pink and white flowers are produced from spring to autumn, but with adequate light they will flower throughout the year. Grows to 6 in (15 cm) but can spread up to 9 in (22.5 cm).

Likes bright light but avoid direct sun which can scorch flowers and leaves. Benefits from humidity.
Compost should be watered thoroughly all year round and allowed almost to dry out before watering again. Excessive moisture causes crown and stem rot. Plants are best watered by immersing the pot in 2 in (5 cm) of water for about half an hour. Avoid wetting leaves, which can be permanently marked.
Feed monthly in spring and summer. Pot-on every two to three years in spring in a peat compost. Change compost for fresh in years between.
Propagate by taking leaf cuttings in spring.

Howea forsteriana

Kentia Palm

Long stems bearing deeply divided, sword-shaped leaflets up to 18 in (45 cm) long. Young fronds grow erect but begin to arch gracefully as they mature. Grows to 7 ft (2.1 m) with a similar spread.

Likes good light but shade from direct sun.
Compost should be moist always in growing period but barely moist during winter rest.
Feed every two weeks in spring and summer. Pot-on every other spring in a loam compost. Change compost for fresh in intervening years.
Propagate from seed sown in spring with bottom heat of 75°F (24°C), but they take many years to reach a decent size.

Washingtonia filifera

Desert Fan Palm

Graceful, fan-shaped, grey green fronds carried on 12 in (30 cm) stalks from a short, reddish trunk. Each frond, up to 2 ft (60 cm) across, is divided into many segments, and from these fine filaments grow. The overall height is 5 ft (1.5 cm).

Likes good light all year round with a certain amount of direct sun every day, when available. A spell out of doors in summer in a sunny sheltered spot does a lot of good. While it can stand dry air, a humid atmosphere keeps the fronds a better colour.
Compost should be moist always in the growing period. In the winter rest period, allow surface to dry out between waterings.
Feed every two weeks in spring and summer. Pot-on every two or three years in spring in a loam compost with the addition of leaf mould.
Propagate from seed; this is not easy and requires considerable bottom heat.

Nephrolepis exaltata 'Rooseveltii'

Boston Fern

Fronds up to 3 ft (90 cm) long bear opposite pairs of deeply-divided pinnae with wavy edges. *N. e.* 'Whitmanii' has closely-packed, pale green pinnae giving an overall lacy effect. Can be displayed in a hanging container.

Likes bright light but away from direct sun.
Compost should be moist always in growing period and just moist during winter rest. If compost dries out completely, fronds will shrivel. Should this happen, cut them away and new growth should appear, provided roots have not been affected.
Feed every two weeks in spring and summer. Pot-on every spring in a peat compost.
Propagate by division when potting-on or root the plantlets which grow on the runners. Pin them down in the compost and sever from the main plant when well-established.

Hanging plants

Callisia elegans

Striped Inch Plant

Close-packed, oval, 1 in (2.5 cm), dark green leaves with white stripes and purple undersides carried on stems up to 2 ft (60 cm) long. Insignificant white flowers appear from spring to autumn.

Likes bright light with direct sun for good leaf colour but shade from scorching sun. Give the plant a winter rest at about 60°F (16°C).
Compost should be moist always in growing period and barely moist in winter.

Feed every two weeks in spring and summer. Pot-on for a second year in loam or peat compost. After two years stems become bare and lanky and it is best to raise new plants. Cut back bare stems to compost level in spring.
Propagate by taking stem cuttings in spring or summer. They will root in compost or water.

Piper ornatum

Ornamental Pepper

Bronzy-green, heart-shaped leaves with veins picked out in silvery pink. Dark maroon undersides. This pepper can be grown as a climber or trailer, but in a hanging basket the trailing stems may have to be cut back to about 18 in (45 cm) if they are not to get out of hand.

Likes bright light, but shade from direct sun. Does best in a humid atmosphere; plants should be sprayed daily, especially in warm spells.
Temperature in winter should be 60°F (16°C) minimum to prevent leaf fall.
Compost should be thoroughly watered all year round, but allow surface to dry out between waterings.
Feed every two weeks in spring and summer. Pot-on every other spring in a peat compost, changing the compost for fresh in the year between.
Propagate by taking stem cuttings in early summer. Plant several together for a bushy effect.

Senecio macroglossus variegata

Variegated Waxvine

Spear-shaped, lobed, mid-green leaves, splashed with cream to yellow markings, and carried on trailing or climbing stems. The leaves closely resemble those of ivy in form. As they mature, the leaves at the end of stems tend to fall off and at that stage it is better to propagate and start off new plants. Watch out for aphids.

Likes bright light with direct sun to maintain good leaf colour.
Compost should be watered thoroughly all year round, but let surface dry out between waterings.
Feed every two weeks in spring and summer. Pot-on once only, in spring, in a mixture of two thirds loam compost and one third coarse sand.
Propagate by taking cuttings from late spring to summer. They will root in water or compost. Plant several stems in the hanging container for a bushy effect.

Stromanthe amabilis

Oval green leaves up to 8 in (20 cm) long, banded with darker green from the central rib. The undersides are grey-green. Leaves will fan over the edge of the container, covering its surface only. This is a compact trailer.

Likes a slightly shaded spot away from direct sunlight which may both bleach the leaves and scorch them, turning them brown.
Compost should be moist all year. Let the surface dry out a little before watering again.
Feed every two weeks in spring and summer. Pot-on every other spring in a peat compost. Change compost for fresh in the year between.
Propagate by dividing the rhizome; each piece should have four or more leaves.

Bulbs

Hippeastrum hybrids

Narrow, strap-shaped leaves which may appear at the same time as the flower spike or when flowering is over. Several trumpet-shaped flowers about 6 in (15 cm) across are carried on the end of a 20 in (50 cm) hollow stem from mid-winter to early spring. Flower colour may be red, orange, pink, white or white streaked pink to red, depending on cultivar. Leaves die down in early autumn and the bulb has a dormant period.

Likes good light with direct sun. Start bulb into growth in winter by bringing into a temperature of 65° to 70°F (18° to 21°C).
Compost should be just moist. When flower stalks and leaves appear, increase frequency of watering so that compost is moist always. In early autumn stop watering and when leaves have completely withered, remove them. Store the bulb in compost at 50°F (10°C) until started into growth later in the year. Repot in early autumn in loam or peat compost with the shoulder of the bulb showing above the compost surface. When flowers have died cut them off, but allow flower stem to wither completely before removing it.
Feed every two weeks in spring and summer.
Propagate by removing offsets when repotting but it will be many years before they reach flowering stage.

Cacti

Rhipsalidopsis gaertneri

Easter Cactus

Narrow, flattened stems about 1½ in (3.75 cm) long, joined together and eventually reaching an overall length of 12 in (30 cm). The stems arch over and the plant is best displayed in a hanging container. In spring, brick-red flowers appear from the end of the latest stem.

Likes good light, but shade from direct sun.
Temperature in winter should be a minimum of 50°F (10°C). In spring, a temperature of at least 65°F (18°C) is needed to bring the cactus into flower.
Compost should be always moist in growing period, but allow it almost to dry out between waterings in winter.
Feed monthly in spring and summer. Pot-on every spring, after flowering, in a mixture of two parts loam compost and one part sand.
Propagate by taking stem cuttings with two or three sections in summer.

Schlumbergera truncata

Christmas Cactus

Flattened, 1½ in (3.75 cm) segments with notched edges, joined together to form trailing stems 12 in (30 cm) long. This is a cactus suitable for a hanging container. Pink to dark red flowers are produced in early winter from the tip of the latest segment. The best form is the hybrid *S.* 'Buckleyi' (syn. *S.* 'Bridgesii').

Likes bright light, but shade from direct sun.
Temperature of 55°F (13°C) needed from early autumn to early winter. Bring into the warmth of the garden room – 65° to 75°F (18° – 24°C) – when flower buds first appear.
Compost should be moist always in spring and summer and barely moist during the rest period before flowering. Increase watering when flower buds appear, but compost must never be soggy.
Feed monthly in spring and summer. Pot-on every spring in two parts loam compost to one part sand.
Propagate in summer from stem cuttings with two or three segments.

Bromeliads

Aechmea fasciata

Urn Plant

Rosette of grey-green, strap-shaped leaves up to 2 ft (60 cm) long and cross-banded with silver. Flower spike of bright pink bracts surrounding small blue flowers appears in summer. Flowers are short-lived but bracts remain colourful for months. After flowering, the rosette dies down but produces offsets for new plants.

Likes bright light with some direct sun but shade from scorching sunlight. Good ventilation and humidity required in periods of warm weather.
Compost should be watered thoroughly in growing period with the top surface allowed to dry out between waterings. Keep the central urn topped up with water, and soft water for preference. In winter the compost should be just moist and the central urn should then be kept dry.
Feed monthly in spring and summer. Potting-on is not necessary since the main plant dies down after flowering.
Propagate from offsets. These should be detached and planted in a mixture of loam, peat and leaf mould. Flower spike will not be produced for three years or more. Change compost for fresh each year in spring.

Billbergia nutans

Queen's Tears

Rosette of close-packed, arching, sword-shaped, dark green, shiny leaves about 20 in (50 cm) long. Green and blue flowers emerge from pink bracts carried on arching stems in summer months. Spreads to 3 ft (90 cm).

Likes bright light with direct sun for flowering but shade from scorching sun.
Compost should be watered thoroughly all year round and the top surface allowed to dry out before watering again.
Feed monthly in spring and summer. Pot-on in spring in peat compost.
Propagate by removing offsets when potting-on; they should be well-established before severing from the main plant.

Dyckia brevifolia

Rosette of sword-shaped, fleshy leaves, up to 6 in (15 cm) long, with barbed edges. The undersides of the leaves are striped silvery white. New rosettes are produced in rapid succession, making a dense cluster covering the surface of the compost. Orange flowers are carried on 20 in (50 cm) stems in summer. Unlike most bromeliads, the rosettes of the dyckia do not die down after producing a flower stalk.

Likes good light with direct sun all year round. If left in shade, leaf colour tends to fade.
Compost should be thoroughly watered all year round, but allow surface to dry out between waterings. If the compost is too dry for a short period the plant draws on water reserves in the fleshy leaves, but it is better not to force it to do this.
Feed monthly in spring and summer. Pot-on in spring after the rosettes have completely covered the surface of the compost. Use two thirds loam compost and one third sharp sand for good drainage. In years between change compost for fresh.
Propagate by removing offsets when potting-on.

Part 4

Care of Conservatory Plants

This simple lean-to recreates a period feel using modern materials. A pinewood frame capped with metal glazing bars is given a convincingly Victorian look by cast aluminium brackets which form lacy arches between the uprights. But for practical purposes these decorative features are placed behind the glass for easy cleaning. Also practical is the high and steeply sloped roof, which is angled to prevent water collecting and causing damage. Inside, the furnishings reinforce the period design with reproduction Regency garden furniture.

Potting

In the previous section on plants suitable for the various types of conservatories and garden room, the individual plant entries give recommendations on when to repot and pot-on plants. The usual time is spring, when plants are starting into new growth.

When repotting, the compost is changed for fresh and the plant is returned to the same size pot. It is best to do this every year since the old compost will have built up excess deposits of mineral salts, from the fertilizer used to feed the plant, and in hard-water areas there will also be a build-up of lime. Excess mineral salts leave brown deposits on the side of clay pots or on the surface of the compost, while excess lime is shown by white deposits. Over the year the compost will also have become compacted, starving the roots of vital oxygen.

Start by removing the soil ball from the pot and gently tease away some of the old compost from the roots, taking care not to damage the delicate root hairs. Return the plant to a clean pot and gently firm fresh compost around the roots. (See next page for which compost to use.)

Plants require potting-on when their roots begin to grow through the drainage hole of the pot, when they start pushing up and showing above the surface of the compost, or when all the roots have completely filled the pot. Pots usually graduate in steps of 1 in (2.5 cm), and plants should be moved up only one size at a time. Do not transfer them to a pot with more than a 1 in (2.5 cm) increase since the roots will take a long time to spread into the new compost. In the meantime there will not be enough roots to take up water and fertilizer and the compost will therefore become sodden and sour.

How to pot-on

The easiest method of potting-on is to fill the bottom of the new pot with compost, so that when the plant is placed inside it will be at the same height level as in the old pot. Remove the soil ball from the old pot; place the pot inside the larger one, resting on the new compost, and fill in the gap with compost. Remove the pot and place the soil ball of the plant in the impression left behind, firming it against the compost. Fill in any space with extra compost if necessary.

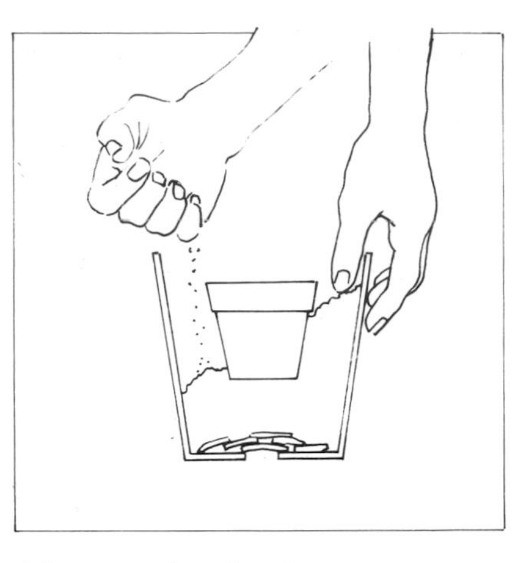

After removing the plant, use the old pot to form a mould in the compost of the new pot.

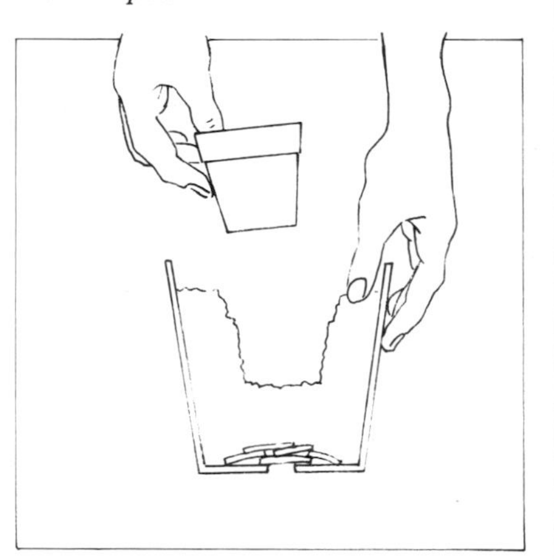

Once the compost is packed down to the right level, carefully remove the old pot.

Lower the soil ball of the plant into the hole, gently firming the compost round it. Add more if needed.

After plants have been repotted or potted-on, water the compost thoroughly until drips run out of the pot drainage hole. Allow the excess water to drain away. Keep the plant in a slightly shaded spot for a week or two until it has recovered from the shock. It will take a little time for roots to spread into the new compost and consequently the plant will require less frequent watering. The new compost will provide nutrients, so additional feeding should not be necessary for another two or three months.

Plants can be potted-on until a 10 in (25 cm) size is reached, and then into tubs, but if you wish to restrict the size of the plant it is best to stop at a 10 in (25 cm) pot and then top-dress annually. This entails removing the top 2 to 3 in (5 to 7.5 cm) of compost from the pot and replacing it with fresh. The plant can stay in the pot during the process, but take care not to damage its roots when removing the compost.

Plants which are grown hydroponically, that is, with their roots in water, require no repotting at all, but the aggregate has to be washed regularly to remove excess salts. Potting-on will be necessary, but far less frequently than with plants grown in compost since the root system spreads less in water. To pot-on, remove the plant from the aggregate, wash both the roots and the aggregate and then plant in a larger container with additional aggregate, as you would in potting-on with compost.

Composts and feeding

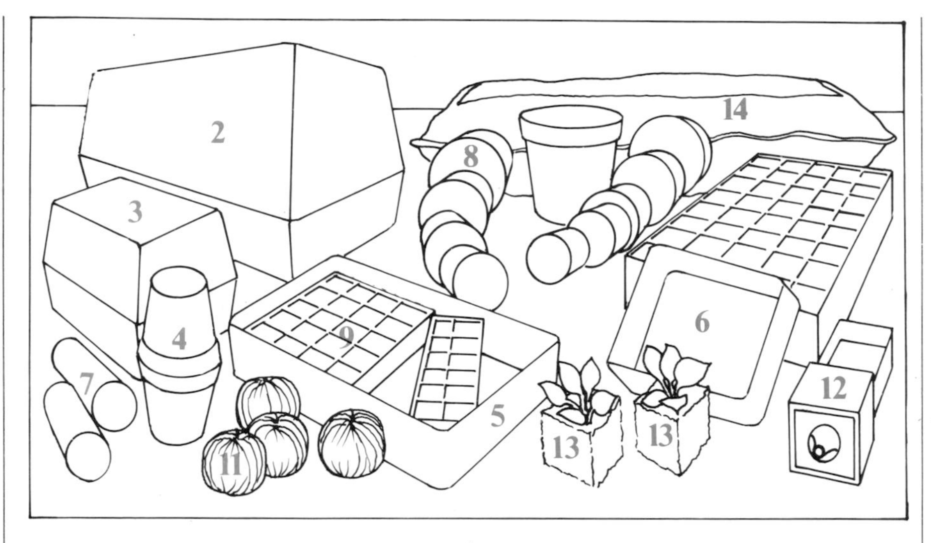

1 Plastic pots 2 Propagating top for standard-size seed trays 3 Propagating top for half-size trays 4 Propagating top for pots (various sizes) 5 Full-size seed trays 6 Half-size seed trays 7 Fibre pots 8 Compressed peat pots 9 Peat strip pots 10 Polystyrene slab pots 11 Jiffy 7s 12 Soil block maker 13 Soil blocks 14 Growbag

Fresh compost, whether loam or peat, will contain nutrients for the plant to use up over a period of two to three months. It is then your job to provide the plant with what it needs – nitrogen, phosphorus, potassium and trace elements – to ensure continued healthy growth. This is best done by using a balanced fertilizer.

Plants should be fed only from the time they start into active growth in spring until late summer or early autumn. Feeding later than this encourages the plant to continue growing when light intensity is poor. The result will be weak growth. Excessive feeding also causes a build-up of salts in the compost which can harm the plant permanently.

The individual plant entries (on pages 72–147) recommend when and how frequently to apply feed. Feeding less often than advised will do the plant no real harm; it will merely discourage exuberant growth, which may be quite acceptable.

Fertilizers are usually sold as liquid or powder, to which water must be added. Always follow precisely the manufacturer's instructions on mixing the proportions of fertilizer to water. Apply it when the compost is moist, to avoid any danger of burning the roots.

Other methods of applying fertilizer include slow-release tablets or spikes. These gradually release food over a period of several weeks, thereby cutting down on the chore of feeding. Tablets should be pushed deep into the compost near the side of the pot. The number of fertilizer spikes needed depends on the size of the pot. Insert them close to the edge of the pot to lessen the possibility of fertilizer burning the roots.

When the time comes for repotting and potting-on the plants in your conservatory, you will have to decide what type of compost to use. This will usually be loam or peat based, but other materials are frequently added to make it more free-draining. The individual plant entries of pages 72–147 suggest the most appropriate compost or mixture to use.

Loam composts consist of mixtures of soil, peat and sand in varying proportions. Mixtures are available for raising seeds and cuttings and for use with established plants. The so-called growing composts include nitrogen, phosphate and potassium fertilizers. Proprietary brands are usually divided into three grades, containing varying amounts of fertilizer in suitable proportions for young plants up to large mature specimens. The soil used is not always of the best quality, often including too much clay, which makes the mixture compacted and sodden.

Peat composts are increasingly used in preference to loam composts because they are lighter in weight and often of better quality. They consist of peat with the addition of sand and, sometimes, perlite or expanded polystyrene, indicated by the presence of white granules, which improve the free-draining qualities of the compost. Peat composts also contain fertilizers to provide for the plant's needs over two to three months. Take care in your choice of peat composts. The best are made of coarsely milled peat with a rough texture and plenty of air spaces, giving a light brown colour. The worst are almost a dust, often made of sedge peat, dark brown in colour and turning nearly black when moist. This compost will grow compacted with watering, excluding vital air from the roots.

Certain plants do better in mixtures made up especially for them. Both cacti and succulents, for example, require a very porous, free-draining compost usually in the proportion of two parts loam compost to one part sand. Palms are grown in two parts peat compost to one part coarse sand, again to make the mixture more porous. Ferns can either be grown in peat compost, to which sand can be added if necessary, or a mixture of equal parts loam, peat and sand. Typical composts for orchids, which can be bought ready mixed, consist of medium-grade bark, perlite and charcoal, or sphagnum moss peat, perlite and coarse sand. A free-draining compost is vital to ensure the roots of epiphytic orchids are surrounded by plenty of air.

Pruning

Plants are pruned to keep growth in check, to achieve a bushier effect, or to retain a pleasing shape. Of the various degrees of pruning, the simplest and lightest is pinching out, which encourages plants to put out bushy growth. With your fingers, or a pair of scissors, take off about 1 in (2.5 cm) of each growing tip just above the node, the point where the leaf joins the main stem. This will signal the dormant leaf axil buds lower down the stem to spring to life.

Once these axil buds have started to put out side shoots, they too can be pinched out. Only pinch out young plants which are not already lanky and do it regularly, about every six weeks or so, once new growth has started up.

Pinching out

The next, more rigorous stage in pruning is cutting back, to retain a good plant shape when a few stems have spurted ahead of the rest. Cutting back may also involve the more drastic but essential step of removing all stems to within a few inches of the compost, again in order to bring to life dormant buds and encourage bushy, as opposed to lanky, growth. Use either a sharp knife or secateurs, making the cut at an upwards angle or straight across just above a node.

Take care when pruning flowering plants. It is important not to remove stems on which that year's blooms are due to appear. Flowers which grow on green stems are appearing on the new season's growth, but flowers growing on a dark brown stem are blooming on the previous season's wood.

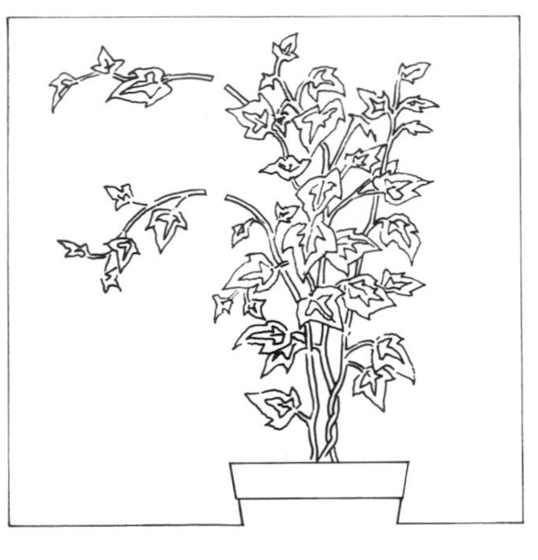

Cutting back

At some stage, plants may pass their best, losing their lower leaves to expose a bare and leggy stem. If they are cut back to within about 6 in (15 cm) of the compost, just above a node, new growth will eventually appear from the dormant buds. Dizygotheca and dieffenbachia are two plants to which this treatment can be applied; but cutting back does alter their shape and natural habit of growth.

When ferns have dried out too much and their foliage has died, they too can be rejuvenated by cutting back all the stems to compost level. Once the stubble has been sprayed regularly, new growth should appear.

Other minor plant-tidying operations will keep your plants looking their best. Leaves which have started to brown at the tips can be trimmed, but be careful not to cut into the green part as this will accelerate the death of the whole leaf. Leaves which are totally brown should be removed, together with their leaf stalk, from the main stem, or at compost level if there is no main stem.

Propagation

'Proceed with caution' is the best advice there is about propagation. Think first not *how* to do it, but *why* you are doing it; otherwise you may find the conservatory taken over by plants in a way you had never envisaged.

Avoid being too eager to propagate just to produce more plants, especially in a conservatory which is already amply provided for. More does not necessarily mean more attractive. Twenty African violets may look more effective than one; twenty giant dieffenbachia do not. Propagation by division demands the most restraint because it is the easiest method.

Planned propagation, on the other hand, is sensible. It means looking ahead, maybe for a year or several years, to the time when a plant will be past its best. You can prepare in advance to replace it with one of its own offspring, by using cuttings, offsets, or in some other way, and thus perpetuate your favourites. Plants may also need replacing not on grounds of age, but because even when young they become straggly and unsightly. In other cases propagation is essential. Most bromeliads die after flowering and need to be replaced by the offsets they leave behind.

Methods to try

It is up to you to decide whether to propagate; here are brief instructions on how it can be done.

Division can be carried out on those plants which throw up several stems from compost level. Remove the compost ball from the pot and gently pull apart the roots, taking care not to damage the fine root hairs. Plants with tough root balls will need to be cut with a knife. It is best to divide a plant in two rather than into several puny pieces. Repot each piece in fresh compost, water well, and keep in a shaded spot for a week or two. Allow the compost almost to dry out before watering again.

Some plants grow from tubers and rhizomes which can be divided. Each piece should have two or more growing points, or eyes. Fill a pot or tray with a layer of compost, followed by a layer of sharp sand, and place the sections on top. Put the container in a heated propagator and pot the sections when growth is well-established.

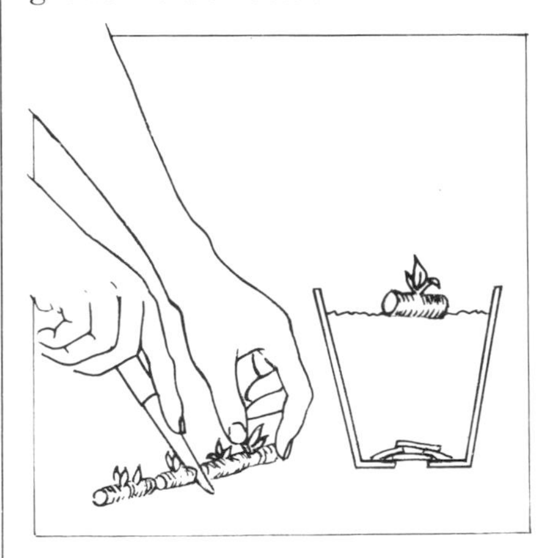

Rhizomes, like these achimenes, can be divided. Each piece should have at least two growing points.

Division of tubers (eg tuberous begonias). The pieces, with two or more growing points, are rooted in moist sand spread over compost.

Removing offsets is another simple method of propagation. Some offsets are thrown up by the main plant at its base; others are carried on the end of runners; and with bulbs, small bulbils are found attached to the base of the bulb. Wait until offsets are a decent size before removing them. When offsets are attached to the main plant at its base you will need to cut them away with a knife, making sure there are enough supporting roots.

Offsets (eg of clivias) should not be cut from the parent plant until they have plenty of roots.

Offsets of bromeliads which die after flowering can be left to grow until the old plant dies.

Offsets of cacti and succulents which have to be cut away should be allowed to dry out for a few days before planting in compost; otherwise they are likely to rot.

Small plants on runners should be pinned down (layered) into a pot of compost and only severed from the main plant when they are growing well.

Tolmiea menziesii reproduces a plantlet at the base of each leaf. Remove a leaf on a stalk, cut down the stalk to 2 in (5 cm) and push it into compost so that the leaf rests on the surface. The plantlet will soon put down its own roots.

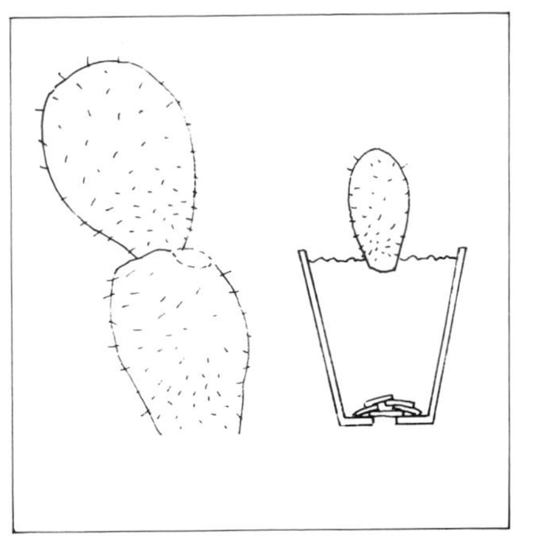

Cuttings of branching cacti, such as opuntia, root easily. Protect hands from the spines.

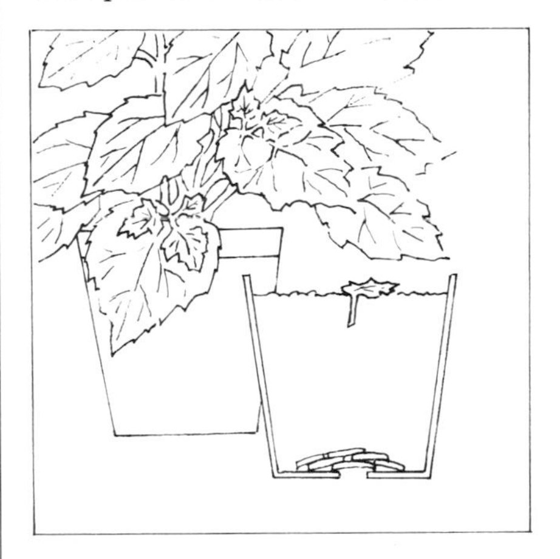

Push the stalk of a tolmiea leaf with plantlet well into the compost so the plantlet can take root.

When repotting a bulb, bulbils can be removed from its base, although it will be many years before they reach flowering size.

Stem cuttings are taken in late spring and early summer when plants are in active growth. Many cuttings will not strike without adequate heat – 70° to 75°F (21° to 24°C) – which is why a propagator providing bottom heat is useful. Even without a propagator, however, cuttings need to be kept moist and humid. Improvise by sticking four canes into a pot of compost, place over the canes a plastic bag punched with a few holes, making sure that the cutting does not touch the sides of the bag, and secure the open end round the rim of the pot with an elastic band. Stem cuttings of cacti and succulents should be allowed to dry out for a few days before planting in compost. They will require a temperature of 70°F (21°C), but no humidity, so do not cover with a plastic bag.

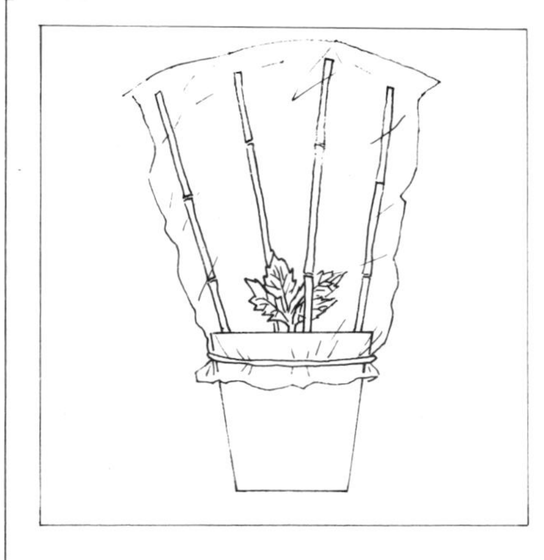

Stem tip cutting planted inside a tent made from a plastic bag and four canes, providing humidity.

Stem tip cuttings, which are taken from soft-stemmed plants, should be about 4 in (10 cm) long with at least three nodes, or points where the leaf joins the main stem. Cut the stem just below a node using a sharp knife; remove the first pair of leaves, dip the stem tip into hormone rooting powder and plant in compost. Place in a propagator or cover with a plastic bag. Some cuttings can be rooted in water and planted in compost when roots have developed.

Hardwood cuttings, taken from hard-stemmed plants, usually need a heel. Hold the main stem and tug the side shoot sharply downwards,

Preparing a cutting for planting — some leaves removed and the stem dipped in hormone rooting powder.

taking away a sliver of the main stem with the shoot. Trim the heel, dip into rooting powder and plant in compost. Place in a propagator or cover with a plastic bag.

Leaf cuttings are the means by which a few plants can be propagated. Break off a leaf and stem of

Cutting with a 'heel' — a small piece of the main stem from which the cutting was taken.

Saintpaulia ionantha, African violet; trim the stem to 1 in (2.5 cm), dip into rooting powder and insert into compost at an angle of 45 degrees. Cover the pot with a plastic bag.

The leaves of *Begonia rex* can be propagated in the same way as African violets, or by pinning down a whole leaf in sand. Remove a leaf,

Dipping the stem of an African violet in hormone rooting powder before planting in compost.

African violet leaf planted and enclosed in plastic bag.

place it underside upwards on a firm surface, and make a few shallow cuts with a sharp knife into the veins. Turn the leaf over and pin it down onto the sand with a few loops of wire. Place in a heated propagator at 70°F (21°C). After several weeks small plants should appear from the cut veins; they can be removed when well-established.

Sowing seed is the cheapest way to obtain annuals, and many other new plants where alternative methods of propagation are not

*Propagating a **Begonia rex** leaf. First make shallow cuts in veins on the underside of the leaf.*

Left: The begonia leaf pinned down on moist sand. Right: Plantlets will appear after several weeks.

always successful. Most seed needs a soil temperature around 65°F (18°C) to germinate, but some of the tropical plants may require temperatures between 70° and 80°F (21° and 27°C). Humidity is also important for these seedlings, so a heated propagator must be used. In a cool conservatory, annuals can be raised from seed without a heated propagator, but trays and pots should be covered with plastic, punched with a few holes, to maintain humidity. Without heat, however, seeds take much longer to germinate.

Fill seed trays or pots with either a loam or peat seed compost to a depth of 2 in (5 cm). Large seeds should be spaced evenly in rows and covered with a thin layer of compost. Fine seed should be scattered sparingly and covered with a thin layer of sand. Immerse the containers in water and wait until moisture beads appear on the surface. Allow the water to drain away and then place in the propagator at the recommended temperature. Seedlings require good light but never exposure to direct sun. Once they have germinated, the seedlings should never be allowed to dry out – it means instant death. Thin them out, removing the weakest, and transplant when the first pair of true leaves appear.

Ferns are the most difficult plants to propagate. The method is to use their spores, which are contained in brown cases found on the undersides of the fronds. Detach a frond, place it in a bag and leave in a dark place until the cases have dried out, releasing the tiny spores. Scatter the spores onto a tray of moist peat moss and enclose in a plastic bag. Place in the warmth in bright light. After a few weeks the compost will be filled with a green film, which is the first stage of a fern's development. Keep the compost moist and maintain high humidity within the bag. With luck, and a great deal of patience, the first recognizable fronds of a tiny fern will eventually appear.

Air-layering is suitable for certain woody-stemmed plants, such as ficus and dracaena, which have lost their lower leaves. A new, leafy plant is created by this method from the top of the old one. Make an upward slanting cut about a third of the way into the stem, a few inches below the lowest remaining leaf. Dust the cut with hormone rooting powder and insert a matchstick into it to prevent it from healing. Pack moist sphagnum moss around the stem, covering the cut area, and secure it with twine. Cover the sphagnum moss with clear plastic, taped at the top and bottom with adhesive tape. Water and feed the plant normally. After two months or so, roots should be visible among the sphagnum moss. Remove the plastic, cut the stem just below the sphagnum moss and plant with the moss in a pot of fresh compost. The bare stem will also put out new growth eventually.

Pests and diseases

Conservatories provide ideal conditions for growing plants. They are also perfect breeding grounds for pests – often encouraged by a warm, dry atmosphere – and for diseases, which thrive in conservatories where humidity is excessive and ventilation poor. Once pests and diseases take a hold they will spread like wildfire through your whole collection; aim to avoid them appearing in the first place.

The first two essentials for a healthy conservatory are to ensure a reasonable level of humidity and good ventilation. Always follow a few simple rules of plant hygiene. Regularly remove dead foliage and flowers. Make sure pots are thoroughly scrubbed out before use and always use sterilized compost. As an added precaution, soak compost with fungicide before potting-on or repotting plants. Do not be tempted to try and save heavily infected plants – throw them away. Inspect plants regularly for signs of pests and diseases. Keep newly purchased plants isolated elsewhere in the house for a week or two before bringing them into the conservatory, checking frequently during that time that they are not harbouring unwanted visitors.

The most common pests and diseases can be treated with pesticides and fungicides. Always stick to the manufacturer's instructions on packets and bottles, using the exact quantities stated. A stronger solution will not rid you of pests and diseases more quickly. On the contrary, you may bring about the plant's speedy death.

Pests

Ants The presence of black ants is often a sign that more serious pests, such as aphids, may be nearby, since ants feed off their honeydew. Ants also carry pests from one plant to another.

Use an ant spray or dust. Spray with malathion but not on ferns, cacti or succulents. It is more important to rid the conservatory of the pests which attract ants.

Aphids Greenfly and blackfly are found on stems, undersides of leaves and flower buds. They suck sap from the plant, resulting in stunted and distorted growth. They also excrete sticky honeydew which encourages sooty mould.

Spray affected plants with dimethoate, malathion or pyrethum. Malathion should not be used on ferns, cacti or succulents.

Aphids are likely to attack a wide variety of plants.

Caterpillars These will attack fleshy, soft, often young, foliage, chewing leaves and leaving behind excrement.

If there are only one or two, pick them off; otherwise spray with derris or resmethrin.

Caterpillars attack a wide variety of plants.

Cyclamen mites These insects are so tiny as to be almost invisible, thriving in cool, humid conditions. They suck sap, scarring foliage and distorting flower buds, eventually causing both to fall. They also spread fungal diseases.

Throw away badly affected plants. Spray mild infestations with dicofol.

They will attack African violets, azaleas, begonias, cyclamen, fuchsia, impatiens and pelargonium.

Earwigs These brown insects are about 1 in (2.5 cm) long with a pair of pincers at their tail. They chew leaves, flower buds and petals. Pick off intruders or spray with malathion, but not on ferns, cacti or succulents.

Fungus gnats Small black flies may be seen on the surface of peat compost in particular, but the real damage is done by the white maggots which eat plant roots. If they are not eliminated the plant will totally collapse.

Drench the compost with diazinon or malathion.

Fungus gnats attack plants where the compost is kept too wet.

Leaf miner Larvae of flies which have laid eggs in the leaves suck the leaf sap and tunnel inside the leaf, leaving behind very obvious white trails.

Remove badly affected foliage and spray with dimethoate or diazinon.

Leaf miners will attack African violets, azaleas, begonias, chrysanthemums, pelargonium, ficus and palms.

Mealy bugs These small insects, related to scale insects, have a white waxy coating. The bugs cocoon themselves in white fluff which is found on leaves and stems. They suck plant sap, causing leaves to yellow, wilt and finally fall, and excrete honeydew which encourages fungal diseases. Some attack roots.

Spray plants with derris, pyrethum, malathion (but not on ferns, cacti or succulents) or the systemic dimethoate.

Favourite targets are cacti, African violets, begonia, dieffenbachia, dracaena, ferns and palms. Root mealy bugs can be treated by soaking the compost with dimethoate.

Red spider mites These tiny red or yellow-green, pinhead-size insects suck sap, leaving yellow spots on the leaves. They cover leaves and stems with fine white webs and whitish powder.

These mites are encouraged by hot, dry conditions in the conservatory, so try to maintain a reasonably humid atmosphere, especially in warm weather, to deter them.

Spray with derris, dicofol or malathion, but do not use malathion on ferns, cacti or succulents.

Plants at risk include aspidistra, cissus, dracaena and schefflera, but they will attack almost any plant given the right dry, warm conditions.

Scale insects Hard oval bumps found on leaf undersides and stems of plants protect these tiny insects. They suck sap, producing yellow spots on leaves and generally stunting the growth of the plant.

Scales can be scraped off lightly infested plants; otherwise spray with malathion. For cacti, succulents and ferns, spray with dimethoate.

Slugs and snails Familiar garden pests may find their way into the conservatory to feed on leaves and tender stems.

Lay down methiocarb or metaldehyde baits. Plants and compost can be sprayed with liquid metaldehyde.

Like caterpillars, slugs and snails are catholic in their plant tastes.

Thrips Brown or black flying insects may be found on leaf undersides. They suck sap, piercing the leaves and distorting growth. Thrips also excrete a reddish honeydew which encourages fungus diseases. They thrive in a warm, dry atmosphere so humidity and good ventilation are both preventatives.

Spray with malathion (but not cacti, succulents or ferns), or dimethoate.

Favourite targets are begonia, croton, cyclamen, ferns, orchids, palms and many other flowering plants.

Whitefly Small flying insects are often found on the undersides of leaves. Shake an infested plant and these moth-like creatures frantically dart about. They suck the leaf sap, causing yellow mottling, and excrete honeydew, which encourages sooty mould.

The most effective treatment is to spray with resmethrin. Malathion may also be used, but not on ferns, cacti or succulents.

Diseases

Blackleg Newly-planted cuttings turn black and rot at their base if the compost is too wet and not sufficiently porous. Cuttings dipped in hormone rooting powder mixed with a little fungicide may help to ward off this disease.

Botrytis This is a fluffy grey mould which grows on stems, leaves, flowers and compost surface. It is caused by too frequent watering, making the compost sodden, and excessive humidity. Remove the diseased areas of the plant. Spray or water into the compost benomyl or thiophanate-methyl. Reduce frequency of watering and humidity, and increase ventilation.

Plants particularly at risk are African violets and pelargoniums.

Crown and stem rot Both stems and, in extreme cases, the crown of the plant turn mushy. Overwatering is the main cause, but excessive humidity contributes. If the whole plant is affected, throw it away. Otherwise remove the rotten stems and dust compost with a fungicide powder. The compost may also be soaked with benomyl, but allow it then to dry out for a few days.

Plants most at risk include African violets, which should be watered from below, begonias, pelargoniums, philodendrons, dieffenbachia, cacti and succulents.

Damping off This disease attacks new seedlings, causing them to collapse at compost level. The culprit here is fungal disease carried in unsterilized compost. Remove dead seedlings and apply zineb to those that remain. Before using seedling compost, soak it with fungicide as a precaution.

Leaf spot Overwatering, poor ventilation and excessive humidity encourage this disease. Leaves are covered with brown and yellow damp spots. Remove infected leaves and spray with benomyl or thiophanate-methyl.

Mildew Poor ventilation encourages this disease, which appears as a white powder mould found on leaves and stems. Remove infected leaves and spray with benomyl.

Root rot Overwatering causes roots to rot. The plant will then be in a total state of collapse, with yellow and curling leaves. If the plant is far gone, throw it away. Otherwise remove the plant from its pot, gently wash off compost and cut away infected roots. Repot in fresh compost soaked with a fungicide.

Plants at risk include African violets, begonias, gloxinias, cacti and succulents.

Sooty mould This black mould, found on leaves, thrives on plants where honeydew has been excreted by insects. Sponge off the deposit and spray the plant to rid it of the insects which deposited the honeydew.

Virus disease This is spread from one plant to another by insects. The result is distorted, stunted growth and leaves mottled with yellow. There is no cure and plants and compost should be thrown away before other plants become infected. Pots should be thoroughly cleaned and sterilized before they are used again.

Index

Amdega 40T: Arcaid/Richard Bryant 46/Tim Soar 45/Robert Wilkinson 22T: BBC Hulton Picture Library 15L: Banbury Homes and Gardens Ltd 37: Alexander Bartholomew Conservatories 40BL, 55B: J-P Bonhommet 24–5, 54–5: Michael Boys Syndication 18: Camera Press/Schone Wohnung 32–3: Angela Coombes 8–9: Country Life 10: Mary Evans Picture Library 15R: Susan Griggs Agency/Michael Boys 19/Ian Yeomans 21R: Fine Art Photographic Library 13B: John Glover 47T: Hall's Homes and Gardens 38: Roger Hammond 56: Jerry Harpur 6–7, 55T, 64–5: Impact/Pamla Toler 11, 13T: Clive Latimer (owner/designer) 46: Machin Designs 30–1: Mansell Collection 12B: National Magazine Co (photo Jan Baldwin) 34, 63, 67T, 148–9: National Monuments Record 14: Marston and Langinger 16–17, 28–9, 39, 40BR, 41, 48–9, 50, 53, 69: Timothy Rendle 61: Royal Botanic Gardens, Kew/(c) H.M.S.O. 12T: Harry Smith Collection 62, 68: Jessica Strang 26–7: Elizabeth Whiting Agency 22B, 66–7: Elizabeth Whiting Agency/Michael Dunne 23/Clive Helm 20–21/Spike Powell 51/Tim Street-Porter 67B.